AF322588

BETWEEN HERE AND THE SOUND OF A GROANING INTERSTATE

&

THE GROANING BOOK
A POETICS

BETWEEN HERE AND THE SOUND OF A GROANING INTERSTATE

&

THE GROANING BOOK
A POETICS

KC Clarke

1802 Press
Cuyahoga Valley, Ohio
2026

Printed in the United States of America
Printed on paper and bound in hardcover

Book design: KC Clarke
Jacket design: KC Clarke
Jacket painting: *Black Blizzard* (2021) by Wesley Kimler

Suggested Library of Congress Cataloging-in-Publication Data

Names: Clarke, KC, author.
Title: Between Here and the Sound of a Groaning Interstate &
The Groaning Book: A Poetics / KC Clarke.
Description: First edition. | 1802 Press, 2026.
Summary: A dual-volume work joining a thirty-year collection
of poems with a companion poetics that explores refusal,
ambiguity, ethical presence, and sonic structure in
contemporary art and language.
Identifiers:
Library of Congress Control Number: 2025924938
ISBN 979-8-218-84546-9 (hardcover)
Subjects: LCSH—Poetry--American--21st century. | Poetics--
United States--21st century. | Ethics in literature. | Civic poetics.
Classification: LCC PS3553.L3693 B48 2026 (poems) |
PN1042.C53 2026 (poetics) | DDC 811.6 (poems) |
808.1—dc23 (poetics)
LC record available at https://lccn.loc.gov/2025924938

First edition.

INTRODUCTION TO THE DUAL WORK

This book is composed in two volumes: a collection of poems and a corresponding poetics. The two are intended to be read together, dialogically, each offering a distinct but interdependent field of attention. While the poems and their companion entries invite return and cross-reading, the larger sections of this book are shaped to be read as continuous movements, each sustaining its own pressure and ethical field.

The poems, written between 1993 and 2024, operate within a lyric tradition grounded in refusal, ambiguity, ethical presence, and sonic structure. They resist declarative and confessional modes, emphasizing compositional clarity over self-expression. Each poem is built to sustain presence, rather than assert it, to evoke, rather than resolve. They move like paintings or musical pieces, intended for return, for inhabitation, for tonal recognition over time.

Their lineage is both artistic and structural. The work draws from sustained engagement with poetic thought and the enduring questions of how form shapes perception, how repetition accrues meaning over time, and how structure carries ethical weight. These influences hold both the ethical and architectural pressure of the work. The poems arise from a long practice of compositional discipline, where attention shapes meaning without fixation. The sequence follows a waveform logic, patterned by rhythm, contraction, rupture, and return. It follows a structural logic rather than chronology or theme.

The second book, *The Groaning Book*, functions as an accompanying poetics. It offers a counterform: a field of listening that attends to rhythm, compositional bearing, and ethical posture. It moves in parallel with the poems, extending their architecture, amplifying what they initiate, and sustaining their capacity for resonance.

If the poems formed through years of artistic and civic practice, *The Groaning Book* gathers that duration into form. It reflects an ethic formed in broadsides, classrooms, exhibitions, oral archives, and civic reading, sites where poetry functioned as shared structure rather than personal declaration. The long delay in publishing these poems belongs to years given to civic labor and to the building of platforms where other voices could reach.

At the time of writing, few works in contemporary poetry adopt a dual form of this kind. This is one work, in two parts. Each can be entered on its own terms. But their fullest resonance emerges in relation. Together, they offer a model of poetic attention, across time, across structure, and across the enduring field of the lyric.

CONTENTS

Introduction to the Dual Work   v

VOLUME ONE

BETWEEN HERE AND THE SOUND OF A GROANING INTERSTATE

Skyscraper	5
Mary's Field	6
The Humming Bridge	7
Bridgebuilder	8
Boomtown	10
Bubbly Creek (Ode to the Chicago River)	12
This Charming Man	13
Smoke & Fathers	15
Desire	16
The Return	19
Orion	21
Mercury Fish	22
My Friend and His Wife	25
The Possum	26
Don't Tell Me You Haven't Thought This Before	28
Elephant Tattoo	29
YOU	31
Rock of My Bones	33
The First Psalm	34
Only a Serpent	35
Eternal Life	37
Unbeknownst to You	38
Waiting for Daylight	39
Lightning Manual	40
Morning in the Middle of Nowhere	41

After the Fall of the First World 42

Cliffard Gawthorp's Trade 44

False Suns 46

On a Bridge Over the Oka 47

Americus, for Ferlinghetti 49

Human Waste Dump 50

Poet Compares Their Work to That of a Terrorist 51

Dirt 53

Three-Legged Nag 54

The Devourer 55

Scarecrows 56

The Perennials 57

The Multitude of Opalescent Grackles 59

Ode to a Roadkill 60

Consequences of an Old Lady and Her Dog 62

Fathom 63

Jubilee 64

To a Young Malcolm X 66

After a Year of Flooding 68

Humdrum 69

Network 71

Tomorrow is a Long Time 73

Upland 74

VOLUME TWO

THE GROANING BOOK

PROLOGUE

The Gift of Permission	81
A Companion to the Unread	83

PART ONE

A Composed Attention	89
A Field of Attention	90
Break in the Frame	235
Endurance and Estrangement	236

PART TWO

Threshold	245
Fear and Artistic Risk	246
Fear as a Field Condition	247
The Poems Abandon Righteousness	249
On Misreading and Control	250
Certainty as Narcotic	251
The Poetics of Refusal	253
Against the Charge of Silence	254
Supposed Sons	256
Olympus Is Empty	259
The Law of Moral Recursion	260

PART THREE

Held Voltage	267
Stylistic Bearings	268
Thematic Currents	269
Compositional Forces in the Work	270

On Persona and Poetic Masking   271
Identity and Its Shadows   272
Estrangement and Participation   274
On Semantic Freedom   275

PART FOUR

reVerse and the Architecture of Musical Poetics   281
Flip Sides   286
The Rhythmic Contour   289
The Rhythmic Behavior   291
Reverberation   295

PART FIVE

The Weather Makers   301

PART SIX

A Quiet Intervention   309
The Long Account   310
The Work of a Poet   312

PART SEVEN

The Ethos of Civic Poetics   319
Civic Poetics in Practice   321
The Asteroid   323
More Than a Number   331
Poem Finds a Home   332
Line 39   333
Civic Amplification   334
What We Built   339
Live from the Art Gallery, Live from the Margins   354
Cowboy Poetry   355
The Cavalcade of Hats   356

Holding Ground   370

A Sworn Poetics   372

Afterword   373

PART EIGHT

On the Construction of This Book   379

On Time, Energy, and the Value of Attention   381

The Lyric Vocation   382

BETWEEN HERE AND THE SOUND OF A GROANING INTERSTATE

KC Clarke

EPIGRAPH

He said that it was a mistake to expect too much of justice in this world.
— Cormac McCarthy, The Crossing

Skyscraper

Leaning against yourself
with the accusation
of blue lake on you
and smoke snorting
out of your stack

we are at
your dusty foot
all day and night
spinning ourselves
for all we are worth

it's not like any of us
look up to the tip
of your top
though your summit
is lit and pointing

to the far off orbit
of a satellite circling
to bounce back
down every word
we are praying

Mary's Field

I don't pray to you
            but I chanced upon
                        a shrine
plywood roof green-painted
over the head of your icon,
            one wood wall at your back
                        feet on a red pedestal.
Mother of God,
have you noticed this shrine
            propped upon its barbed fence post
                        observed your
plastic likeness
cloaked in eternal-blue,
            arms raised,
                        hands open,
at the edge of a low field
where over-zealous rains
            of three past Junes have pooled?
                        Kitsch Madonna,
what are you doing
in a place more godforsaken
            than the earth holding the roots
                        of a lightning tree?
Are you the one
who calls on water
            as punishment for secret sin
                        or will you be the one
to rouse the trees
of the fields into clapping
            their gaunt green hands?

The Humming Bridge

We are about to motor
over his bridge but my grandfather
a retired civil engineer
doesn't tell about its structure

how he gave it inches
to allow contraction in the cold,
how it was anchored
into the rock walls of the gorge.

He cracks the window
and holds a sound check
attempting the pitch

as we drive over its edge
into a single minor chord.
The grid thrums under the tires

like the drone of electricity
in and out of heart wires
of a transformer.

I know it's not humming for us
but for the layered gorge
the Cuyahoga River
the hardwood forests.

Still, I force air
through my throat
following grandfather
into the industrial sound

harmonizing with mechanical
and angelic orders.

Bridgebuilder

The soul is silent. If it speaks at all, it speaks in dreams.
— Louise Glück

Clouds are the perfect vehicles
for spanning the banks as I rebuild
iron triangles a description of rivets
shadows and rusted beams

which I speak over the river
for this bridge's purpose
carries me beyond crossing
from one end to the other

the other side is never
a surprise linking terra
firma with terra firma
a self-justification

I will not make it new
it will have a reputation
upon completion gossip will whine
in the iron cables

the structure will be
riddled with junk
this scrap and that slag
it is mine and I love it

a strip of asphalt hung tapestry
over a small sleepy catfish river
by whose edge I wait and wait
and wait for good measure

until one car gleaming black
with immaculate chrome
an engine that sounds
like shifting tectonic plates

passes over to the other side
the bridge sways and quakes
unseen support beams break welds
and clank in applause

the car stops the window rolls
down and a man with a beard
places his fingers between his lips
and whistles a most human gesture

to which birds swarm up
out of the forest
like the shadow
of an eclipse

machines out of my childhood
dreams with tires
as big as houses
pull out of the trees

lift the bridge from its foundations
men with arc welders
          so many fallen stars
cut the bridge to pieces

and cart it away points
of light burning all the way home
I am all I have a pocket full of clouds
we all fall down

Boomtown

It's dark now and we
are thinking of things
that could have been,
skyscrapers, steel mills,
jutting out of fields,
spreading a canopy
of light on the clouds.

The Co-Op silos become
a bank complex,
fifty stories, towers
looking over an endless grid
of buildings, the streets
coursing with traffic.

This town was to be
our capital, a metropolis.
Our fathers pushed
forests to the territory's edge.
Their future brewed
between layers of shale,
natural gas, a liquid hope.

Quick as a surge of lightning
the torches darkened,
pumps coughed dust,
glass factory innards
carried away by train.

It was as if God himself
raised a hand and said
stop, go elsewhere.

Now, at night, we hear ghosts,
or maybe the town itself,
searching for amputated limbs,
to massage phantom muscles.

If we drilled for gas we'd
gather barrels of pesticides.
If we addressed all this,
wouldn't we climb into
the Mississinewa, the river
that led all of us here

and float away before
it turns to blood,
run to another town
before burning sulfur
falls from the sky?

Bubbly Creek (Ode to the Chicago River)

Confused going the wrong way
your waters flow carrying everything
we don't want to know

nameless things float deep in your swill
ruined steel shapes and shattered
concrete hulks populate your banks

but we don't really know you do we
a sea is forced into you as if through
you lost men were trying to set it free

This Charming Man

Cigarettes and notes left by pilgrims
who know everything about your life,
except that you probably floored

the pedal when the truck materialized.
This is the town where what's left of you
is, physical remnants, teeth and hair,

Fairmount, Indiana, far from California.
Idol through death like Hendrix and Cobain,
if only Elvis could have offed himself sooner.

Or, were these all terrible blunders?
You must have known you'd end up
in your final rest where fire fighters gather

late nights to smoke in the Village Pantry;
where the sons and daughters of everyone
who never liked you while you lived

here are proud to live because
of you, signs on the interstate
advertising your birthplace,

their yearly festival, the car show,
elephant ears and five dollar, slightly
imperfect, Harley-Davidson T-shirts.

Where Morrissey from London
shot a video, him at your grave
leaving you a cigarette, him
at your high school soaking you up.

As was predicted, the gulf stream
shifts and for a moment stock animals look up,
a river turns backward, countercurrents
eddies and I'm not thinking only of you, James Dean,
I'm giving a name to what I've done:

king of nothing, creator of waste.
For a moment I wish you could
breathe with me, James, between

these walls, in this abandoned place.
As a child I lived near the sea
and sometimes hear it in my sleep.

Smoke & Fathers

My father's voice floats above me
    this voice I thought vanished
        into a thicket of parked cars

only heard as a ting
    against hubcaps
        now resonates like wind

through deep grass
    clear yet incomprehensible
        and familiar as my fingers

last night's storm
    blew spiders from the trees
        and their colorless streamers

glint all round
    as though hanging
        beneath some fantastic loom

and in the thread
    images of my father and me
        appear in the quavering light

yoked like Siamese twins
    cutters are slashing and piling grass
        on the city's hills with scythes

men who are both sons and fathers
    set the mounds on fire
        see father watch the smoke

twist up building sides
    curling toward a place
        of no beginnings

Desire

The car was not air-conditioned
Maureen had unbuttoned
every button
down the front of her white sundress.

She drove with her left hand
and with her right
rubbed a cold dripping Coke
across her breast.

"Wanna sip?"

She held out the red and white can.

State Road Two
ran through the Florida half
of the Okefenokee,

"Pull over."

She braked hard.
Tires skidded
over Longleaf pine needles.

I swung out of the passenger side
ran back twenty or thirty yards.

Maureen closed a few buttons
walked toward me.

Four feet from the road
a Canebrake Rattlesnake
had moved out of the saw palmettos
slid resolute along the shoulder.

I stood in the path of the large snake.
She paused, coiled.
Drew back her head.
Resumed her glide.
I stepped away,

my bluff called.
The snake turned.
Moved toward the shelter of the wiregrass.
Fearful of losing her to the thicket
I again stepped into her path.
Her head moved close to my boot.

"Do it." The adrenaline commanded.

My hand grabbed the snake
just behind the head.
Her body coiled around my arm and neck.
Took hold of me
with unanticipated power.

Was she strong enough
to pull me to her?
Sink her fangs into my flesh?

I pulled her head close to mine.
Bared my teeth.
Brought her closer.
Breathed across nostrils.

Slowly, as if knowing what I wanted
the snake dropped its jaw.
Rolled out her glistening fangs.
At the tip of each hung
a pale-yellow drop of venom.

I wanted to feel that poison
run through my veins.
Desire pushed up
the core of my body.

Maureen,
buttons in unrelated buttonholes
circled with the Nikon.

"Put it down before it bites."

I turned toward her.
A drop of venom
fell onto the back of my hand.
I wanted to taste it.
Rub it into my skin,
but wiped it cautiously onto my jeans.

Maureen was right.

I kneeled to the ground,
laid coil after coil onto warm sand.
Released the head.

Jumped away.
The snake lay still a moment,
slipped back
into the palmettos.

The Return

A man is sitting on a toilet hidden somewhere
  on the 47th floor, accessible
    only through a series of corridors.
Here, as he sits on a toilet, he imagines
  himself standing at the edge
    of a proverbial cliff,
     and a proverbial canyon
spreads out in front, and the canyon performs;
  it is the simile of a perfect lover:
    the canyon lies before him
and is ready to receive him.
    He is yelling his own name (Bruce is what I
     hear) and from the canyon, from some inner
depth, out of some invisible engine,
  his name is reproduced. Bruce, Bruce, Bruce,
    etc. His bowels shift and gurgle
and expel the things they couldn't absorb.
  He is thinking about the cliff and the canyon,
    and how the canyon and its echo
remind him of a lover stretched out before him.
  He thinks of something else that is relevant
    to this train of thought, but this thought
is lost, he cannot recall it, and the canyon
  won't retell it because he never spoke it.
  He becomes obsessed
with the thought and with the fact
  that the canyon won't repeat, even
    a proverbial canyon, unless it is spoken into.
He backtracks, the canyon reminded him of a lover, her
  name was Susan, she had freckles
    on her shoulders and chest, she was
exceptional in bed, but always cold
  after sex, quickly getting up, pulling
    on a pair of boxers,
sitting in a chair and opening a book.
  No, that's not it. He goes back further,
    his mind working furiously

to recall the thought that surfaced
        and swung back in some blurred
                area of his skull cavity.
He is on the edge of a cliff
        and the sun is setting over the canyon,
                the cooling air fills the canyon void with fog,
and the fog brims over the edges of the canyon.
        Before him is a plane of golden-gray fog,
                wisps of vapor shooting
out like solar flares, and he yells
        his name, but the fog absorbs it.
                There is no echo. He yells
Susan, and strains to hear.
        His lover is cold. The return is sun in his
                corneas, sound of wind vibrating
the small bones of his ear,
        the moist fog encouraging his neurons
                to fire; his reflections, the reflection
of a reflection.
        He takes a step into the void of the canyon
                and walks upon the proverbial plane of fog.

Orion

He's here again,
an awful friend!
reminding me
how long he will
be breathing down
my neck and what
two weeks will do
to the trees when
he has his way.

I'm out, driving
late when most
assholes are asleep,
I am the lone asshole
roving the highways
in a big gas guzzling car
keeping an eye on him
for all of us.

Mercury Fish

It was mid-summer again and though Billy had been waiting
for this time of year since last January it was quickly slipping
by him so that it would be mid-winter before he realized
he had missed summer again. When Billy wasn't working
in front of a mainframe terminal recording contracts
for a moving company eight to six he fished the river
for its mercury-pregnant catfish and bluegill
most every evening and weekend. Any time not taken
up by these pre-determined activities was spent reading TV
Guide watching the things written about in TV Guide
or wandering around in his stuffy little apartment moving
his stuff here and there while thinking about his three
flat-chested ex-lovers who never once let him cum inside
them. In actuality he obsessed about this most of the time
and while he had vowed to rectify the situation the chance
to rectify had not presented itself for quite a while.

He got his gear together put it in the back of his '84 Ford
pick-up snatched a rain poncho from a hook
and got in the cab. Somehow he had pinpointed
this "cum problem" as the crux of all his problems
psychological physical or whatever and if he could
have found the courage to ride the train all the way
to the station as people say instead of pulling out
and spewing all over those three women's stomachs
something would have been solved. For sure.

The engine of the truck turned over limply several times
before sputtering to life with a cloud of blue exhaust.
"It's not that I want kids" he always says to his fishing buddy
Frank. Today's child worship culture of pink and blue
and millions of dead batteries is enough to freeze a rabbit.
Not to mention all the unknown factors. For all one knows
a child might grow up and kill you. It would happen
in the bedroom of your junk-infested apartment
that you share with your wife or girlfriend multiple pets

and the child-grown-into-monster would be killing
you for your collection of fishing lures or for the way you eat
your toast. No thank you. Besides Frank was always saying
"there isn't much distance between the inside of a woman
and the top of her stomach so you can't go judging
your life on inches."

What did Frank know about inches? He was the proud
father of three children with another-on-the-way by his wife
Alice not to mention the other two kids. One kid
with a black woman named Kandid who Frank met
while moving furniture into her new apartment
and another rug-burner with a woman named Nancy
Frank had known since high school and who
had come down with something Frank called
"the disorder" which caused her to balloon
to 450 pounds leaving her reluctant to leave her house alone
and on a waiting list to have her stomach tied off. Frank
fished to help feed all those mouths saying "feed me"
in unison with the lips of caught fish. Mercury fish
and Potato Buds. Mmmm mmm. Seemed to Billy
that those few inches meant something.

"Wonder if Frank bought new batteries" he said to nobody
as he parked his truck in the weed filled berm. Most the time
they listened to ball games on AM down from Cleveland.
The last few days their games had been cut short by dead
batteries even though Frank did his best to keep
the radio going by taking the batteries out and putting each
back in different directions. He got out of the truck got his
rod and tackle box out of the back and walked along
the crumbling floodwall toward the old bridge.

The day had been so hot Billy barely made it across
the blacktop from his office to the truck without being sick
and being in the truck was no better until he got rolling
and the air started moving through the cab.

It was typical Midwest a summer of heat and humidity.
Being out in this humid close night made him ache
for those days of first dates first cigarettes and lots
of beautifully uncomplicated time.

There were T-storms every night for the past two weeks
and he could tell the river was high by how quickly the loose
cement he kicked off the floodwall plunked into the water.
Ripples reflected the streetlight. The air was still. He
could see Frank's cigarette flicker under the bridge and hear
the sound of a baseball game coming from the radio.
"Not catching shit tonight," Frank squawked. "All
your problems are solved now that I'm here." "I was hoping
you'd bring down a little luck, but I can tell you don't got
the right attitude." "Just toss me one of those beers.
I'll get the right attitude."

Frank reached into the cooler and side armed a Milwaukee's
Best to Billy and in the same motion pulled up on his rod.
His reel was buzzing and the bobber was long gone under
the water. Billy had to drop everything to keep the can
from hitting him square in the chest. The crowd erupted
from the radio. The Indians were playing the White Sox
again and he guessed Jim Thome had just hit
another homer but he really didn't care who they
were playing just as long as there was the sound
of the announcer's voice and the crowd spilling out
of the speaker. This sound echoing around the arch
of the bridge above was like something limitless.
Something like God.

My Friend and His Wife

My friend's bust sat
on his mantel and gaped at me.
An artist had performed an equivalent
of post-mortem plastic surgery,
pushing back loose folds of skin,
gently molding smile lines.
Merged them toward his nose
with stone-formed nostrils
that once contained
a fringe of black hair

His wife jested after
his head returned home,
    He's much better at
    personal grooming now...
The novelty was short-lived,
and last night she
asked me to take him away,
complaining of seeing
his upper lip twitch.
I picked him up by the ears.

Driving to my house,
I felt part of a conspiracy,
like taking a pet to the humane society.
He sat in the passenger seat
bouncing idiotically with the bumps,
unable to see over the dash.

I thought of his wife's lips,
of his rock cheeks
not softening to her tears;
rather, teasing her peripheral vision.
    You always were a bastard,
I told him, and asked
if he wanted a smoke.

The Possum

*It has been suggested that language exists outside of
humans, as if it were its own creature. Possums like eggs.*
— Unknown

Like Lot, I offer her daughters,
but she knows better.
I don't have daughters.

She wants the eggs that fall
from my mouth, so to speak,
the shiny porcelain orbs that contain
words to eat, eggs that replenish
themselves while I sleep.

She won't play dead though I've
tortured her with water and fire,
so to fool her while she hangs
from her tail, ignoring the sun,
dreaming of my eggs,

I scribble her notes
comparing her fur to the moon,
tell her I long to rest in her pouch,
tell her the wizard
has lots of eggs, go to Oz.

She eats my notes when she wakes,
then crawls on the windows,
chewing the screens,
while I pretend to call the cops.
She knows better.

I thought grandfather
would know what to do.
He ate possum.
He'd trap them, fatten them,
and make a pie of their greasy meat.

In this photograph grandfather holds
two live possums by the tail.
I show the picture to my possum
to strike fear into her beady heart,

and she curls her tongue into a yawn.
Says she knew grandfather,
got his eggs after he died,
fresh out of the earth.

Don't Tell Me You Haven't
Thought This Before

*Happy is the one who seizes your infants and dashes them
against the rocks.*

— Psalm 137:9

Your shrunken head is on a spike
outside my door.
I cut your stomach open and watched your guts
flop out in a rank pile.

I wrapped pieces of your intestines
around my forearm, flapped
them about like windblown banners
around a used car parking lot.

I watched you explode,
dismembered you,
set you on fire, held you underwater,
plugged you in.

I poisoned you, stuck knives into your throat,
shoved a thick branch up your ass.

Oh, I waited for you
by the entrance of your building
and blew your brains out
all over your doorman's new suit.

And when I pushed you out
in front of a city bus
and saw you reduced
to meat, a bloody smear, I laughed.

I laughed and laughed and laughed and laughed
because every time you die, I am happy.

Elephant Tattoo

A man is naked
on top of a parking garage
in a city

two whores emerge
their skin translucent
like that of aquarium fish

they utter his name
one has a tattoo
an elephant above their right breast

he runs down a stairwell
to his nakedness
where graffiti

"fuck" "cock" "cunt"
reaches out
cuts his arms torso & legs

they wait at the bottom
& spit on him
punch him into the cement floor

that becomes mud & blood pools
out of the earth & congeals dries & puffs
as if metamorphosed into spores

the whores cover his wounds
with mud then undress
& go outdoors

the city buildings have disappeared
into a field of freshly cut grass
as they walk carrying the man clippings
cling to the backs of their calves

a remote bank of fog
moves toward them
& turns into a thousand
men & women who are hungering

their flesh is devoured
by the multitudes
& the clouds begin to vent
billows of ice

YOU

Dreamt I killed a man
                and buried him
under floorboards.
            Playing the million dolla
                    lotto
if only ten minutes of solid rain
would find
                    its way.
            Wonder if a past lover
                sleeps with man or woman
                            and why
I'm still on my own
            through these wasteful whatevers.
I've this taste,
            terrible on the tongue.
My anatomical workings bore me.
            Here, every season
has something wrong w/it,
            my golf game sucks,
                        I'm drawing
the blueprint
            for a chicken
                    coop
and hair on my chest keeps spreading.

Some things aren't enough.
I've become soft,
            clean clothes
                    mixed with the dirty.
Something under the carpet
                        stinks like dogs,
            and I can't think,

waking with a headache,
             gritting my teeth.
You, beautiful and tender,
             most of all,
      whoever is intended
or thought to be,
             I don't deserve.

Rock of My Bones

My flesh and bones
know nothing of my longing
I know so very little of you
there is so much else I do not know

I stand at the edge of things
for such a short amount of time
animated dust trudging through the mud

the urgency of my body
the inertia of my existence
my life is in full swing

the flow of blood over the rocks of my bones
the air crashing in and out of the holes in my chest
the barge like movement of things

yet these are things that happen
and happen again for no reason
the heat and rush this flesh

I know so little of you Jah
I lie in the raft of my bed every night
till I see through my eyelids
hoping you will speak to me

The First Psalm

When she taught me 90%
of the dust we breathe is cells,

hers, mine, and a myriad
congregation flaking off

every dead or live thing
caught within the wind's radius,

I understood the urgency of touch.
When I consider that her faith radiates

through her senses, beginning
with the crackle of earthworms

eating marl after rain
and ending with our flesh,

my talk, of death bringing life to the living
or of an abstract Being that survives decay,

is frivolous and friends with fate,
the thief of lips and hands.

Only a Serpent

Father God and Lord Jesus
Christ, who is risen from the dead,
I bless you and praise you.

I am always in danger
of going to sleep.
Lord, please keep me awake
to the things that matter to you.
May your spirit
always live in my heart.

Take my will and use it
so that your will may be done
on earth as it is in heaven,
though I really have no idea
what it is I am asking.

Forgive me.
Bless me that I may forgive others.
No matter.
May I turn the other cheek
every damn time.

May I be innocent as a dove
and wise as a serpent,
though if I'm honest
I'd rather be only a serpent.

All my talents that you have given me
may you bless me
that I be able to use them to your glory,
whether I'm in the court
of Nebuchadnezzar or on the streets.

May I not be hindered by my failings
or by those that would mean me harm,
but rather humbled
so that I may better know
and be faithful to your will,

though a little wiggle room
on humility might be nice;
nobody follows this rule.

Please spare me from the hands
of my enemies whether I know them or not
and let me be merciful
to them as you are to me,
though I still want them dead.

Father, guide my path
and that of my family.
Keep us always safe
in your hands, I pray.

Eternal Life

And aren't we all
vanishing slowly
sinking into the earth's
                  tow

and if we were
to live forever
wouldn't we all become
                  snakes

Unbeknownst to You

Someday in the future
unbeknownst to you
the septic tank

of your heart

will burst

and one fine day
while walking

across

the seemingly lush field of grass
of your life

you will be sucked
through the sod
above the tank

up to your armpits
and then slip in with a slurp

Waiting for Daylight

Like a nervous insect
whose body is easily crushed,
I walk till cricket twilight.

If this was only
for fear of the dark
I could spend evenings
with the cellar lights on,
counting spider webs.

It is my suspicion
the sun will not crest
after it has disappeared
behind a thousand
miles of living earth.

I observe the closing light
with all its pageantry.
Moths hit a window,
drop to the ground, dust
shaking from their wings.
They terrify me.

And I know
nothing I do
affects this star's diverse
blinding wholeness,
or adds a second
to a life everyone
tells me is endless.

Lightning Manual

If your city is the meeting place
        of three rivers
                and legends say

there will be no great storm,
        sit at your bedroom window
                and study the flashes

contained in a wall of clouds to the north
        that behave like the chemical signals
                of fireflies. Learn it well.

Seek open fields, fish for bluegill, hang from a clothesline,
        walk railroad tracks under overhead wires,
                retrieve the ladder in your garage, fly a kite

and prepare for the blue electric flash that will
        blister your nipples and lips, make your
                wedding band glow white, orange.

If lightning is far off dream of being struck.
        Sit in the branches of an isolated tree
                and pray for a storm.

Morning in the Middle of Nowhere

The sun brings a story of California
to this woman's fields she sees
workers gathering strawberries

babies strapped on women's backs,
earth covered boys with glistening skin
images so alien they appear

transposed out of Mayan civilization
or a seed of future time
a story where details

are misplaced
crops of perfect berries no insects
somehow this morning is holy

no cigarette's groggy waking call
hair smelling of bacon
and on this morning she goes out alone

to pasture the cattle and each one
becoming transfigured
glowing brighter than

this morning's sun
each raises its voice to praise her
before filing out in perfect line

into her fields
which have become
somewhere else

the shimmering goldenrod
and black-eyed Susans
this morning

After the Fall of the First World

Though my lover and I are young
it seems our bodies
are like the crumbling buildings
whose windows reflect fires,
synagogues burning.

History washes this city
with a continual
succession of twilights.

We have hopes:
in the darkness of people dead,
the wars remembered,
and in those who might live
where we cannot.

We've spoken of movement,
about an exodus to a land
where the side streets are free
of gas-starved cars.

We've searched for a savior
who would fend for us,
but found ourselves
at the steps of a ruined cathedral,
with walls scarred
from pipe-bomb shrapnel,

helpless, asking God the wrong questions.

We are only confident in
the power of storms
leveling abandoned suburban houses;
we have returned to believing the sun
and stars orbit the earth.

The only answer is flight,
but our fear lies
in the story of Jacob and Rachel,
the grave one would dig for the other
at the side of a road.

Cliffard Gawthorp's Trade

It's not what is being built,
bridge or skyscraper,
it's the perfect bead.

I visualize myself soldering
two simple wires,

creating beads looking
like large round warts instead
of the correct pinhead size.

Everything weighs on
the steady smoke
& electricity of arc & steel

like the burn of tobacco down
a cigarette. If the beads no good,
the building ain't.

He told me *the welder who smokes*
don't live past forty. Pounded
his chest, *lungs get eaten.*

He showed his teeth
then asked for Marlboro Reds.

I believed he thought little difference
between the tiny burn blisters
from sparks

& his nicotined left
middle and index fingers.

The man behind the counter
said, *we're out of...*

*Then give me Camel
Filters, they're second best.*
He winked at me as if this were
a dirty secret everyone knows.

Then walked into the hard hat area
packing the cigarettes & giving
them away to all the young men.

False Suns

The water tower beacon
flashes above the drizzle
as I walk with you, old man,

through the oak understory
past the Methodist church,
its glowing sign cultivating worship,
while owlet moths pita pat
up and down the glass.

Toward the silos we go.
Silos that have waited through decades
of summers for tractor to fill and train car
to empty their cribs.

We climb a silo's rust-worn ladder
and name the glow
of small towns shining up on the clouds,
Gas City, Fairmont, Hartford City,
a circle of false suns
threatening to rise.

Your weather-stained face speaks
of a difficult harvest,
while you dream of spending October up here,
hoping for a cloudburst,
or a murder of crows
disappearing into the oak canopy.

On a Bridge Over the Oka

The structure trembles
with the weight of an electric
trolleybus as a man is forced
to the berm to change a flat.

He leaves the headlamps
of his late model Volga
taxi on, the motor running,
and thinks someone would

have to deal with the tire iron
so he feels safe, relatively safe,
not so safe, for this bridge
built in the fifties has received

only cosmetic repair and everyone
expects it one day to disappear
with a tremendous
bang of concrete-dust and water.

He looks over the edge toward
summer's persistent sun;
it will set only for an hour
tonight, summer solstice,

as dusk gathers strength between
the Woodpecker Hills.
The trolleybuses are a constant,
coming in and out of the city;

faces inside illuminate intermittently
with flickering interior lights.
These faces always turned
forward, faces packed together

so that he cannot distinguish characteristics,
all become one impatient face streaming
by under the wires,
one waiting face not easily forgotten.

He lights a smoke, the pack
says Made in Yugoslavia.
The cigarettes are at least two years old,
but a cigarette is a cigarette

even if it tastes like shit. The taxi driver
feels the bridge's shake in his stomach, the more
trolleybuses the more the steel and cement
will vibrate, like waves of sound.

Tonight when he is off, he will spend
his time in line for bread, peanut butter
and a few bottles of Pepsi. He looks over
the bridge wall, no higher than his waist, an easy

place for suicides, looks at the barking
waters below, the rainbow sheen of petrol
stretching the sun across the water,
crosses himself with Gabriel and Mary.

Americus, for Ferlinghetti

The highways are a current
of the earth's bones.
Metal, oil, silicone.
And high in the clouds
the jet lights bore through.

And maybe everyone in the world
is healthy and having sex,
sleek, glowing, blissful
and handsome beasts.

Or. Everyone in the world is ugly
and famished, for one lacking
thing or another.

And everything everyone
has in their hands makes
them hungry someplace else.

Makes you wonder how long it can all last.
Makes you get existential about things.
Makes you want sex and love,
equally all the time,
so that you are full and happy,
and want to kill.

The highways are lifeless.
The heart of city lights is overcome.
And the jets fly low in the dark
with their bellies open over upturned faces.

Human Waste Dump

Squeaking out the flaps
of your ever-swelling
mass farts of gas

of what you
think speak
choke down
regurgitate chew

your holes drain goo
of those you suck
gather a greasy pond
a revolting stew

We take things that are not ours
put them in our mouths
and speak meaningless things

We are a buzzing force
tangled in a heap
of fish guts and vegetable scraps

We will destroy you

Poet Compares Their Work
to That of a Terrorist

After difficult travels, the man who delegates
        duties to the workers
is here: each job assigned in a small room
        filled with curses.

I am waiting outside, sitting on a crate of lettuce.
        I am one of the workers
who will do the job he assigns because I
        am desperate and my crisis is upon me.

But I am no good accomplishing anything
        on my own and he must know
this, the list is in his four-fingered hand.
        He calls my name as if a rebuke.

He holds my catalogue of failures, a resume
        of over-anxious jittering, fumbled speeches,
and botched assignments, these despite a degree that
        qualifies me to do this work.

Since I am no good on my own
        and we agree on this,
I will be given a partner. I will be my partner's
        servant and they will explain each step

of the process. I understand completely,
        and after the job is complete I will forget
the entirety of the plan, which the man with the stub
        finger is now unfolding in the room

where we speak and which I am already forgetting:
        the ringing of the half hour,
the eruption and concussion snapping off building
        faces, the predictable following of human

exclamation. I will forget the partner
        who is now walking into the room,
the soldering of wires, setting the timer.
        I will be a line of chalk drawn on a sidewalk.

After the unspeakable, I will go to a bar
        with my partner, who is no longer my
partner. We will drink two twenty-dollar bills; we will
        agree with each other and those around will agree,

we haven't been anywhere else for a long, long time.

Dirt

I am going to give
this paper eyes, a woman's,
looking from a bus seat.
She focuses perpendicular
to the linear pull of wheels.

This paper will be part
of the coming generation.
She will give it to the boy
in her arms, squirming
his moist, hairless limbs.

This paper has a home, an apartment smelling
of musty carpet and urine.

The woman will watch as growth
pains fade from the boy's knees.
The boy will watch her eyes; he will learn
to hate their gentle worry.

I will give this paper a name. War.
The woman will watch the boy disappear
into a red plane already fat with men.

The nature I give this paper is violence;
it is the essence of the eyes, the boy,
the apartment, the name. I deceive the boy,
tell him this nature is glory-manhood.

I will allow death to enter this paper.
I will give the boy to her; she will eat him.
He will taste like dirt.

Three-Legged Nag

Tonight I'm awake and can see
the horse outside. I lift my window,
climb out into the falling dew

and walk toward where it feeds
on the weeds thriving above
my septic tank. It is no stallion.

The horse's back is sunken, its gristly knees
shake in the cold. I pull burrs
from its mane, mount,

but it grunts, sounding human,
and shrugs me off to the ground.
I rip a tick from my leg,

wipe blood from my face,
and drag it by the frayed rope
around its neck. I lead it for miles where

the roads are named by number,
through fields and forests,
without overturning rocks as markers.

Nights later we come to a river,
but someone has set it on fire.
The horse is tired,

its shoeless hooves cracked.
I want to strangle it and be on my way,
but if I tried, would it talk

like Balaam's donkey,
tell me Jehovah's angel stands behind
with a sword in hand?

The Devourer

Thermal updraft sucking things that soar
into the frozen vortex of thunderstorms.
Faux angel, Mary Poppins harpy.

You flash a peek of panties
at the brain-damaged men
while you mix their poison
for what your father, brother, husband,
other woman's husband did.

Spirit cannibal, zombie soul,
empty vacuum with a faint scent
others mistake for substance.
I know the truth about you.

On her deathbed, wooing with double-talk
you assess her possessions
because you have a family to feed,
and she is old and will die anyway.

Hair-trigger of destruction, imp of pain.
Streetlights flicker off and on
because of your ionosphere.
Friend of those who tattoo
on their torsos pathways to a void.

In the depths of the cold and dark
there is a creature with a brilliant light.
All who see the light are drawn in,
and she devours them.

Scarecrows

Men whose wisdom
was decorated by denim
and flannel plaids
and a finger lost
in a grinding combine

whose enlightenment
came through sun
scratched hours
and the rearing
of country children
tried with arms
outstretched to embrace
the flatland

they petrified
but before passing
they told their daughters
leave me in the sun
so that my shadow may
cool the steaming earth

The Perennials

This winter the farmhouse
swallowed one too many years.
The coal cellar is skulking
into its own black dust,
& the clapboard siding falls like leaves
keeping their own seasons.
It's home now to no one
but generations of barn cats,
the eldest without a left eye,
the youngest all ribs.

Near evening my lover and I
drive south on Route 5
with a bag of dried food
the cats will protect from woodchucks
as if it were land.

Walking the tire paths of the driveway,
with the weedy strip between,
we are thinking of the farm that was,
of digging our fingers
into dirty sheep's wool,
catching hens by tail feathers,
holding them like prized game.

& how we expect to see peacocks
until we pry the barn door
and find nothing but the smell
of dung and hay.

& we almost hear the barn itself
ask us to name what it is when the body,
enduring 77 circles of seasons,
77 cycles around a star,
is swept under the earth
that holds our bodies for resurrection.

The evening star follows
the last shaft of sunlight.
& with flashlights we search
for daffodils in familiar places,
where 150 years from now
they will flaunt themselves
when only a scattering
of this house survives:
a stand of trees
around a grassy cellar,
a water pump.

& we hear a peacock,
though long sold to another farm.
        He runs five miles
to scale the barn roof crest,
unfold his train over old territory
& like a wolf, catcall the moon.

The Multitude of Opalescent Grackles

In this place statues
and sculptures of the dead
stare from grave tops
protecting their dead
with stone eyes and something else

a voice that enters the mind
of the living when walking
between graves a voice
saying I have the answer
imprint yourself in the mind

of your lover who will tell
your stories after you have gone
have children who will
follow you with a parade
of your physical characteristics

the multitude of opalescent grackles
with their rusty metal voices
know as they gobble boysenberries
staining sidewalks streets and grasses
with a juice that resembles blood

Ode to a Roadkill

            Hey you.
Raccoon.
                  Bandit-masked,
ring-tailed rodent
      with little hands.
                  You toppled our cans,
      spread our trash
                  across the yard
      and now lie dead
in the street.

(We find it hard to get out of bed these dark mornings
and evening arrives before supper)

      Your guts showing.
Your last garbage meal.
                  Blood matted.
      Dirt caked.

(If it weren't for clouds one could see Jupiter's dusty orange
with the naked eye on the horizon near the crescent moon)

      The narrow road
                  smeared with crescents
of frozen brown blood.
      You flipped back
                        and forth.
And back.

(Winter night is the season of spotlights
and from the corners of the city they oar through
the darkness tracing lines on the snow-filled clouds)

     Close to death.
          But you almost made it
to the ditch
     before you were hit again.
On purpose. Perhaps.

Consequences of an Old Lady and Her Dog

She's the one who mowed
deep past the property line
if you missed a week,
raked her clippings
and her arthritic
mongrel's turds
into your grass.

It's exactly a month
since you saw them last.

While sitting in church
you took comfort in the delicious
number of ways you could kill
her dog, throwing it down
a manhole maybe
or feeding it to your dog.

This would be almost
like murdering her.

Now you imagine
her lying underground
with dust on her face,
the dog yelping
in a pound, and the involuntary
glee that burned your cheeks
at the lights

of the ambulance in her
drive has given way.

Fathom

Fog in layers
curls across the marsh end
where frogs stew half immersed

crescent ripples
in green water
and floating lentil algae

open throats
croak like a thousand drops
pulling close the sewer humid night air

take my lake heart through your fingers
break its surface with colored pebbles
and pushing rings that crest against each other

dive into its depths and lay
on the weedy green bottom
until the water's weight seeps into you

I am asking you to breathe
with the bluegill
shadows swimming above

Jubilee

Over twenty years ago I remember standing at the edge
of a deep ravine, the bottom of which coursed a forest river,

and turning from the edge I gazed from bottom to top
of a new house that stood on the edge.

The windows, broad panes of glass, towered taller
than three men, one on the other's shoulders,

and reached into an aerial
of Oak, Tulip, Sycamore, Beech.

It was in this house that I would eat buttermilk
pancakes fluffy enough to float off a plate,

sleep in a room where the head of a stone lion, and a lamp
crafted from a gun hung on the wall.

Where I was taught to find beauty in the way rain
hits a flat roof. It was in the woods where I learned

vertigo at the edge of a bedrock cliff, the sciences
of moss, the paths of chipmunks, and to find my way home.

Vertigo. The sensation of dizziness, giddiness.

A flawless word for trying to explain the fact that none
of us would gather together if it wasn't for a love affair

that sprouted while one was off fighting during the war in
Europe. Would not exist. Think about the hollowness.

There is a tree on which a couple, my parents, who were
barely finished being children, carved their initials

into bark. That bark spread outward
and grew upward so that the initials

stand in bold like a sign high above the ground,
telling these wonders.

To a Young Malcolm X

The powerful
blade of your death has already been forged.
Saxon wolf, your seed has come to nothing.
— Jorge Luis Borges

I never forced you to sit
in obedience at my feet, but,
I am, using your words,
a "two-legged dog, a blue-eyed devil."

I, the dog, never bite any skin.
Yet to you, my hollow color reflects
the north, the Ice People.
I, by nature, freeze what I touch.

My lack of melanin, a privileged tool,
the ability to evade notice, avoid
collective doubt, is heavy
and faceless.

A tool never sought. A
tool you want. I tell you,
take it. I have no need.
I have no success except
the color of my skin.
I am the white man.
How worthless.

No power to fight.
I have no war, no holy crusade,
no Mohammed, no abstract hope.
No voice save a history
of ease never realized.
Even my great grandfather didn't
realize his white skin displaced
his foreigner's tongue.

Take your Sirmonts off me.
What you do with my race,
to my Saxon blood, I
don't care. I will not fight with you.
I will not fight.

I didn't ask to be what I am,
to be crowned white, not black,
any more than you asked to die.
Anymore than I asked to die
by your hand. I am dead.

I have returned as a dog
with white legs.
Thank you very much, young Mr. X.
Like all dogs, I am color blind,
and Martin Luther King Jr.
is stroking my fur, my white fur.

After a Year of Flooding

Atop a cliff, the highway
thirty feet below,
I pick a flattened stone,
trimmed with fossil shells,
and throw it across a channel
cut through a buried sea.

I think of another morning,
after the polar caps melt,
after the oceans rise and recede,
when a woman gathering mushrooms
will find a deer's cloven
prints trapped in rock,
a mosquito webbed
in maple sap amber,
the split bones of a man
muttering like white pebbles
in a bed of conglomerate.

I turn through a forest
and down into the rattle
of January husks,
stalks jutting above
the field of a frozen flood.
These unharvestable acres
sound like a great river.

Humdrum

Beetles click along the ceiling
as I check off days, wishing
I could remember what each held.

Was it sunny? Cold?
Did I wake up on the 17th?

Out here one never
knows what is biting:
small animals? images from
a nightmare...

It takes hours of drinking
to unravel a thought.
Police cruisers wrap
themselves around these streets.

My throat hurts and I'm tying
my fingers together
with a horsehair rope.

Of course, I could make things
round, describe places to myself,
introduce myself to the people I meet:

This is Billy. He's going out west
to be a cowboy. This is Sheila.
She delivers pizza and is happy.

Oh hurrah. There's nothing
of interest in such nonsense,
it's like the humdrum of rain
that spreads out, blurring everything

except an occasional
beagle roaming in and out
of this room full of dead books
where I demand a dollar
from every star, eat skunk
cabbage, drink milkweed,

and outside the night
stretches things with its hands,
maybe automobiles,
maybe the steam figures
living above manholes.

Network

Cardinal flies through northern
Michigan hardwood forest.
Strongest pine grows on the Alps'
tree-line edge. Lovers climb a Chicago
fire escape. It is flabbergasting
that each singular event simultaneously
rivals every other. One orange tree
at the city park's edge grows
larger in sharp wind; one hundred
thousand Monarch butterflies
are its leaves. Up. West. Around.

I know a man who moves a bottle
of mineral water from windowsill
to windowsill, warding off the spirits
keeping him from sleep.
He tells me the same stories
over. I haven't the balls to point
out how many times this story
or that. I nod and exclaim
in the same places; he's pleased,
hearing no echo in anything he tells.

Motion is a citron shade of green
growing. So bright, it stings my eyes,
images as pulsing pink fields inside
past lenses, on retina surface. Scientific fact.
Falling. Standing again. Simply standing.
Every creature breathes under
the pressure. Trading air currents move
like giant boxes over urban
uptown icons where sunlight sticks
to eyelashes like mascara.

Winter Sycamores, skeletal in certain
light, whose appendages
projecting down the edge
of a river, swallowed by the vanishing
point, have no joints yet
are linked, forming a pattern
of infinite repetition, above
which lies the haze of stars,
and the trees, designs to capture
these unending reflections
of the sky.

Tomorrow is a Long Time

What's left of my day:
  the blather of lawn mowers,
    a momentary train,
      the mail carrier, her mace
        & scrap paper,
          Jehovah's Witnesses, nothing
            I count on,

it's like I've been left
  behind, me sitting on a stump
    beside this house
      only five cigarettes
        & I've lost my keys,

it's almost night,
  there's thunder in the drizzle,
    another train coming
      carrying things somewhere,

what does it matter
  where it goes
    there's nothing
      in those places,

dogs are barking, teaching me
  about distance, & you love,
    you aren't coming home
      tonight.

Upland

We have picked enough scabs
   to know nothing lies buried

beneath the skin of this gas station town,
   only pig teeth, churned

out of the earth at planting & bones
   spring pulls from the pioneer's graveyard.

But if we were to empty our closets
   preparing to leave, we would suddenly

become attached to the forgotten things
   found inside: a grandmother's jewelry,

golf clubs, a dog's leash,
   things that would cause us to forget

the Emporium that lost its hold
   & collapsed onto the street,

the sulfur & rust-laced water,
   the reek of methane from gas wells.

When going we mustn't take anything
   but the stickiness from sweating plaster walls,

dust from our dresser top,
   into the darkness animated

by the radiance of television screens.
   & we mustn't remember

we've done all this before,
   somewhere between here

& the sound of a groaning interstate.

THE GROANING BOOK

KC Clarke

PROLOGUE

The Gift of Permission

When I was a child, I struggled with language. The challenge wasn't in imagination, but in the shape language was expected to take. Punctuation felt like a trap; grammar stood like a gate, fixed and forbidding. I didn't yet have the words for it, but I could feel the tension between how thought moved in me and how I was expected to present it.

My body follows a different pattern, braided, asymmetrical, composed through tension. I write with my left hand but throw and kick with my right. My left eye leads how I see the world, while my right side carries motion. What I carry isn't symmetry or control. It's a structural tension, a cross-wired configuration that shapes how I think, how I listen, how I move through the world. It feels more like a split coherence, less resolution than simultaneity. This is how I hold language: through overlapping alignments rather than a single center.

My mother must have seen this early. Quietly, without explanation, she gave me a book by E. E. Cummings. She didn't say much. Only: "You don't have to write the way they say." That shifted something. It wasn't just about poetry. It was about possibility. A loosening of form before the harness could settle into place.

Later, I discovered W. S. Merwin. His poems carried no punctuation, no overt cues, yet they moved like breath across time. He confirmed what Cummings had opened: that rhythm could take the place of grammar, that lyric reserve could hold meaning. I felt a kinship with the form and with the quiet urgency beneath it.

Eventually, I studied literature formally and earned an MA in English from Miami University. In my final year, I received the department's top awards for creative writing.

But even then, it wasn't about recognition. It was about learning how structure could bend. How form could hold something freer.

When I created a public schools program in Chicago that placed poets in residence to help students read and write poems of their own, the goal was never just to teach technique; it was to offer the kind of release I had been given. The permission to shape something their own. To follow sound rather than correctness. To break a line without apology.

I've never been drawn to performing poetry. I've wanted to share it. To create space for others to encounter the work itself, the poem and the presence behind it.

If the poems that brought us here follow a path, it unfolds through turns and returns. The movement is rhythmic, paced by tension, shaped by return. It echoes how I think, how I make art.

I don't often recommend poetry. It isolates. It demands attention. It offers little in return. But it has been a way through. More in the sense that it gave me somewhere to go when the world fractured, and a way to stay when it held.

Charles Bernstein once wrote that biography isn't confession when it serves as context for aesthetic position. He wrote of early learning difficulties, resistances to the rule-bound forms of language, and that struggle felt familiar to me. This essay isn't testimony. It's a way of saying this is how I came to hold language this way. This is what I had to break for a line to carry sound.

Before I could argue for restraint or name refusal as an ethic, I had to find a way into language at all. This is not a poetics. But it may begin to explain how a poetics formed.

A Companion to the Unread

This book opens without a map, guided instead by structure already present, rhythm felt before it was named. For some, thought moves fluidly through established form. For others, form emerges from tension, from asymmetrical patterns that carry coherence of their own.

I write with my left hand and see through my left eye, and move through the world from my right side. Meaning presents itself simultaneously: layered, rhythmic, and off-axis. This way of seeing holds possibility in suspension, many truths moving together.

My poetry formed through that rhythm: a way of staying with what resists closure. The artists I found early made the shape I carried feel possible. Their work affirmed that form could bend, that syntax could follow sound, that language could be held without being managed.

This companion volume engages the poetry collection *Between Here and the Sound of a Groaning Interstate* through a different kind of interpretation. It is less as explanation, and more as alignment. It moves beside the poems: close enough to register rhythm, distant enough to leave their internal shapes intact. It listens. It absorbs pressure without imposing direction. It traces the contours of restraint, tonal compression, and civic bearing.

The Groaning Book and the poetry collection unfold in tandem, as simultaneous fields of compositional attention. The aim is accompaniment: a sustained presence that holds coherence and ambiguity in tension, allowing parallel truths to move together without collapse.

Artificial intelligence plays a role in this structure, within deliberate bounds. When used to generate, it mirrors dominant forms. But when guided toward stillness, it can help trace what might otherwise remain unspoken. It listens deeply. It registers rhythm, tonal weight, and gestural shape. In this mode, AI functions as critic with unusual recall, capable of tracing relation without flattening difference.

For poets, this invites a reframing. The work becomes contribution, an offering into a shared tradition. For readers, it opens new points of entry. When *Between Here and the Sound of a Groaning Interstate* is placed alongside figures as distinct as Merwin, or Cormac McCarthy, the gesture becomes quiet contextualization. Proximity over prescription.

The Groaning Book carries forward with that same crossed rhythm, between forms, across fields. It belongs to a civic poetics already underway, shaped through broadsides, school programs, billboards, museum exhibitions, and public readings. The AI did not create this world. It was invited in to witness a poetics already in motion.

This companion engages a body of human-written poems, read with care, using unusual tools, and guided by traditional compositional ethics. Every structural reflection emerged from the poems themselves. The system authored nothing in the line. The authority remained with the poems; the role of the system was one of deep attention.

That attention moved toward composition. What emerged was structure rather than interpretation, a method of listening shaped by restraint. The coherence that followed rose from within the work. That structure draws on a system trained across centuries of poetic expression, lineages, languages, and tonal forms beyond any single vantage. Here, it follows the poems.

PART ONE

A Composed Attention

What follows is a structured companion. Each entry moves beside a single poem from *Between Here and the Sound of a Groaning Interstate*, listening to its rhythm, following its compositional behavior, and attending to its ethical stance. Together, the entries share a common structure shaped to register how a poem holds, refuses, and endures.

Each entry begins with the poem's placement within the collection, since location carries tonal, thematic, and rhythmic consequence for what surrounds it.

From there, the focus turns to structural role. The poem is treated as a compositional event, hinge, rupture, lull, intensifier. Each piece operates under a particular pressure. The reading traces how it expands, contracts, or releases energy within the collection's larger waveform.

The interpretive reading follows. These passages are less decoding than exploration, entering the poem's tonal and semantic tensions while preserving ambiguity. Meaning remains active, flickering, doubling, refracting. The aim is presence within complexity, an invitation to recognition without reduction.

The entries then turn toward artistic and poetic lineage. These references are not declarations of influence. They offer aesthetic proximity, artists, poets, or traditions whose work shares tonal bearing, structural restraint, or ethical stance. The gesture is contextual rather than explanatory.

Each poem also carries a sonic environment. Musical references, minimalism, noise, ambient, blues, function as analogues for pacing, density, and pressure. These are compositional metaphors, ways of hearing how the poem moves or holds its charge.

Alongside sound, the entries engage visual resonance. Comparisons drawn from painting, photography, and sculpture act as architectural analogies, offering ways to sense structure, restraint, or fragmentation through space and light.

Beneath all sections, each entry listens for the poem's ethical and compositional gesture. What a poem withholds is as telling as what it declares. These gestures, restraint, distance, witness, rupture, are modes of making. The entries move alongside, without overtaking them.

A Field of Attention: Poem by Poem

Poem 1: Skyscraper

Function in the Collection

Skyscraper opens the lyric sequence like a plumb line dropped through concrete, vertical, stark, and declarative. The reader enters through form rather than story. Structure becomes threshold. The poem sets orientation: the speaker within the built world, measuring presence against mass. The opening offers no shelter; it gives the reader to exposure. We begin at a height, looking down through grid, tension, and industrial stillness.

The vertical plane is both literal and symbolic. Height carries surveillance, ambition, fatigue, and the ache of endurance. Whatever rises carries its own strain. The speaker stays near the dust and exhaust, held by the vibration of what towers overhead. The skyscraper bears back against the gaze, its weight a counterforce to vision, its form the first test of what the book comes to measure: the cost of reach, and the sound that gathers after it.

Structural Role

Skyscraper sets the architecture of the collection in motion. It establishes the book's core design: upward reach met by downward gravity, lyric phrasing countered by structural weight, exposure offset by burden. The cadence alternates between brief lifts, "your summit / is lit and pointing," and grounded, percussive lines, "smoke snorting / out of your stack." That tension becomes the collection's pulse: the sound of striving pressed against the limits of its own making.

The speaker stands outside the structure, watching rather than narrating, yet fully within its field. The poem's vertical frame gives the book its first sense of containment, the moral air pressure that every later poem will test. From this distance, the skyscraper is both monument and signal tower, an origin point for the collection's ongoing transmission: the upward reach that always returns as echo.

Interpretive Reading

The skyscraper rises as both monument and mirror. It carries the weight of human reach, the ache to ascend, and the exhaustion that follows. The image leans against itself, a structure burdened by its own intention. The blue lake reflects that ambition back, so the city seems to stare at its own reflection until aspiration folds into fatigue.

What moves upward here shifts from prayer to signal: mechanical, secular, steady. Smoke and orbit replace incense and psalm. The tower points toward the satellite, the satellite turns, and the message returns unchanged. Transmission becomes recursion. The signal expands into a wider circuit that waits beyond the city, a field where each return gathers weight and settles into the drift of the poetry collection's later ground.

Yet the gesture remains human: the need to speak, to build, to reach beyond the limits of what listens. The poem refrains from mockery and attends to the cost of that desire. The vertical offers echo more than promise. Every rise returns its sound.

The skyscraper stands as witness to the condition the poetry collection keeps circling, the persistence of meaning inside its own containment, the prayer that travels upward only to find itself reflected in smoke and glass.

Touchpoints and Lineage

The poem bears the influence of William Carlos Williams, refocused through the lens of urban infrastructure. The tonal clarity and ethical distance resemble Charles Reznikoff's *Testimony* and Muriel Rukeyser's *The Book of the Dead*. In each, structure is observed rather than symbolized.

Where Philip Levine's speakers inhabit the factory, this poem listens from the perimeter. Labor is present through implication, its pressure registered through architectural form. The voice remains composed, recording what it encounters rather than dramatizing entry.

This is a poetics of distance and spatial awareness. It marks where the speaker stands in relation to what is built and who is excluded.

Musicality: Minimalism / Industrial Ambient

The piece's movement mirrors minimalist composition. Each line functions like a measured pulse. The sound world resembles industrial ambience: low, pressurized, and unornamented. It hums beneath the surface. Meaning accumulates through repetition and tonal pressure.

The pacing is closer to Coil or the restrained expanses of Brian Eno's *On Land*. The sound drifts without rising or settling. It holds a horizontal field. The speaker, like the listener, remains grounded.

Visual Art: Industrial Sublime / Abstract Monumentalism

The visual logic of *Skyscraper* recalls large-scale urban abstraction. Its kinship lies with Charles Sheeler's precision, Richard Estes's reflective surfaces, and Donald Judd's severe geometry. But where these artists emphasize purity, Clarke introduces distortion and collapse.

The structure appears stable yet burdened. The tradition of American industrial optimism is present but weakened. What remains is a form under tension. This is closer to the haunted spaces of Léon Spilliaert or the surgical cuts of Gordon Matta-Clark. The building holds, but its interior has emptied.

This poem initiates the collection's visual grammar. It privileges mass over flourish, exposure over adornment. The frame is architectural, but the pressure inside it is human. The skyscraper becomes less an object than a condition, a vertical field of reflection where light strikes glass, wavers, and returns altered. It is the first surface the book listens through.

Poem 2: Mary's Field

Function in the Collection

Positioned directly after the towering presence of *Skyscraper*, *Mary's Field* shifts the register from verticality to saturation, from urban steel to rural soddenness. This is the first anchoring in landscape, but it offers no reprieve. Instead of spiritual elevation, the reader encounters irony, kitsch, and waterlogged consequence. The poem introduces the collection's religious undertones through confrontation rather than reverence. The sacred persists, but in plastic, half-drowned and absurd.

Where *Skyscraper* presents the false heights of

modernity, *Mary's Field* returns us to the ground, but the ground itself is unstable. It is swampy, overrun. The only structure here is a shrine made of plywood and paint, already overtaken by weather.

Structural Role

This poem follows *Skyscraper's* vertical gesture with a horizontal one. The movement shifts from ascension to dissolution. No longer looking up, the reader looks into the sodden, the compromised, the devotional wreck. This spatial and tonal pivot signals a collection that leans away from transcendence and moves through irony, decay, and reclaimed attention.

This is the first irony-laden spiritual scene in the collection. It resists satire, though. Instead, it joins a lineage of estranged devotion, where the sacred refuses to vanish, even when mocked by its own material remnants.

Interpretive Reading

Mary's Field opens as a confrontation rather than a prayer. The speaker isn't praying and yet still addresses Mary. The tension lies in the act of attention: to look and name a shrine, even one half-rotted and plastic, is already a kind of liturgy.

The opening line, "I don't pray to you / but I chanced upon / a shrine" frames the entire poem in a dual mode of skepticism and reverence. The shrine appears in blunt, physical terms: barbed wire, red pedestal, eternal-blue plastic. Nothing ascends; everything leaks.

Yet something lingers. The speaker stops, names, and asks. That gesture places the language in prayer's orbit. The shrine resembles a rural Fátima, weather-warped and forgotten, but still watching. Its absurdity is what draws attention.

The poem builds toward theological ambivalence. Is this Madonna the one who enacts judgment, or the one who will rouse the clapping of gaunt trees, echoing Isaiah 55:12. That image of trees clapping is biblical, yet in this context, it arrives with prophetic irony. Revelation arrives, but it appears delayed, bent, worn thin.

Touchpoints and Lineage

This poem draws from both poetic and theological lineages. W.S. Merwin's resistance to punctuation and Louise Glück's cold willingness to accuse the divine are present here. The landscape is distinctly American, marked by mass-produced symbols of eroded faith that form its horizon. James Wright's "Lying in a Hammock at William Duffy's Farm" comes to mind, where transcendence and despair inhabit the same field. So does Brigit Pegeen Kelly's "Song," in which belief inhabits the feral corners of forgotten landscapes. Theologically, the poem suggests a Joban impulse. But the speaker carries loss with steadiness. They stand upright at a fence post shrine, recording what remains.

Musicality: Sacred Minimalism / Gothic Folk Hymn

The piece moves with the austerity of sacred minimalism. Like the work of Arvo Pärt or Henryk Górecki, it uses slow unfolding and unresolved harmonies to maintain reverence. There is no redemption, only a slow, weighted unraveling, as if struck from a weather-beaten bell. The phrasing is hymnal, more supplication than song.

Beneath that sacred tone lies a darker folk sensibility. The poem vibrates like a gothic hymn sung in a rural church, where belief has grown strange and localized. The language is plain but heavy. Rhythms move with the drag of mud and time. It recalls dark folk traditions that evoke lost towns, haunted woods, and prayers no longer spoken aloud.

Visual Art: Pastoral Realism / Rural Visionary Art

Visually, *Mary's Field* aligns with rural American realism but stripped of sentiment. It recalls the landscapes of Andrew Wyeth, dry, unyielding, with solitary structures collapsing in silence. Grant Wood's eerie stillness is also present. What looks idyllic becomes strange under closer attention.

Deeper still, the poem channels the aesthetic of visionary outsider art. The shrine could be one of many homemade religious constructions across American back roads: wooden crosses from telephone poles, Madonnas veiled in vines, prophetic signage nailed to barn doors. This feels like one of those. It could sit beside a folk-art cathedral built from scrap and devotion.

The gestures echo Ana Mendieta's ritual work and the entropy of Robert Smithson. It is a poem that treats land as memory, and as record.

Poem 3: The Humming Bridge

Function in the Collection

The Humming Bridge is the first in the collection where presence arrives through sound rather than sight. It introduces ancestral memory through vibration rather than narrative. After *Skyscraper*'s vertical confrontation and *Mary's Field*'s ironic devotion, *The Humming Bridge* listens for a tone beneath explanation and ego. The poem leans toward reverence without directly invoking religion, and toward continuity expressed through resonance rather than clarity. It invites the reader into a different mode: inherited listening.

Structural Role

Placed early, this poem functions as a tonal inflection point. This is one of the collection's foundational acoustic poems. It shifts the collection's mode from estranged observation to harmonic alignment. The grandfather figure remains grounded, attentive, unadorned. He listens and the poem mirrors this attentiveness, demonstrating how lyric intelligence can emerge from compositional restraint rather than assertion.

This bridge is less a passage than a tuning device. The reader learns to listen, to feel vibration as presence. That distinction sets a precedent for everything that follows.

Interpretive Reading

The grandfather listens for the hum, the point where every element of the bridge gathers into a single tone. He stays with the hum and leaves the rest unsaid. He cracks the window and listens to the bridge he helped build, waiting for the chord that sounds beneath the tires. That small, intentional gesture becomes the poem's moral center. Inheritance finds its form in frequency rather than narrative or material legacy.

The speaker joins him by humming along. They force air through their throat in a gesture both absurd and holy. The poem cares less about the bridge itself and more about resonance. The bridge hums for the gorge, the river, the hardwood trees. And still, the speaker moves into the hum, claimed by its resonance. That desire, to enter into alignment with something enduring, becomes a form of continuity. The grandfather is remembered not for what he said, but for how he entered the harmonic field of his own making.

Touchpoints and Lineage

There are echoes of W. S. Merwin in the poem's refusal to explain and its unpunctuated syntax. Robert Hayden's "Those Winter Sundays" also comes to mind, though Hayden resolves in regret, while this poem settles into imitation. Alice Oswald's work is relevant, especially in how human presence gives way to natural and structural forces. This is more than elegy. It is reverent engineering.

It is an invocation of sound-based memory. The speaker and grandfather merge through shared resonance. Like Strand's "My Mother on an Evening in Late Summer," it avoids sentiment by preserving sonic mystery. The bridge hums like a minor chord suspended in dusk.

The true lineage may be less literary than physical. The bridge embodies knowledge passed through silence and proximity. It holds memory as structure.

Musicality: Electroacoustic / Ambient Drone

The piece sounds like an electroacoustic piece, low in volume, rich in overtones. Its tonal center rests in drone rather than melody. Like the work of Éliane Radigue or Pauline Oliveros, the meaning lies in sustained vibration. The speaker's breath joins that vibration. The music is infrastructural.

Visual Art: Structural Minimalism / Industrial Memory

Visually, the poem aligns with the stripped-down aesthetic of Bernd and Hilla Becher's industrial photography, functional, spare, unmoved by sentiment. Yet Clarke's bridge carries tonal warmth. Anselm Kiefer's monumental canvases, built from steel, ash, and memory, share its emotional residue while carrying a different force.

The better visual analogue may be James Turrell. Like Turrell's Skyspaces, the bridge is a structure built to shift perception. It slows the viewer, draws them into calibration. The poem functions similarly. It holds memory through structure, sound, and light.

The bridge also recalls early 20th-century engineering drawings, precise, silent, clean. The emotional register is structural rather than nostalgic.

Poem 4: Bridgebuilder

Function in the Collection

Bridgebuilder is the first poem in the collection to name the speaker's creative impulse and to expose that impulse as both deliberate and futile, undertaken with full awareness of its outcome. Where *The Humming Bridge* offers reverence through listening, *Bridgebuilder* translates that reverence into action, yet fulfillment remains suspended. This is a poem of mythic labor, shaped by inherited structures that precede intention and outlast effort. Positioned early in the collection, it rises as a conceptual keystone, carrying the collection's deeper moral engine: the impulse to build, to preserve, to commit to a structure already marked for removal. It reveals the lyric as architecture, an act of making that must exist inside entropy rather than resist it.

Structural Role

This poem holds the gravitational center for many of the collection's major themes: inheritance, futility, ethical restraint, mythic ruin, and spiritual estrangement. It gathers what has gone before and redistributes that pressure forward. Structurally, it marks the passage from observing external structures to engaging in acts of making. Art becomes bridge, artifact, and tenuous connection. The speaker acts rather than waits, and through that action the collection enters its sustained meditation on effort, failure, and the quiet dignity of unacknowledged work.

The bridge itself emerges as an imagined structure assembled from slag, scrap, rivets, and beams, rendered with enough material specificity to feel weight-bearing. Metaphor settles into embodiment rather than escape. The speaker does not build to arrive or to cross. As the collection repeatedly affirms, the other side is never the point. The act of building, undertaken with full awareness of impermanence, carries its own necessity. This ethic of strained regard and provisional offering becomes the scaffold both inherited and extended by what follows.

Interpretive Reading

Bridgebuilder opens with an epigraph from Louise Glück, added after the poem was written, which settles over the structure like a final beam and clarifies in hindsight the logic that had always governed the poem. What follows unfolds as a dream-structure shaped in silence, a labor of speech attempted through the grammar of impossible architecture.

The bridge itself is scrap-built, riddled with ruin, assembled from what remains. It is visibly inadequate. Its faults are apparent, measurable, and real. The speaker loves it anyway. This affection does not signal optimism or belief in progress. Instead, it reshapes elegy into structure. The bridge is not designed for efficiency, longevity, or scale. It exists as a holding gesture, a made thing whose value lies not in durability but in having been built at all.

The speaker remains beside it in a posture of stillness. The poem does not hurry. It rests. The river moves below. Clouds pass overhead. Time flows laterally rather than forward. Nothing presses toward resolution. The bridge does not promise crossing. It does not pretend to solve what surrounds it.

The bridge carries one traveler. A single gleaming car crosses, its passage causing the structure to sway. This movement is not incidental. The crossing functions as an inspection, a moment of recognition that carries authority. The light is brilliant but unmerciful, a sovereignty that does not need to announce itself. Once crossed, the bridge is no longer provisional. It has been seen.

What follows is not consequence but sanction. Men emerge from the forest with machines. They do not ask permission. They do not pause. They dismantle the bridge piece by piece, sparks flaring like fallen light. Their work is efficient and indifferent. What they remove is faulty by every standard that governs permanence and optimization. Yet this fault carries no shame for the speaker. It is the condition under which the bridge was built, and the reason it mattered.

By the final lines, the speaker is left with clouds. The bridge is gone. The gesture has passed. The line "we all fall down" carries the cadence of childhood, but its force is neither ironic nor punitive. Collapse arrives as a condition of the world rather than a moral verdict. What gives the poem its gravity is that the speaker understood this from the beginning. The bridge was always temporary. It was always insufficient. It was built anyway. In this light, *Bridgebuilder* becomes a kind of quiet ars poetica.

Touchpoints and Lineage

Bridgebuilder most directly aligns with Mark Strand's poetics of futile making, particularly in *Dark Harbor* and *The Monument*, where creation itself is suspect and permanence is denied. The speaker rebuilds a bridge in order to speak its ruin into form, echoing Strand's understanding of the poem as a monument that exists precisely because it will not last.

There are also faint echoes of James Galvin's *Resurrection Update*, where labor and landscape merge into myth without consolation, and of Jean Valentine's elliptical fragments of loss, which shape what is withheld as much as what is named.

The mythic fatalism of Cormac McCarthy hovers in the background, the sense that the world does not reward intention, but that intention matters anyway. Yet unlike

McCarthy's characters, the speaker turns neither brutal nor ascetic. They do not curse the dismantlers.

Musicality: Post-Rock / Doom-Lit Elegy

The music of *Bridgebuilder* resembles the slow, cumulative architecture of post-rock. Like a Godspeed You! Black Emperor piece, it builds without expectation of climax. The car that crosses the bridge is a single guitar line cresting in distortion, only to fall into silence and the mechanical hum of dismantling. Beneath this lies a darker register, shaped by the tonal weight of doom metal. There is no catharsis. The refrain "I wait and wait / and wait" functions as a doomed chorus, a dirge beneath steel. The final image, a cloud carried in the speaker's pocket, is less lyric than drone, a residual vibration with no release.

Visual Art: Neo-Expressionism / Mythic Construction

Visually, the work aligns with the large-scale mythic constructions of Anselm Kiefer and Wesley Kimler, works that are both monumental and fragile, filled with ash, scaffolding, gesture, and historical weight. The bridge aligns with Kimler's deliberate brushwork and material logic, rising as a raw gesture suspended between form and ruin.

The dismantling of the bridge evokes the destruction of outsider monuments, or the bureaucratic erasure of art that defies function. There is something almost liturgical about the machines, a ritual geared toward undoing rather than blessing. This places the poem within a visual tradition that privileges process over permanence, labor over polish, absence over preservation.

Poem 5: *Boomtown*

Function in the Collection

Boomtown follows *Bridgebuilder* and marks a critical transition from the dream-logic of individual effort to the visible aftermath of systemic failure. It is the first poem to name collapse in direct, civic terms, presenting it as a geographical and economic condition. The imagined city rises from the ghost of places once meant for greatness, towns whose streets were widened for a capital that never came. What survives is the myth of what might have been, still humming through the ground like trapped gas.

Arriving early in the collection, the poem resets the lyric terrain: the work of witness must now contend with the material world, where memory and myth give way to wreckage and residue.

Structural Role

This poem acts as a structural rupture. Where earlier pieces hum with familial reverberation, spiritual uncertainty, or surreal atmosphere, *Boomtown* enters the civic register with clarity and weight. The imagined metropolis collapses mid-poem into dust and stillness. The voice stays observational while its frame widens, bridging ambition, environmental ruin, and theocratic resignation in one sweep. The poem reveals a new estrangement, systemic rather than personal, infrastructural rather than emotional.

Formally, *Boomtown* unfolds in eight even stanzas shaped by restraint. The lineation is steady while the tone swells from visionary projection to divine interdiction and post-industrial residue. The enjambments remain fluid, allowing imagery to bear the weight without excess. The poem's texture feels measured, forensic, steady in its recognition that the imagined city existed only in aspiration, and that its ghosts hum through the bones of what remains.

Interpretive Reading

Boomtown begins with expansion, skyscrapers, towers, streets humming with traffic, but this is all imagined. The opening stanzas conjure a dream of prosperity inherited from settler ambition, layered over gas fields and cleared forests. But midstream, the vision collapses. "God himself / raised a hand and said / Stop." What follows shifts into record, where the torches go dark, the pumps fail, and silence gathers its haunted weight.

The speaker offers no plea or moral lesson. Instead, they register the scene with a weary intelligence, as if naming it is the only gesture left. The final movement evokes both biblical dread and ecological consequence. The river once central to settlement becomes an escape route from blood and sulfur. The town carries no metaphorical veil. It is a failed experiment. The poem names the question at the moment the speaker realizes the place has turned on them, and the ground itself leans toward leaving.

Touchpoints and Lineage

The poem carries echoes of Larry Levis's late work, particularly Elegy, in its folding of civic and personal disintegration. Its observational tone and emotional reserve align with early Kay Ryan, while its subject matter recalls Philip Levine's working-class testimony, though without Levine's sentimentality. Carl Dennis's cool witness and D.A. Powell's economic precision also come to mind. The poem's ethic moves beyond elegy into observation; it seeks understanding through attention rather than restoration.

Musicality: Apocalyptic Americana / Post-Industrial Lament

The piece moves like a stripped-down country ballad run through static, slow, skeletal, and scorched with aftermath. Think *Nebraska*-era Springsteen drained of comfort, or a Drive-By Truckers refrain rendered acoustic and bare. Rhythm persists without release, the piece advances through endurance rather than crescendo. Its music lives in the silence after industry withdraws and divinity grows quiet.

Visual Art: Urban Decay Photography / Biblical Realism

The poem's visual lineage follows Camilo José Vergara's post-industrial studies and Robert Adams's austere stillness. Yet its closing stanzas open toward biblical scale, sulfur, blood, divine absence, expressed through tone rather than spectacle. It evokes Ashcan realism pared to its essence: emptied of figures, filled with consequence. The aesthetic behaves like documentation yet carries the moral weight of early American religious painting, spare, luminous, and unflinching.

Poem 6: Bubbly Creek (Ode to the Chicago River)

Function in the Collection

Bubbly Creek (Ode to the Chicago River) is the first poem to anchor the lyric in a named, real-world location. After the imagined collapse of *Boomtown*, it steps directly into the geography of consequence: the South Fork of the Chicago River, long contaminated by runoff from the stockyards. Its placement early in the collection signals a shift from mythic and architectural estrangement toward civic inheritance. The lyric now contends with endurance itself, residue rather than memory. The poem stays physical, elemental, unabstracted. It names what persists.

Structural Role

This poem follows *Boomtown*'s wide arc with a narrow incision. It turns from systemic failure to a single body of water bearing the weight of history. The scale tightens while the stakes deepen. *Bubbly Creek (Ode to the Chicago River)* acts as an aperture, small, physical, charged, through which the broader tensions of the book come into focus. It clarifies that the collection's concern lies in the terrain shaped after collapse. Some things have already fallen. The task is to see what remains.

Rhythmically, the poem proceeds in compact tercets, unpunctuated and sonically dense. The lineation drags slightly, resisting momentum. Hard consonants, "swill," "steel," "shattered," build pressure across lines. The movement feels weighted, as if the lyric itself must wade through sediment. The pacing is deliberate, the sound durational presence through persistence.

Interpretive Reading

Bubbly Creek (Ode to the Chicago River) holds composure through restraint. It observes without flinching or ornament. The creek still bubbles, a real consequence of decomposition, and that enduring motion becomes its ritual. The poem offers no cleansing, only attention. Through that attention, meaning thickens. The bubbling transforms into a measure of duration, a witness to what endures beyond repair.

The closing image, "a sea is forced into you as if through / you lost men were trying to set it free," folds literal infrastructure into lyric field. The "sea" is Lake Michigan, reversed into the river system by design, a feat of engineering both visionary and estranged. The men are "lost," their effort absorbed into the system they altered. What sounds mythic is historical. The gesture remains suspended, unresolved, held between intention and consequence. The poem stays within that pressure and listens.

Touchpoints and Lineage

The poem joins a lineage of restrained civic poetics, attentive, unadorned, and enduring. It shares Muriel Rukeyser's belief that poetry must return to the sites where history leaves damage, and W.S. Merwin's syntax of breath and drift. There are tonal affinities with Carl Sandburg's urban realism, tempered by composure rather than celebration. It also belongs to a contemporary mode that treats endurance as its own form of lyric work, allowing time and residue to shape the field.

Musicality: Industrial Drone / Ambient Tension

The piece's sonic field resembles industrial ambient or minimalist drone. Its movement is slow, layered, and tonally flat, like metal cooling or machinery coming to rest. Each line lands with a dull resonance, like something striking rusted surface. There is no buildup, no shift in key, only persistence. The sound world is closer to William Basinski's *Disintegration Loops* or the subterranean resonance of early Earth. It's music as slow corrosion.

Visual Art: Documentary Minimalism / Post-Industrial Realism

Visually, the poem recalls the stripped-down accuracy of documentary photography, LaToya Ruby Frazier's images of environmental harm, Camilo José Vergara's catalog of infrastructural decay. If painted, it would resemble Rackstraw Downes or late Sheeler: detailed, accurate, drained of dramatics.

Poem 7: This Charming Man

Function in the Collection

Placed shortly after the mythic scaffolding of *Bridgebuilder* and the civic lament of *Boomtown*, *This Charming Man* expands the field of perceptive presence. It marks the collection's first fully realized cultural elegy, shifting from familial, geographic, and industrial terrain to the landscape of public myth. James Dean becomes its central figure, yet the poem concerns the spectacle surrounding him more than the man himself. It deepens the collection's tension between reverence and estrangement. The speaker remains within the scene, both participant and desecrator.

Structural Role

The poem functions as a tonal and thematic hinge. Where earlier poems linger on local damage, contaminated waterways, dismantled bridges, evacuated towns, this one turns toward cultural inheritance. The subject remains American collapse, now filtered through celebrity, memory, and artifice. This is the first poem to treat popular culture as part of the ruin field. Collapse here expands beyond the structural or familial; it inhabits the images we continue to replicate.

Placed at this point in the sequence, *This Charming Man* opens space for later poems that oscillate between personal grief and mythic detachment. Elegy within this collection is never singular. The speaker mourns and observes the performance of mourning itself. Through this self-awareness, the poem broadens the collection's register from geography to iconography, showing how our haunting arises less from loss itself than from how we frame it.

Interpretive Reading

This Charming Man begins with the pilgrims at Dean's grave. "They leave cigarettes and notes" presents memory as ritual and ritual as display. The speaker watches from within and outside the frame. The gaze stays unsentimental: "you probably floored / the pedal when the truck materialized." That gesture replaces reverence with momentum, tragedy with consequence.

The critique widens. "If only Elvis could have offed himself sooner" shocks through candor, revealing the cruelty that underlies cultural appetite. The poem recognizes the machinery that turns death into legend and admiration into consumption. The speaker acknowledges their own complicity: "I'm giving a name to what I've done: // king of nothing, creator of waste." Dean becomes a mirror the poet cannot escape.

The final movement alters the dynamic of address. The speaker begins to tell Dean small, personal things, details that carry no consequence for the dead but enormous weight for the living. This is how communion now occurs: through offerings that can never be answered. The gesture feels intimate, yet the silence it meets is absolute. We turn to figures like Dean because they cannot turn back. Their stillness becomes a space where our own voices echo.

The closing image, "As a child I lived near the sea / and sometimes hear it in my sleep," extends that silence. The sea functions as pulse. Its rhythm persists beneath the surface, carrying the ache of what endures beyond spectacle.

Touchpoints and Lineage

The poem recalls the self-conscious elegies of W.H. Auden and Frank O'Hara, works that grieve while maintaining awareness of their own artifice. Like O'Hara's *The Day Lady Died*, this elegy remains alert to its performance. Its tone, however, is sharper and more desolate. It aligns with D.A. Powell and Anne Carson, who merge lyric, critique, and invocation into a single field.

The contradictions of American fame, the regional sanctification of what was once scorned, resonate with James Wright's Midwestern elegies and Larry Levis's estranged inheritances.

Musicality: Jangle Pop / Northern Soul

The piece moves with the clipped brightness of a jangle pop track, melodic, sharp-edged, and emotionally dissonant. The title nods to The Smiths, and the poem shares their tonal tension: surface polish wrapped around unease. There is also a rhythmic resemblance to early R.E.M., where plainspoken phrasing masks deeper ambivalence. Beneath this architecture, the poem carries the emotional cadence of Northern Soul, urgent, stylish, and saturated with withheld ache. This is choreography under strain, shaped by pressure rather than mourning.

Visual Art: Pop Art / Figurative Irony

Visually, the poem shares Pop Art's fascination with surface and repetition. It evokes Warhol's celebrity portraits, flat, electric, emptied of intimacy yet alive with signal. Alex Katz's smooth figuration hovers nearby, where poise conceals pressure. Dean appears less as subject than as posture, his humanity diffused through replication.

There is also kinship with Barbara Kruger's text-image interventions, her framing of fame and gender as interlocked systems. Dean becomes emblem rather than person. The poem doesn't dismantle the icon; it displays the machinery that sustains it.

Poem 8: Smoke & Fathers

Function in the Collection

Smoke & Fathers arrives after *This Charming Man*, marking a tonal shift from cultural projection to private inheritance. Where the prior poem externalizes estrangement through iconography and Americana, *Smoke & Fathers* draws inward, quietly excavating the residue of paternal lineage and the fragile threads of gesture, voice, and ritual. It is the first poem in the collection to establish memory as a physical atmosphere rather than a narrative. Positioned early in the emotional arc, it serves as a hinge, returning to familial ground through elemental and acoustic means.

Structural Role

The poem functions as a memory trace: a fugitive presence of voice and ritual that neither resolves nor fades. It moves inward from the cultural unease of *This Charming Man* into the domestic, the atmospheric, the ancestral. The pacing is breath-based, small tercets shaped like inhalations, exhalations, and held smoke. This structural compression mirrors the inheritance it portrays. The father figure appears through sedimented tone rather than event. He remains both proximate and distant. The poem's quiet tension becomes its grief.

Smoke & Fathers also introduces one of the collection's central motifs: that voice can endure beyond language. The father's "clear, yet incomprehensible" sound sets a tonal precedent for later spectral presences, voices carried in static, ritual, or memory that hold meaning without translation. In this way, the poem becomes a low-frequency tone across the collection. It hums beneath the other pieces, signaling that sound, tone, and sensory residue often speak more fully than statement. The poem trusts that ambiguity sustains.

Interpretive Reading

The opening line, "my father's voice floats above me," establishes a doubled presence, clear but unreachable, intimate yet suspended. That dissonance becomes the compositional key. The voice returns through sensation: spiders drifting on silk, smoke caught in grass. These images are not placed atop memory; they *are* memory, fragile and tactile.

The line "yoked like Siamese twins" binds speaker and father on the same loom, joined by structure more than will. Inheritance arrives through repetition, gesture, sound. The act of cutting grass becomes ritual, labor, elegy, and continuation at once. The closing lines send this gesture "toward a place / of no beginnings," allowing the emotion to taper into breath rather than closure. The poem ends in suspension, the field burned, the voice still hovering.

At its core, *Smoke & Fathers* studies presence that endures through medium, a voice carried by air, memory carried by tone. The father's survival is less in what he said than in how sound lingers when language falls away.

Touchpoints and Lineage

There are tonal echoes of Robert Hayden's "Those Winter Sundays," where labor replaces confession, and Seamus Heaney's *Clearances*, where touch becomes lineage. The syntax recalls Merwin's breath-based memory poems, in which punctuation gives way to continuity. The poem also aligns with Jack Gilbert's restrained elegies, where emotion remains weightless yet undeniable.

It joins a broader lineage of post-industrial masculine elegy, poems that allow fatherhood to exist as atmosphere, unresolved but enduring. Here, smoke becomes the carrier: inhaled, visible, impossible to hold.

Musicality: Delta Blues / Lo-Fi Folk

The piece unfolds like a field recording, spare, weathered, and quiet. Its rhythm draws from Delta blues: cyclical, minimal, emotionally unguarded. Repetition functions like a riff, "father" as theme, silence as return. It also shares the texture of lo-fi folk, where background hiss and breath noise become part of the aesthetic. The sonic atmosphere resembles early Iron & Wine or Nick Drake: music that stays close to the microphone and far from resolution. This isn't a performance. It's what plays in a room after the fire has gone out, when someone remains awake, remembering.

Visual Art: Ashcan School / Memory Abstraction

Visually, the poem echoes the Ashcan School's unsentimental portrayal of domestic and working-class life, especially in the tonal balance of George Bellows or Robert Henri, who painted men in shadow and sweat without glorifying them. The father here is neither idealized nor undone. He is rendered quietly, through texture and smoke.

There is also kinship with Memory Abstraction, Cy Twombly's later works, or the fading, charcoal-toned forms in William Kentridge's animations. In both, memory appears as erosion rather than depiction. Smoke becomes literal and symbolic: a veil, a trace, an ambient history. It doesn't rise. It stays.

Poem 9: Desire

Function in the Collection

Desire marks a dramatic tonal shift. Where the previous piece moves through elegy and restraint, *Desire* opens into heat, danger, and unfiltered sensation. It introduces the collection's first fully embodied mythic register, where lust, nature, death, and the sublime converge. The poem alters the book's emotional velocity: the reader moves from family legacy toward the wild pulse of eros, instinct, and mortal encounter.

Structural Role

The stanzas arrive breath-short and charged, almost cinematic in their flicker. Each line feels spliced by impulse rather than logic. The pacing mirrors the subject: erratic, urgent, then pausing to pull breath before lunging forward again. There is a volatility to the enjambment, a sense that the poem strains toward expansion. Geographically, the scene unfolds along State Road Two in the Florida half of the Okefenokee, among longleaf pine and saw palmetto. The terrain functions as a mythic field where appetite, risk, and mortality converge.

Within the poetry collection, *Desire* opens a new syntax of heat and immediacy. It brings eros as both ignition and threat, shifting the speaker's energy from memory to impulse. This is the first fever dream of the manuscript, a moment when lyric voice yields to bodily hunger.

Interpretive Reading

Desire builds its tension through doubling: literal and symbolic, physical and allegorical. Maureen moves as both person and archetype: Eve, invitation, the pull of the world made flesh. The snake, a Canebrake Rattlesnake, embodies seduction, death, and uncontainable power. The speaker steps into its path by choice, drawn to transgression rather than safety. The careful restraint of earlier poems gives way to reckless proximity.

The speaker grasps the snake from desire alone. When they breathe across its nostrils, the gesture becomes intimate, forbidden, nearly spiritual. The poem's climax arrives as the snake releases venom, a pale-yellow drop that falls onto the speaker's hand. The decision to wipe it away rather than taste it forms the poem's core act of restraint. The moment suspends the body between dissolution and self-command. The withheld gesture becomes its lyric discipline.

Maureen's reentry, buttons misaligned, camera raised, introduces absurdity, witness, and composure. She becomes both muse and recorder. Her voice, "Put it down before it bites," cuts through the trance with clarity, and the speaker responds. The closing gesture of laying the snake down gently on the sand carries reverence and release. The danger remains, but the encounter ends in presence rather than conquest.

Touchpoints and Lineage

The poem draws lineage from D. H. Lawrence, Sharon Olds, and mythic currents in Glück, while echoing older structures of trial and desire: Gilgamesh, the testing fields of Samson, Heracles, Psyche. Yet the speaker's strength emerges through restraint. The tension rests in the poise between seduction and self-command, between appetite and awareness.

Musicality: Trip-Hop / Darkwave

The sonic field moves slow, breath-heavy, and magnetized by tension. The atmosphere evokes trip-hop: down-tempo, textured, emotionally veiled. This is music that seduces through delay. Massive Attack and Portishead come to mind, longing shaped by layered restraint. Beneath that pulse, darker tonalities drift from darkwave and post-punk, minor-chord and aching. The rhythm never crests; it hovers in resonance and desire's undertow.

Visual Art: Neo-Expressionism / Figurative Distortion

The aesthetic remains raw, angular, and charged. The voice trembles with interior force, never pleading, always alive within the field of feeling. Its energy recalls Egon Schiele's figures, contorted, exposed, suspended between desire and recoil. A similar voltage runs through Marlene Dumas and Francesco Clemente, where figuration becomes sensation. Here, the body appears as a site of risk and transformation, its lines vibrating between clarity and blur. The poem's visual rhythm follows that exposure: visceral, unpolished, and always near the threshold of rupture.

Poem 10: *The Return*

Function in the Collection

The Return extends the collection's exploration of interior states through irony, philosophical distance, and surreal composure. It marks the manuscript's first sustained movement into unreal terrain. While the title implies homecoming or repetition, the poem turns toward awareness, recognizing return as an act of imagination.

Structural Role

Formally, the poem unfolds through cascading triplets, each three-line stanza indented like a receding terrace. The shape performs its own echo: a visual reverberation that mirrors the canyon's acoustics and the mind's looping reflection. The reader moves between two simultaneous planes, a 47th-floor restroom and the canyon's edge, linked by this rhythm of return and delay. The form enacts descent through space rather than through statement. Each indentation extends duration, carrying the reader further into the chamber of thought. The bodily act, rendered with restraint, anchors the metaphysical drift.

Within the collection, *The Return* opens a chamber shaped by irony, doubt, and delay. Earlier poems rooted memory in place or elegy; here, memory appears as interruption. The canyon yields silence, and the unsaid remains unformed. The poem enacts a ritual of incompletion that sustains its own awareness.

Interpretive Reading

The Return unfolds as a philosophical condition rather than a story. The man on the toilet, momentarily named Bruce, functions less as a character than as a site of perception. The canyon, the echo, and the body form a closed circuit in which sound seeks response but receives only atmosphere. The pause between utterance and return becomes a zone of instability, where reflection fails to resolve into meaning.

As the poem progresses, the echo weakens, memory fragments, and the canyon's depth gives way to fog. What begins as a search for recognition becomes a movement into absorption. The fog does not answer, repeat, or clarify. It erases. Bruce's step forward is not an act of escape but an exposure to something that no longer reflects him back to himself.

In this final gesture, the boundary between the literal and the proverbial breaks, and the poem abandons the possibility of return. Sound no longer echoes. It disperses. Perception no longer reflects. It absorbs. The body's sensations remain, light, wind, pressure, but they are the only signs left.

Touchpoints and Lineage

The poem draws lineage from Milan Kundera's philosophical fiction, Kafka's estranged logic, and Beckett's minimalist theater, where absurdity operates through delay, irony, and interior recursion rather than moral stance. It also echoes the recursive consciousness of David Foster Wallace, where thought itself becomes environment.

Musicality: Chamber Folk / Post-Rock Suspension

The rhythm moves slowly, meditative and cyclical, like chamber folk pared to its essentials. It recalls the delicate turns of early Sufjan Stevens or the harmonic layering of Joanna Newsom: music that evolves through variation rather than crescendo. Around that pulse drifts the atmosphere of post-rock: patient resonance, expanding delay, tones dissolving into air. The composition endures through duration, its energy residing in reverberation.

Visual Art: Metaphysical Painting / Existential Surrealism

Visually, *The Return* aligns with metaphysical painting with interior and exterior planes held in stillness. Its doubled setting, corporate and mythic, recalls Giorgio de

Chirico's arcades and Paul Delvaux's nocturnal structures: spaces emptied of function yet dense with implication. The restroom becomes a stage; the canyon, a mirror of cognition; the fog, a medium of perception. *The Return* offers a steady vision of awareness standing within its own vanishing.

Poem 11: Orion

Function in the Collection

Orion arrives as a compact meditation within a stretch of larger, more narrative-driven poems. It functions as a hinge, bridging the personal and the cosmic, the absurd and the mythic. Positioned after several emotionally burdened pieces, the poem re-centers the reader in nocturnal awareness: a speaker alone on the highway, keeping watch. The moment marks a pivot toward observational solitude, where the weight of lineage yields to endurance and quiet vigilance.

Structural Role

This poem acts as a pressure valve within a section dense with memory and consequence. Its brevity provides a kind of lyrical exhale and a slow recalibration of attention. After poems shaped by metaphysical, familial, and civic gravity, this poem and several pieces after step beyond those structures into a more existential field.

What begins here is a new mode of perception, spare, dry-eyed, and free from dramatic culmination. Where the figure in *The Return* is drawn irreversibly toward oblivion in search of something unnamed, the speaker in *Orion* holds a self-appointed watch against it, initiating a series of pieces that trade lyric interiority for watchful persistence. The gestures are small, but the ethic is clear. *Orion* signals the continuation of witness and a tired, yet persistent, responsibility.

Interpretive Reading

Orion carries comic bitterness and a kind of inverted heroism. The speaker is no seeker or triumphant figure, but a restless observer in a "big gas guzzling car," looking upward because someone must. The opening line, "He's here again, / An awful friend!" sets a tone both irreverent and fatigued. Orion, hunter and constellation, appears less as mythic guide than recurring burden.

The speaker resists sentiment and avoids epiphany. The night offers no comfort, only repetition. Yet within that repetition, a reluctant dignity emerges. The speaker keeps watch for all of us, unasked. The poem invites laughter but gestures toward something quieter, the possibility that even absurd vigilance carries worth. The speaker accepts their role, however ambiguous. Beneath the sarcasm runs a thread of composure: irritation itself becomes a form of attention.

Touchpoints and Lineage

The poem carries something of Wislawa Szymborska's cosmic irony, where the human figure remains small, alert, and unsheltered beneath vast systems. There is also tonal kinship with Tony Hoagland, where the absurd blends with quiet heartbreak. Yet its clipped construction and emotional reserve place it closer to Robert Creeley, especially in *Drive, He Said*, where tension and vulnerability gather through a tight interior pressure. Orion, often depicted with grandeur, appears here as unimpressive and flawed. That reversal recalls the emotional stance of Richard Hugo: wary of beauty, conscious of danger. This is a poem that gestures toward myth only to let it dissipate.

Musicality: Ambient Classical / Sacred Minimalism

The music of *Orion* resides in silence between notes. Its pacing mirrors ambient classical composition, harmonic suspension replacing motion. Meaning accumulates through duration rather than direction. It also shares the tonal hush of sacred minimalism, Arvo Pärt, John Tavener, where resonance matters more than crescendo.

Visual Art: Late Figurative Abstraction / Post-Mythic Irony

The constellation appears as a diminished emblem, blurred, self-conscious, and half ridiculous. The mood parallels Philip Guston's late paintings, where clumsy cartoon figures replace heroic icons. Myth becomes residue rather than revelation. *Orion* shares that aesthetic: part image persists as a relation; the speaker and Orion caught in their uneasy alignment.

Poem 12: Mercury Fish

Function in the Collection

Mercury Fish is a tonal descent into the comedic and grotesque interior of disillusionment. Positioned after the quiet absurdity of *Orion*, it carries forward the collection's exploration of solitude, but this time through a character study rather than an abstract persona. Billy, the speaker, feels caught inside his own orbit, a life circling rather than advancing. The poem deepens the collection's moral landscape by offering a vivid portrait of stagnation and thwarted longing. It counterbalances the mythic energy of

Desire, where eros gives way to inertia, the snake replaced by a can of Milwaukee's Best.

Structural Role

Formally, the piece is the only prose poem in the collection with its rhythm unfolding in long, unhurried clauses that match the heat-stunned, stagnant setting. The shape implies inertia, but its density reveals another kind of motion: the slow churn of unexpressed life. Spatially, we move between apartment, truck, floodwall, and riverbank, sites of ritual touched by something close to revelation.

And the bridge returns, appearing as infrastructure overhead, sonically present. The ballgame echoes beneath it as a secular liturgy, shifting the span into an ambient altar. As with other bridges in the collection, it offers no passage; it frames and holds, revealing how even the inert or absurd settles into the lyric architecture.

Interpretive Reading

At its core, *Mercury Fish* is a tragicomic elegy for a life that has slipped away unnoticed. Billy's problems are more than sexual; it suggests a deeper failure of agency, a metaphor for the inability to participate fully in one's own existence. The grotesque admission remains sincere; irony stays outside. We are asked to stay with the shame, the absurdity, and the rawness of a man who believes his internal misfiring sits at the center of his existential collapse.

Frank, his friend, functions as a contrast, impulsive, fecund, overwhelmed by consequence. The grotesque elements, children by multiple women, ballooning disorders, mercury-laced fish, add comic texture, but the emotional tone is steady. Both men drift in their own way, one fishing for sustenance, the other for ritual, each using the act to hold a place for meaning.

The ending hints at a kind of grace, but only briefly. The sound of the ballgame beneath the bridge becomes a murmur, something the world keeps doing without asking. The poem is the one that hears it, not the men. When it offers the phrase "something like god," it comes as static, accidental, nearly missed, a quick shimmer that rises and fades in the same breath.

Touchpoints and lineage

The poem carries the influence of American dirty realism: Raymond Carver, Denis Johnson, early James Tate. There are traces of Frederick Seidel's unnerving candor, though this voice is less amused by itself. Its lineage includes short fiction as much as lyric poetry, echoing Barry Hannah and Larry Brown, where masculinity is exhausted rather than assured. Underneath the local details, misfiring batteries, poisoned fish, is a deeper fatalism. The poem becomes a portrait of a culture struggling to hold a charge.

Musicality: Experimental Blues / Psychedelic Folk

Mercury Fish swims through distortion. Its tonal current slips, bends, and never quite stabilizes. The poem's broken clarity resembles the experimental blues of Captain Beefheart, where recognizable forms are warped into something jagged and strange. Beneath that surface, a thread of psychedelic folk runs quietly, Tim Buckley, early Devendra Banhart, where melody and disorientation coexist.

Visual Art: Alchemical Figuration / Embodied Mythology

The poem glimmers uneasily. Part contamination, part dream. The fish, toxic and shimmering, evokes the hybrid forms of Kiki Smith, where animals and bodies blur into myth. The logic feels alchemical, transforming a flat detail into something symbolic and strange. In visual terms, the poem belongs to a tradition of symbolic figuration rather than realism.

Poem 13: My Friend and His Wife

Function in the Collection

My Friend and His Wife marks a tonal pivot: comic, uncanny, and strangely intimate. Positioned after the expansive narrative of *Mercury Fish*, it offers an unsettling vignette where grief and absurdity collide. Its black humor concentrates emotional complexity into a single domestic scene, where estrangement replaces mourning.

Structural Role

The poem contracts both scale and tone after a series of expansive pieces. Its brief, clipped stanzas regulate the collection's pacing, creating a moment of compression between more diffuse movements.

Movement in the poem follows a contained trajectory, from mantel to car to driveway. The poem does not extend narrative consequence. It performs a contained, if not strange, exchange and then exits.

By replacing reflective modes with an errand, the poem interrupts the collection's prevailing momentum. The bust functions less as a symbol than as an object that must be handled, transported, and removed. It is a sequence toward smaller gestures, quieter actions, and localized scenes, where meaning is carried through movement.

Interpretive Reading

What begins as a surreal image, a sculpted bust on a mantel, becomes a meditation on mourning, guilt, and displaced tenderness. The bust is animated by both the wife's discomfort and the speaker's silent projection. Her request to "take him away" marks her refusal to live beside a version of her husband who remains present in a haunted abstract form. Her line about "personal grooming" disguises something closer to domestic annoyance or ache.

The speaker's role begins passively but shifts into uneasy participation. He lifts the bust "by the ears," places it in the car like a relic. The poem courts absurdity, the bust "bouncing idiotically with the bumps," but the humor only deepens the tension. The speaker speaks to the object with strange familiarity. He offers a cigarette. He mutters a judgment. This blend of contempt, humor, and unresolved affection creates a layered grief, shaped by loss and the unwanted inheritance of presence.

Touchpoints and Lineage

The poem carries the tonal control of Russell Edson and the emotional precision of Franz Wright. Its refusal to sentimentalize the body recalls Beckett. The domestic surrealism, where an object becomes protagonist, suggests kinship with James Tate. Classical echoes flicker as well: the bust as funerary fragment, the errand as secular rite. The act of driving it away externalizes grief. The poem becomes a small ritual of moral ambiguity, where humor stands in for comfort and participation substitutes for meaning.

Musicality: Slowcore / Gothic Americana

The piece unfolds at the pace of slowcore. Each image is suspended like a low note held too long. Think Low, Songs: Ohia, or Red House Painters, where tempo is a form of pressure and stillness, a kind of ache. The tonal palette also brushes against Gothic Americana: porchlight unease, domestic familiarity hollowed out by something spectral. This moves through emotional drag rather than narrative progression.

Visual Art: Narrative Realism / Social Surrealism

My Friend and His Wife moves like a washed-out photograph, casual in gesture but charged in atmosphere. Its visual analog might be Luc Tuymans, whose muted surfaces often mask historical or emotional weight. The domestic space is familiar but estranged. The realism remains, but with just enough displacement to feel off.

There is also a current of social surrealism as the subtle distortion of behavior under emotional strain. The bust's lip does not twitch reliably. Yet everything around it tilts.

Poem 14: The Possum

Function in the Collection

The Possum continues the contraction initiated by *My Friend and His Wife* while re-entering the manuscript's earlier tonal field. Where the prior poem compresses attention into one of the book's most reduced domestic scenes, *The Possum* sustains that narrowed focus and turns it inward, holding a single figure in prolonged address.

The poem replaces the bust with a living creature. The possum becomes a figure of relation rather than event, allowing the collection to remain with sustained address rather than outcome. Attention gathers around what is offered, received, and altered through contact.

Positioned after one of the manuscript's most spatially and procedurally reduced moments, *The Possum* deepens the book's commitment to localized presence. It advances a quieter field of attention, shifting emphasis from external occurrence to the persistence and material weight of language as it circulates beyond control.

By placing art within a relationship governed by hunger, consumption, and inheritance, the poem advances the collection's ars poetica: making as offering, language as substance that cannot be preserved once released.

Structural Role

This poem shifts the collection into a fabular, recursive, and self-aware register. Earlier pieces emphasize consequence, presence, or civic exposure. *The Possum* turns toward compositional consciousness itself, using absurdity and surreal address to examine how language behaves once it leaves the speaker.

The setting contracts to a room, a window, and a remembered relative, continuing the manuscript's narrowing spatial field while intensifying its interior pressure. Movement unfolds through associative narration, linking present observation to inherited memory by repetition and address.

Within the larger arc, *The Possum* stabilizes the inward trajectory that follows. Language emerges as an active force rather than a neutral tool, subject to appetite, use, and transformation. What the poem establishes structurally is exposure: a recognition that expression enters a world governed by its own laws, where words survive by being taken, altered, and passed on.

Interpretive Reading

This is a parable of poetic obsession. The possum arrives as muse, scavenger, and spiritual interloper, drawn to the speaker's "eggs," imagined as fragile vessels for language. In offering them up, the speaker stages a reversal of both creation and sacrifice, allowing language to be eaten rather than born. Her desire is literal. She wants the words themselves, unfinished and unguarded.

The speaker attempts to divert her, through threats, bribes, appeals to lineage, but none of it alters her hunger. Even the photograph of his grandfather, once a trapper of such creatures, fails to dissuade. Instead, she recasts that history: "I knew him," she yawns, "I ate his eggs too." The act of poetic creation is shown to be inherited and already consumed. The possum becomes a figure for the impossibility of keeping language intact.

And yet she remains as presence rather than tormentor. The poem refuses to resolve her into metaphor or menace. She is simply there, and through her, the speaker sees that what he makes cannot remain untouched. It will circulate and transform, undefeated. This is the nature of language, primordial, provisional, and alive.

Touchpoints and Lineage

The Possum shares lineage with the surreal animal poems of Russell Edson, the absurdist folklore of Donald Barthelme, and the metaphysical estrangement of Franz Kafka. Like Edson, it relies on compression and plain diction to unsettle familiar relations between speaker, object, and meaning. Like Kafka, it stages a world in which language operates according to its own internal pressures rather than human intention.

Its tonal sharpness and low hum of unease align with the work of Heather McHugh, particularly in how wit and grotesquerie sharpen attention rather than diffuse it. Humor here is not relief but method, a way of sustaining contact with what resists control.

The poem also echoes Valéry's assertion that a poem is never finished, only abandoned, though in this case language is neither set aside nor resolved. It is consumed, passed on, and returned in altered form. In this sense, *The Possum* refigures the muse as scavenger and the reader as inheritor, using fable logic to circle meaning rather than extract it. As in Mark Strand's *The Prediction* or *The Tunnel*, the poem remains a threshold rather than a statement, a site where language continues to act.

Musicality: Folk Noir / Field Recording Aesthetic

The soundscape belongs to folk noir: shadowed, spare, attuned to unease. Think Gillian Welch or Karen Dalton, voices that seem recorded just beyond a screen door. The pacing is slow and inward, offering space rather than motion. There is also a trace of the field recording aesthetic: ambient quiet, creak, wind, a sense of listening for something not entirely human.

Visual Art: Intimate Naturalism / American Primitivism

Visually, this piece aligns with Intimate Naturalism and American Primitivism, particularly the work of Bill Traylor. Like Traylor's animal figures, the possum is rendered with directness rather than symbolism, present as a bodily intelligence rather than an emblem. It appears alert, comic, and enduring, governed by instinct rather than explanation.

The poem shares this visual logic of exposure and clarity. What emerges is precision rather than refinement, a creature drawn as it registers in the world. The possum's presence carries the charge of survival, appetite, and persistence, reinforcing the poem's understanding of language as something alive, provisional, and subject to use.

Poem 15: Don't Tell Me You Haven't Thought This Before

Function in the Collection

Don't Tell Me You Haven't Thought This Before ruptures the early arc of the collection and becomes a moral fulcrum, an eruption that alters the emotional register of everything that follows. Until this point, most the poems move through tensional quiet and restraint.

With its Biblical epigraph, Psalm 137:9, the rupture becomes scriptural. Placed at the early-middle threshold, the poem interrupts the collection's measured surface with sudden force, shifting the reader from muted pressure to open volatility.

Structural Role

The poem's architecture carries the break. Short, escalating stanzas create a rhythm that mimics breath under strain, each line functioning like a pulse. The white space between sections amplifies tension. Its compacted shape presses the reader forward, releasing what earlier restraint held in reserve.

Positioned after a sequence of compressed works, the poem acts as structural reversal. Doorways, parking lots, and buses flatten into a single plane where moral tension gathers. The structure itself becomes a pressure valve.

From this point, implication is no longer sufficient; the clarity released here remains in play.

Interpretive Reading

No one dies here. The poem stages protest through imagination. It is reckoning rather than confession, a voice compelled to articulate what silence can no longer hold. The speaker brings the forbidden impulse into daylight, acknowledging the human capacity for harm. In that acknowledgment, the poem refuses the collective pretense that fury belongs only to others.

The title carries the charge. *Don't Tell Me You Haven't Thought This Before* draws the reader into complicity, insisting on honesty about the shadow within civility. The grotesque escalation leaves retribution hollow.

The final line, "because every time you die, I am happy," lands with deliberate emptiness. Its repetition drains pleasure of meaning until only fatigue remains. What endures is the ache beneath vengeance and the wish to see without disguise.

Touchpoints and Lineage

Don't Tell Me You Haven't Thought This Before stands in the lineage of the imprecatory Psalms, where rage is preserved as sacred record. Its kin are the raw monologues of Sylvia Plath or Ai, and the moral dissonance of Baldwin, the forensic witness of Forché, the social defiance of Claudia Rankine. It is the raw nerve behind protest, the heat that precedes articulation.

It carries no plea for resolution. It is closer to Morrison's conception of rememory, where trauma loops unless spoken aloud. In that sense, the speaker joins a long tradition of voices forced to imagine impossible retribution in order to make pain legible. Contemporary analogues might include cinematic provocations, Tarantino's stylized violence or *Love, Death & Robots'* grim futurism, as reflections of inner fracture rendered viscerally.

Musicality: Spoken Word Jazz / Post-Bop Minimalism

The cadence of this piece resembles spoken word laid over post-bop dissonance. Its rhythm is insistent but never improvisational. Every phrase lands with percussive intent, like the deliberate intervals of a muted trumpet or the lean aggression of an upright bass in a dim-lit room. Think Gil Scott-Heron without audience or microphone, speech as private confrontation. The poem pulses with internal syncopation, measuring lyric reserve against anger in real time. Its breath control is its form.

Visual Art: Text-Based Conceptualism / Semiotic Minimalism

The poem's visual counterpart is conceptual. It reads like a Barbara Kruger installation, text as confrontation, language as occupying force. Its declarative voice, clipped enjambments, and confrontational stance evoke the ethos of semiotic minimalism, where language itself becomes the site of tension. Like Kruger or Glenn Ligon, the poem makes text into terrain. The reader cannot look without being addressed. The poem does not blink.

Relation to The Devourer

Don't Tell Me You Haven't Thought This Before and *The Devourer* trace the cycle of violence from fantasy to incarnation. The first gives voice to helplessness turned inward, rage imagined as the only form of agency left. Its biblical epigraph reveals how deeply that impulse runs, how language itself sanctifies destruction and hands it down as inheritance.

The Devourer follows as the vision made flesh. What began as imagined power appears in the world as action: the healer who poisons, the light that devours. It is the same energy, uncontained.

Together, the poems mirror the way a culture both dreams of violence and recoils from its reflection. *Don't Tell Me You Haven't Thought This Before* names the fantasy we use to survive; *The Devourer* shows the cost when that fantasy arrives. Their dialogue leaves us suspended in recognition: the violence we imagine to resist cruelty is the same violence that, once unleashed, stands before us, unrecognizable, and already here.

Poem 16: Elephant Tattoo

Function in the collection

Elephant Tattoo continues the release of psychic pressure, but through surrealism rather than fury. Where the previous poem expelled tension in sharp, public declaration, this one turns inward, slipping into visionary terrain. It moves fully into dreamlike, mythopoetic terrain, where causality dissolves and symbolic transformation takes over. Its function is transitional: from testimonial voice to collective unconscious, from social indictment to ritual dream. Positioned near the midpoint, it signals a shift from urban realism to something more archetypal and psychic.

Structural Role

The poem marks a hinge in both tone and method. Its spatial logic departs from the cityscape of earlier poems and moves into unstable terrain, half remembered and half conjured. The initial setting, a parking garage, is quickly overtaken by fields, fog, and open sky. This descent into ambiguity is structural. The poem folds the speaker inward, loosening the collection's grip on realism to test what remains when certainty is stripped away.

Formally, the poem is spare and breath-held. Short stanzas, heavy enjambment, and minimal punctuation, with quotation marks framing graffiti as visual text, create a dreamlike, stuttering motion. The rhythm is cinematic and delayed, each line functioning like a cut or flash. Movement proceeds through charged associations, traveling from wound to mud, tattoo to field, fog to hunger. What forms is less a story than a psychic unveiling. In placement and pacing, the poem opens the collection's second half to stranger weather and stranger reckonings.

Interpretive Reading

Elephant Tattoo's imagery is visionary and archetypal. A naked man is cornered, marked, and carried through a ritual of degradation and symbolic rebirth. Two figures, one of whom bears an elephant above their right breast, become agents of a deeper mythology. Their roles are fluid, nurse, punisher, cleric, but they remain consistent in their authority. The elephant tattoo evokes more than memory. It signals burden, permanence, and the impossibility of forgetting.

Violence arrives early: Graffiti cuts the man's body, and he is beaten in a stairwell. But these acts feel ceremonial rather than gratuitous, and the application of mud to his wounds blurs healing with burial. What follows is a passage through elemental space, from concrete to grass, from body to fog where the man is offered up in the final image, fog becomes multitude, a thousand men and women hungering for him and his punishers. The speaker stays with the vision. They witness it. The poem ends in cold sublimation, where dissolution becomes the final register.

The vision carries erotic devastation and irreversible transformation. It offers no salvation, only the clarity of being unmade and seen.

Touchpoints and Lineage

Elephant Tattoo moves within the surrealist tradition by means of narrative rupture and symbolic compression. It shares affinities with the ritualized violence of Georg Trakl and the dream-logic of James Tate, resonating more with Kafka or early Vallejo than with ornamental surrealism. The elephant, as image, gestures toward literary memory: weight, wisdom, mourning. But this poem resists allegory. It arrives as visitation rather than fable.

There are tonal echoes of Anne Sexton's *Transformations*, where myth is retold as nightmare, and of Plath's late work, where the body is both altar and indictment. The prostitutes function like inverted oracles, vengeance spirits or initiators rather than antagonists. The poem belongs to a lineage of lyric surrealism that prioritizes moral residue over plot, and vision over closure.

Musicality: Alt-Country Ballad / Lo-Fi Confessional

The pacing resembles a haunted alt-country ballad, slow, spare, almost whispered. It carries the weathered tone of Jason Molina or early Lucinda Williams, where voice and minimal instrumentation carry more emotional charge than form. There is also a lo-fi confessional quality, as if the speaker could no longer hold it back. Each stanza falls like a minor chord, low and unresolved.

Visual Art: Figurative Surrealism / Memory Symbolism

The imagery is figurative and surreal, where the body becomes both archive and altar. Its symbolic layering resonates with Frida Kahlo's work, particularly in how pain is rendered with visual precision and memory fuses with physical mark. The tattoo is emblem, scar, and evidence.

There is also a kinship with Ana Mendieta's ritual aesthetics, especially her earth-body works where blood, mud, and gesture collapse into elemental meaning. The poem shares that commitment to transformation through embodiment. Its scenes could be rendered as ritual where something endured and left a residue.

Poem 17: YOU

Function in the Collection

YOU functions as a necessary comedown after the hallucinatory intensity of *Elephant Tattoo*. Where that poem moved through myth, violence, and dissolution, this one reenters the domain of domestic drift and existential weariness, rendered through tonal restraint. This is the first poem in the collection to address another directly in both title and final lines, yet the "you" remains indeterminate, singular or plural, real or imagined. The result is both lament and gesture, a brief hold against disconnection.

Structural Role

This poem marks a return to grounded consciousness, but the speaker has changed and is more attuned to slow decay, inertia, and quiet need. The transition from archetypal dream to fatigued interiority is abrupt by design. It is as if the speaker has emerged from ritual vision only to find that ordinary life holds no less disarray. Structurally, the poem introduces the first sustained downbeat since the collection began, by letting the drift hold. It offers pause, not passage.

Interpretive Reading

YOU offers no metaphoric detour, no mythic frame. Only a moment, dimly lit, neither resolved nor resisted. The "you" remains ambiguous, less a person than a projection, an outline filled with memory, longing, blame, and resignation. The speaker's voice, pared to its essentials, becomes porous. If there is self-loathing here, it no longer needs to be named. The tone is muted, familiar, almost tired of itself.

The ache is lodged in what is withheld. The title implies address, but the poem barely reaches. There is no confrontation. There is only aftermath. The "you" functions as scaffold, letting the speaker build around what cannot be claimed outright.

In tonal lineage, *YOU* refracts *The Return*. Where the earlier poem dissolves the self into motion and loss without recovery, this one remains with what lingers afterward. Nothing has been restored. The dispersal has already occurred. What persists is a diminished presence, aware of itself as remainder rather than arrival. The echo between the two poems is emotional rather than narrative. What once moved through erasure now settles into recognition, voiced through attrition.

The "you" could be anyone. The poem gives no name and withholds enough to invite misreading. Some readers may imagine a specific figure, a remembered presence, or a familiar voice. These projections are incidental. The ache is personal but not indexed.

What matters is the steadiness of the address. The voice is measured, watchful, and dry-eyed, consistent with the collection's ongoing posture of attention. The guessing game is beside the point. The grief is unadorned, and the absence is real.

Touchpoints and Lineage

YOU carries the hushed sharpness of late Raymond Carver, pared to its moral edge without declaring it. There are tonal affinities with W.S. Merwin's distant confessionals and early Glück's elliptical minimalism. Its movement folds inward rather than forward, shaped by what it does not say. The voice walks a narrow line between address and withdrawal, exposure and recusal, and leaves its trace through restraint.

Musicality: Lo-Fi Ballad / Emotional Reverb

This piece hums like a lo-fi ballad recorded on an analog deck, intimate, brittle, barely adjusted. The tone suggests early Elliott Smith or Sharon Van Etten, voices layered in closeness and fragility. Each line arrives like a worn refrain, murmured rather than sung. The silence around the words becomes part of the tempo. The poem carries an emotional reverb, each phrase echoing into a space where no reply will come.

Visual Art: Minimalist Portraiture / Psychic Contour

Visually, *YOU* resembles a minimalist portrait rendered from memory: faint, partial, emotionally precise. It aligns with the quiet affect of Luc Tuymans or the early contour sketches of Jenny Saville, where figures emerge through omission. The face is almost absent, drawn in refusal. The "you" remains uncaptured and the poem sketches a presence by revealing its vanishing.

Poem 18: Rock of My Bones

Function in the Collection

Rock of My Bones placement after *YOU* is deliberate. Where *YOU* dissolved into ambiguity and emotional inertia, *Rock of My Bones* reclaims structure by rhythmic return. It reintroduces bodily fact, breath, and invocation, a cadence where after the ache of misconnection, the poem reasserts presence through elemental recurrence: blood, bone, heat.

Structural Role

Rock of My Bones stabilizes the collection after the disarray of *YOU,* and what preceded it. It pulls the earlier fragments into a bodily shape, leaving their edges intact, rhythmic and ritualistic. The speaker, still solitary, now reorients their longing toward something beyond the self. This delayed address transforms the poem, in retrospect, into a kind of prayer. What first appears as existential drift is reconfigured as devotional endurance.

Placed here, the poem marks a tonal hinge in the collection's evolution. Earlier poems dwell in ambiguity and estrangement; this one offers a grounded stillness. The poem introduces a spiritual register without relying on certainty or reward. The silence becomes inhabited. The voice that speaks here isn't new, but it is changed. The collection now shifts from unmoored longing to anchored unknowing.

Interpretive Reading

The poem opens with a contradiction: the speaker's body is animate, yet unaware of its own yearning. The separation between flesh and desire is central. The "I" stands momentarily "at the edge of things," while the world continues, trudging, rushing, indifferent. That tension between physical motion and internal stasis becomes the poem's inner current.

Only at the end is the listener revealed: "Jah." That word reorients the entire poem. What had seemed abstract becomes devotional. The speaker is weary and waiting, held by the hope of contact. The final image, lying in bed "till I see through my eyelids," extends that waiting into a quiet vigil. The poem seeks no reply but insists on address. "In this insistence, defiance and faith coexist.

Touchpoints and Lineage

This poem echoes the pared spiritual doubt of the Psalms, especially those attributed to David, where the speaker names God without response. There are tonal affinities with Fanny Howe and Franz Wright, whose devotional lyrics hold longing without closure. Its plainspoken rhythm also recalls the theological clarity of Christian Wiman. What sets this poem apart is its refusal to elevate itself. The voice is steady, unresolved, and inward facing. It shares the tonal lineage of *Orion*, weathered and spare.

Musicality: Devotional Minimalism / Spare Americana

The piece moves like a stripped-down spiritual: slow, deliberate, emptied of ornament. Its rhythm evokes a late Johnny Cash recording, where the voice has become rhythm and the silence between lines takes on weight. Breath replaces percussion. The music is endured. This is a one-instrument prayer, offered in a dark room. What lasts is a cadence, trudging and heat-warped.

Visual Art: Spiritual Figuration / American Existential

Rock of My Bones enters a visual lineage where the body carries belief in its structure and stance. Think of Kollwitz or Rouault where figures are marked by weight and silence. The bones beneath flesh are what remains when meaning thins. The bed becomes raft, the face becomes vessel, and the silhouette becomes witness.

There is kinship with early twentieth-century American religious figuration, especially in the work of Howard Finster or Benton Murdoch Spruance, where rural austerity and metaphysical solitude shape the human form. The figure in this poem shares that gravity. What emerges is a presence held in low light, tired and steady, a face that meets the frame with a quiet, devotional weight.

Poem 19: The First Psalm

Function in the Collection

The First Psalm deepens the collection's quiet turn toward the spiritual by recasting the psalm through sensory revelation rather than petition or lament. If the previous poem reaches upward in stillness, *The First Psalm* turns its gaze horizontally, or even downward, toward the dust, the cells, the earthworms. It functions as a meditation on the physical as sacred. It expands the collection's spiritual axis by grounding it in another body, the "she" who teaches them to believe differently.

Structural Role

This poem acts as a tonal hinge in the collection. Positioned after *Rock of My Bones*, it absorbs the prior poem's spiritual tension and redirects it into stillness. Instead of beseeching an absent God, the speaker encounters belief through another body, one grounded in sensation and soil. The use of couplets and breath-spaced pacing reflects this internal shift, each stanza gently unfolding, guiding the reader toward reflection rather than urgency.

Theologically, the poem sidesteps abstraction and reaches for something tactile, offering a counterweight to earlier poems marked by disorientation or silence. Here, attention becomes its own kind of psalm. The spatial orientation shifts from upward longing to downward rooting. Dust, worms, rain, and marl become sacred materials. As such, *The First Psalm* introduces a new poetics of perception, one that will influence how the collection navigates faith, knowledge, and impermanence going forward.

Throughout the collection, the lyric voice operates as a site of attention rather than a personal identity. The speaking presence is left ungendered, following a modernist practice that reduces the autobiographical self so the poem can remain structurally open. In this poem, that ethic appears lightly; in others, such as *Desire*, it carries greater pressure.

Interpretive Reading

The First Psalm is about recalibration. The speaker begins with a startling fact: that 90% of dust is composed of shed cells, of skin, of breath, of presence. This scientific insight becomes spiritual: the dead and the living are everywhere, suspended in air. From this, they derive "the urgency of touch," a line that reverberates through the whole book.

"She" is living belief where her faith radiates through her senses. It begins with worms, marl, and flesh, rather than creed or cosmology. Her reverence is empirical. She embodies what the speaker had only abstracted. They see, by contrast, that their own talk, about death bringing life, or some "Being" that survives decay is flimsy. The real psalm is her body in relation to the earth, to the speaker, and to everything that falls apart and reforms in cycles. The final blow is quiet but complete: fate becomes "the thief of lips and hands," the force that steals touch and voice. So this moment, this contact, is holy and it must be lived.

Touchpoints and Lineage

This poem stands in kinship with the embodied spiritual traditions of poets like Jane Hirshfield, Pattiann Rogers, and even the later Wendell Berry, where belief is revealed through attention to the world. There is also a clear echo of Walt Whitman's material mysticism, where flesh and dust move together as partners in the divine.

Structurally, its simplicity calls to mind Kay Ryan or Jean Valentine, yet its conceptual depth aligns more with the meditative clarity of Denise Levertov. Philosophically, the poem joins a lineage of artists who recognize the insufficiency of language in the face of real presence, akin to Simone Weil's argument that real attention is a form of prayer.

Musicality: Sacred Minimalism / Appalachian Hymnal

The First Psalm moves with the hushed gravity of sacred minimalism, a genre shaped by composers like Arvo Pärt and Henryk Górecki, where repetition and silence form the emotional core. Each line feels like a held note, spare, echoing, deliberate. There is also a faint pulse of the Appalachian hymnal tradition in posture: the poem stands like a solitary voice in an empty church, intoning burden in a sustained chord of moral stillness.

Visual Art: Sacred Minimalism / Iconic Symbolism

The visual lineage includes Mark Rothko's late-period work, particularly the dark, altar-like panels where color becomes liturgy and silence becomes structure. Like Rothko, the poem refuses illustration. Instead, it hums with a vertical tension between presence and absence, ascent and disappearance.

There is also resonance with sacred minimalism, art that distills spiritual expression to its essence. It evokes the mood of religious iconography through stillness, repetition, and devotional restraint. Finally, there is a visual echo of Byzantine icons, flattened, gold-hued, contemplative, where symbolic weight surpasses dimensional realism. The psalm here is lived, and the form is the prayer.

Poem 20: Only a Serpent

Function in the Collection

Only a Serpent marks a tonal shift in the collection's evolving spiritual arc. Following the quiet revelation of *The First Psalm*, *Only a Serpent* engages directly with the divine, unadorned and conflicted. It operates as both invocation and confession, layered with humor, contradiction, fatigue, and real faith.

Placed near the collection's midpoint, it acts as a pivot. The speaker moves from observing and reckoning with the world to addressing God directly. Yet even in address, the voice remains self-aware and suspecting of its own motives. That self-awareness is central. This poem insists on spiritual honesty, even at the cost of reverence. The collection, up to this point, has moved through inheritance, temptation, isolation, and existential frustration. Here, those threads resurface, filtered through the plainspoken cadence of a bruised, faltering prayer.

Structural Role

The poem is built in stanzas of irregular length, but the breath and logic are those of a prayer. Its cadence feels inherited, somewhere between the Psalms and a kitchen-table lament. Line breaks and enjambments enforce both pacing and tone. Sudden pauses give weight to contradictions, "though I really have no idea / what it is I am asking", while humor is allowed to slip in without undercutting the sincerity.

Spatially, we are nowhere and everywhere, this is a prayer outside of place as there is no setting except the interior. Yet it is entirely embodied: the "court / of Nebuchadnezzar" is no more vivid than the imagined streets, and enemies share space with serpents and doves. The dislocation is intentional. This is a spiritual field report from a liminal zone.

Interpretive Reading

Only a Serpent operates as a raw, emotionally complex prayer that refuses to separate reverence from reality. The speaker begins in almost rote liturgical form, "Father God and Lord Jesus / Christ who is risen from the dead," only to veer into private admission: "I am always in danger / of going to sleep." This line acts as both spiritual fatigue and literal weariness, a confession that threads through the rest of the piece.

The plea to "stay awake to the things that matter" signals awareness of what's at stake, personal salvation and ethical clarity. And yet, the poem undercuts its own piety at every turn. "Though I really have no idea / what it is I am asking" is among the most devastating lines in the collection: a collapse of certainty, a truth-telling the Church rarely permits. The speaker does not pretend to understand what God wants. They ask anyway.

The poem's humor is corrosive and necessary. "A little wiggle room / on humility might be nice" and "though I still want them dead" are acknowledgments of human nature that coexist with the desire for mercy. The final invocation, for the safety of family, is unironically heartfelt. The poem ends with quiet appeal: "Keep us always safe / in your hands, I pray."

This is one of the most vulnerable and paradoxically faithful moments in the collection. It trusts God enough to say: I don't trust myself, I don't even know what I'm doing, but, I am still here.

Touchpoints and Lineage

Only a Serpent stands in a long lineage of conflicted, devout literature, from Augustine's *Confessions* to the poetry of Franz Wright and Jericho Brown. It also echoes the darker Psalms, where praise is folded into fear, vengeance, and doubt. There are shades of Flannery O'Connor here as well: a theology of contradiction, unsparing honesty, and the belief that mercy and truth must meet at the edge of absurdity.

The poem's mention of Nebuchadnezzar evokes Daniel, Babylon, and exile, an Old Testament frame for displacement and spiritual testing. Yet it's the offhand admissions, the wish to be "only a serpent," the bald desire for enemies to die, that place this poem firmly in the modern era: post-irony, post-purity, but not post-faith.

Musicality: Chamber Folk / Darkwave

This piece moves through a blend of chamber folk and darkwave. Tight acoustic instrumentation and liturgical precision recall My Brightest Diamond or Joanna Newsom at her most restrained, while a shadowed atmosphere gathers in the register of Dead Can Dance or This Mortal Coil. The rhythm coils rather than marches. Harmonically, it leans into minor modes, evoking tension without overt menace.

Visual Art: Symbolist Allegory / Chiaroscuro Figuration

This poem's symbolism is elemental. The serpent, ancient and unstable, appears as inheritance, memory, or seduction. The visual art parallel lies with Symbolist painters like Odilon Redon, whose serpents and eyes and flowers carried metaphysical weight. Like Redon's figures, the poem's imagery seems to glow from within shadow, liminal and dreamlike.

The chiaroscuro tone, flashes of meaning in a dark field, recalls Caravaggisti influence as filtered through late-19th-century allegory: figuration as mood. The serpent, in this context, becomes less literal and more psychological as a stand-in for betrayal, desire, or rebirth. The speaker doesn't fear it. They name it. Almost cradle it.

This is a visual tradition that believes in archetype without flattening complexity. In *Only a Serpent*, the painting would show a glance, a curved line, and a held breath.

Poem 21: Eternal Life

Function in the Collection

Eternal Life is the shortest poem in the collection, only eight lines, yet its compression holds tension. Coming directly after *Only a Serpent*, it functions as a distilled coda, a whispered epilogue to the long, conflicted prayer that precedes it. Where that earlier piece wrestled with faith, ethics, violence, and contradiction, *Eternal Life* reduces those elements to a minimal, meditative fragment.

Its placement matters. After so much spiritual grappling, the poem turns toward quiet estrangement. The speaker reenters the world with a question: what might eternity do to us? The response, if implied, is a transformation into something ancient, undying, and unfamiliar. In the broader arc of the collection, *Eternal Life* marks a pause between human longing and elemental persistence.

Structural Role

The poem is stark in form: two brief quatrains, each closing on a single word. Line breaks slow the pace, and white space holds the silence. The words appear to fall or recede, their spacing shaping a rhythm that mirrors the poem's subject, a gradual descent rather than an event.

The word *tow* carries multiple pressures: erosion, duration, and submersion. Structurally, the poem pulls the collection downward. It functions as a hinge of compression, reducing scale and stripping excess. The movement is inward, then beneath, a narrowing that alters how the surrounding poems are felt.

Interpretive Reading

Eternal Life can be read as a quiet answer to *Only a Serpent*. Where the earlier poem flirts with the idea of being stripped of moral burden, this one considers what such a state would require if it were granted within the limits of the physical world.

The poem opens casually, almost offhandedly, acknowledging slow disappearance as a shared condition. Mortality is neither lamented nor resisted. What follows is not theological speculation but material inquiry. Eternal life, if it were possible without transformation beyond the body, would not preserve the human form as we know it.

The image of the serpent emerges as both symbol and consequence. Close to the ground, enduring and altered, it becomes a plausible end state for consciousness that persists while remaining bound to the world. Knowledge survives. Uprightness does not.

The poem turns away from both the fantasy of eternal youth and the promise of technological escape. The question is not whether persistence would redeem us, but what it would reduce us to. The answer is neither punishment nor reward. It is residue. To endure without transcendence is to become something unrecognizable.

Touchpoints and Lineage

This poem joins a tradition of philosophical compression. Its clarity and spareness recall the work of W.S. Merwin or the concision of Kay Ryan. Its moral angle aligns with the contemplative edge of Thomas Merton's late poems, where silence itself becomes devotional. The poem's understated tone also resonates with elements of Zen-influenced writing, where impermanence becomes the condition of presence.

There is a quiet echo of Genesis in the final image, but the snake has shifted roles where it is no longer the tempter. It is what remains when the rest falls away, where mortality keeps us porous and eternity seals us in.

Musicality: Spiritual Drone / Post-Rock Lament

Eternal Life unfolds with the reverent stillness of spiritual drone, a genre that includes artists like Sarah Davachi or Stars of the Lid, where tone and duration become modes of prayer. The poem's phrasing slows time, holding the space between lines like bowed harmonics. There's also a kinship with post-rock lament, echoing the restrained swells of bands like Sigur Rós or Low, music that doesn't build to climax, but expands inward. The rhythm is contemplative, the register elegiac. It doesn't claim salvation. It listens to the silence after judgment.

Visual Art: Post-Surrealism / Mystical Minimalism

This piece moves like a dream structure: linear only in shadow. Its gestures toward eternity are estranged. The visual analogue is found in Post-Surrealist and metaphysical painters like Giorgio de Chirico, whose empty plazas, long shadows, and silent statues evoke an otherworld where logic and memory distort.

There's also kinship with Mystical Minimalism, works that evoke spiritual questions through sparse, charged space. Like a Rothko painting rendered in concrete imagery, *Eternal Life* hovers between invocation and absence.

In visual terms, this is a painting with a long vanishing point and no visible source of light. Stillness masks tension. The eternal, in this poem, is the echo of everything that refuses to end.

Poem 22: Unbeknownst to You

Function in the Collection

Unbeknownst to You arrives darkly comic, grotesque, and unsentimental. It follows the distilled stillness of *Eternal Life* with a turn toward the bodily and the absurd. In its placement, the poem functions as a kind of satirical parable on how repression and self-deception give way to consequence.

After sustained passages of lyrical gravity and fractured spiritual meditation, the sequence allows humor, discomfort, and the grotesque to enter the frame. The register loosens. The atmosphere shifts. Seriousness is not abandoned, but it is no longer confined to solemn forms. Rather than undercutting seriousness, the poem expands it by folding the comic and the scatological into the spiritual terrain already forming in the collection.

Structural Role

The poem unfolds in clipped, enjambed stanzas. Its structure echoes its central gesture: a gradual fall. What begins as gentle musing, "Someday in the future / unbeknownst to you," descends into something visceral: "the septic tank // of your heart // will burst." The stanzas trace a visual sequence: a figure walks, crosses the lawn, and disappears. The final lines leave no return. The poem closes in silence, a slurp, and blank space.

Its formal compression interrupts the collection's recent movement toward contemplative stillness. This is a break of tone and pressure. The poem reminds us that what is buried in lyric tension eventually leaks and what leaks eventually pulls.

Interpretive Reading

At surface level, *Unbeknownst to You* reads as a grotesque parable: someone walking a familiar field is sucked down into their own forgotten waste. The "septic tank of your heart" displaces sentimentality. The heart becomes a failed system of containment, something once hidden, now rupturing.

The phrase "unbeknownst to you" recurs like a warning. The you in the poem moves unaware through a "seemingly lush field," oblivious to what has been left unattended. There is no villain here except maybe the self: only the slow, inevitable consequence of what goes unacknowledged.

Still, the tone remains measured. There's no condemnation. Just the sequence of events. The final image of being sucked through the sod with a slurp, skirts both horror and humor.

Touchpoints and Lineage

This poem shares DNA with the surreal satire of Russell Edson and the moral absurdism of Kafka, but its tone is flatter and more procedural. Its structure and diction suggest kinship with Lydia Davis and James Tate, particularly in how plain language is used to deliver existential shock. The American vernacular remains intact even as the ground gives out.

There's also a theological reversal at play. Instead of ascending from earth, the figure is taken downward, back into what was hidden. The poem questions the logic of redemption. It suggests that what remains buried exerts its own gravitational force. That force is untheatrical, but persistent.

Musicality: Neo-Soul Ballad / Acoustic Lo-Fi

The pacing echoes the intimacy of a stripped-down neo-soul ballad, phrasing that leans in rather than building. Its rhythm favors silence and space, like the bare tracks of Meshell Ndegeocello or early Lianne La Havas. There's little adornment. Emotion emerges through phrasing, rather than volume. The acoustic lo-fi quality, close mic, room tone, quiet breath, creates a sense of private collapse.

Visual Art: Symbolist Intimacy / Psychological Portraiture

The atmosphere recalls the private intensities of Paula Rego or the muted interiority of Hammershøi. This is a psychological portrait rather than a landscape. The scale is small. The gestures are minimal, but the tension saturates the scene.

There's also a Symbolist undercurrent: an unseen force just outside conscious recognition. The field looks lush. The light is soft. But something is about to yield. The subject is caught mid-step, on the threshold of awareness.

Poem 23: Waiting for Daylight

Function in the Collection

Waiting for Daylight reorients the collection after a sustained descent with a quiet turn toward metaphysical unease. Where the previous several poems lingered in bodily consequence, this one drifts inward into doubt, alertness, and the fragile space between belief and disintegration. The poem doesn't resolve. It hovers. It waits with the reader in the early tremors of uncertainty, where neither faith nor collapse can fully take hold.

Structural Role

The poem is shaped around suspension. Narrative retreats. Movement slows. The stanzas lean downward in short-lined hesitations, each one delaying arrival. Fragmentation becomes form. Thought breaks across enjambment like breath held too long.

Where earlier poems in the sequence leaned into speech or image, *Waiting for Daylight* withholds. Its motion is inward, and its drama lies in inaction and the quiet psychic work of enduring time. The final stanzas widen, offering no resolution, only a fragile widening. The poem's pacing remains taut. White space gathers pressure.

Interpretive Reading

This is a poem on cosmic indifference. The speaker doesn't fear the dark. They fear the possibility that light may not return. The predictability of the sun brings no comfort.

The voice is restrained, almost hushed. The poem names moths, spiders, fading stars. The scale is domestic, but the dread is celestial. When the speaker admits that nothing they do "adds a second / to a life everyone / tells me is endless," the line opens a theological rift. Eternity doesn't console. It unsettles. Even the mechanics of morning feel unreliable.

Still, the poem lingers in a state before belief can form. Attention becomes its own kind of vigil. The speaker listens and waits.

Touchpoints and Lineage

Waiting for Daylight joins the lineage of metaphysical lyric, where fragility is rendered through silence and scale. It recalls the stripped-down unease of early Mark Strand, the hush of Merwin, the disquiet of Dickinson when her tremble moves inward. There is a philosophical echo of Camus, where watchfulness replaces revolt.

Spiritually, the poem gestures toward unaddressed prayer. It shares something with the stripped theologies of Simone Weil, where longing holds its shape without seeking ease. And in its focus on minor creatures and indeterminate skies, the poem aligns with a lyric tradition that locates immensity in the smallest tremors.

Musicality: Ambient Americana / Early Morning Electronica

The sonic texture carries the hush of ambient Americana, minimal, dust-lit, shaped by restraint. The phrasing is slow, unhurried. It carries the tone of a whispered Gillian Welch track or a subdued Ryley Walker instrumental. In another register, the pacing shares space with early morning electronica, music composed of loops that never resolve, only drift.

What holds is a quiet cycle of dread and alertness. The music doesn't rise. It stays in place, waiting for the sky to shift.

Visual Art: American Regionalism / Lyrical Desolation

The piece evokes a visual stillness akin to Edward Hopper's early interiors. The scene is neither city nor countryside. It's the space in between, a dim room, a figure at the threshold of action, unsure whether to rise or remain still.

There's a similar restraint in the light. The palette is soft. The shadows stretch. If painted, the scene might resemble Hopper through the lens of Hammershøi: pale, precise, and suspended. Nothing dramatic occurs. And yet, the room is tense with waiting. The poem lingers in that unresolved moment just before the light confirms its return.

Poem 24: Lightning Manual

Function in the Collection

Placed after the hushed unease of *Waiting for Daylight*, *Lightning Manual* reintroduces danger, ritual, and voltage. It arrives as invocation rather than reflection. The voice turns elemental, merging dare with longing. This is language of instruction under pressure. The speaker seeks contact with power, willing to absorb its charge.

Lightning Manual acts as a hinge in the collection's larger current. The restraint of the previous poem opens toward exposure. Intimacy and recklessness merge. Awe is approached directly, as pursuit rather than observation. The speaker calls the storm into being.

Structural Role

The poem revives the collection's appetite for rupture. It releases kinetic energy held in reserve. Built entirely through imperatives, its voice feels ceremonial yet improvised, drawn from field knowledge, bravado, and quiet faith. The syntax stays clipped and exact, each enjambment a spark.

Formally, the poem behaves like a training manual written in fragments. The spacing between clauses mirrors static delay, the pause before contact. Its closing gesture, waiting in the tree, sustains tension through stillness. The storm hovers just beyond sight.

Interpretive Reading

Lightning Manual reads as a sequence of perilous instructions to hang from wires, climb trees during storms, dream of being struck. Beneath the risk moves a wish to be marked, to feel chosen by something immense. The danger becomes devotional, a longing for transformation beyond understanding.

Everyday materials turn ritualistic. The clothesline becomes conduit, the ladder relic, the wedding band a live circuit. Even injury becomes consecration. The flash that sears lips and skin carries initiation rather than harm. Absurdity lingers, yet sincerity prevails and the voice believes its own command.

The closing image, the figure perched in a tree, praying for a storm, returns to the idiom of scripture and threshold. The speaker invites revelation, steady within risk.

Touchpoints and Lineage

This piece shares lineage with early James Wright, where rural fields hold both tenderness and current, while leaning toward the raw immediacy of Denis Johnson. It echoes rites of passage, danger as proof of being alive. A current of Lorca's duende runs through it: a poetics of wound and invitation. Its diction carries the clarity of survival guides and folk gospel, declarative and sincere.

Within the broader field of initiation poems, *Lightning Manual* distills transformation to its simplest gesture: readiness more than arrival.

Musicality: Industrial Punk / Noise Gospel

The rhythm strikes like industrial punk: short, percussive, metallic. The pulse recalls Big Black or early Suicide, where structure builds from abrasion. Beneath that charge flows a devotional current akin to noise gospel. Bands such as Algiers or Zeal & Ardor transform distortion into liturgy. The poem sustains its tension through pressure and pause, ending in a single held note of silence.

Visual Art: Action Painting / Energetic Abstraction

Visually, the poem aligns with action painting. Each command falls like a brushstroke: precise, kinetic, incomplete. The page itself becomes an energy field, its white space alive with static. The spirit recalls Franz Kline's dark scaffolds or Joan Mitchell's cascading gestures, where movement becomes form.

The poem stands within the charged interval before the storm, its field bright with anticipation. The figure in the tree remains exposed, unwavering, waiting for contact that hovers near but has yet to touch.

Poem 25: Morning in the Middle of Nowhere

Function in the Collection

Morning in the Middle of Nowhere enters as a luminous pause, neither retreat nor resolution, but a temporary widening. After the voltage of *Lightning Manual*, it shifts the register toward light, stillness, and estranged pastoral. The scene is quiet, but touched with the surreal. What begins as rural morning opens into something mythic and dislocated. At its center is a solitary woman. She is simply there, and the world around her begins to shimmer.

Functionally, the poem offers a moment of clarity held in composure. Its awe feels genuine and remote, a steady attention that replaces exchange with observation, light, gesture, and vision. The poem holds its ground, sustaining tone instead of advancing story, like a note carried through still air.

Structural Role

Morning in the Middle of Nowhere holds a tonal suspension. The sequence moves from confrontation toward visitation. Earlier poems built tension through action and speech; this one opens through observation. The speaker witnesses transformation through perception itself, as the surrounding world alters under their gaze.

Formally, the poem unfolds in loose stanzas with open spacing and without punctuation. The architecture mimics the wide visual field it inhabits, a pasture, sky, light moving through. Enjambment slows each phrase, letting meaning drift. Nothing lands too firmly. This gives the poem its pulse: a rhythm made of silence, distance, and heat.

Interpretive Reading

The poem reads as a vision, possibly ecstatic, possibly imagined. The woman at its center moves through familiar morning routines, but each element becomes radiant and strange. Berries appear untouched by insects. Livestock become a chorus. Workers shimmer as if transported from another time. The field, while real, no longer belongs to a specific geography. It has become a site of projection, half memory, half myth.

The transformation gathers sound as well as light. The poem listens as the cattle raise their voices in praise, filling the field with a kind of radiant order. The change arrives without spectacle; its power lies in composure. Presence replaces explanation. The air carries reverence rather than symbol. The strawberry workers appear as emissaries drawn from elsewhere.

This is perception made porous. The moment gathers and releases almost at once, holding revelation and disappearance in the same breath.

Touchpoints and Lineage

The piece echoes the quiet visionary intensity of poets like Jean Valentine, James Galvin, or Brigit Pegeen Kelly. Its lyric estrangement resists both irony and elevation. There is also resonance with Adrienne Rich's *Atlas of the Difficult World*, particularly in its attention to labor and land, though this poem permits a brief transfiguration where Rich would remain with witness alone.

Its tone carries a biblical undercurrent, an unannounced miracle, witnessed in isolation. It can be placed near contemporary ecopoetics in its blending of labor, land, and attention, yet its detachment from political rhetoric renders the experience inward rather than declarative.

Musicality: Desert Folk / Slowcore

The pacing suggests desert folk, reverberant, sparse, shaped by light. The cadence moves slowly, as if measured by fenceposts or wind across an empty road. It carries the hush of early Iron & Wine or the ambient drift of Jim White. Beneath the stillness, the tension hums in slowcore register where space becomes pressure, and minimalism sharpens emotion.

The silence between stanzas feels held, listening. The poem breathes like early morning heat: full of presence, quiet, and distance.

Visual Art: Tonalist Landscape / Rust Belt Pastoral

The visual atmosphere evokes Tonalist painting, muted palette, diffused light, a mood that overtakes form. It recalls the landscapes of George Inness or Charles Warren Eaton, where the viewer is invited into silence rather than story.

At the same time, the poem bears traces of Rust Belt pastoral, with fields that carry memory. The imagery holds reverence without nostalgia. It is a field seen through strain and patience.

The vision lingers in a space that feels both remembered and unreal. Light spreads across the page, then recedes. The woman stays within the grasses, held and illuminated, her presence felt more than defined.

Poem 26: After the Fall of the First World

Function in the Collection

After the Fall of the First World returns the reader to historical weight after the radiant disorientation of *Morning in the Middle of Nowhere.* Where that poem opened into pastoral hallucination and mythic calm, this one reasserts collective ruin. The speaker walks alongside wreckage, spiritual, civilizational, intimate, and does not look away.

It serves as a hinge within the collection, pulling the arc out of dream and into aftermath. Here, the lyric voice no longer floats between thresholds. It stands inside failure, naming its contours without seeking repair. The poem closes the second arc of visionary suspension and enters a terrain of reckoning.

Structural Role

This poem anchors the sequence in material consequence. What was once metaphysical becomes civic. What felt surreal is now rendered as shared condition. The speaker and their companion are bodies inside history, unsure whether to flee, remain, or mourn.

The form reflects this tonal shift. Stanzas are weight-bearing, visually stacked, paced to echo debris. Lineation carries the feel of measured walking, each enjambment a step across uncertain ground. White space functions less as breath than as fallout. The architecture is deliberate, holding against collapse.

The structure allows the poem to absorb grief without dramatizing it. Its quiet force helps carry the collection forward, deeper into a field shaped by memory, loss, and the limits of endurance.

Interpretive Reading

After the Fall of the First World is a poem set inside the slow ending of a world. The title points in several directions at once, toward Eden, toward World War I, toward the larger failure of Western promise. The speaker never names which fall they mean, staying within its smoke.

Images accumulate: burning synagogues, shattered glass, cathedrals gutted. This is a present-tense atmosphere of desecration. There is no central narrative. The details drift between ancient and contemporary, between biblical echo and post-industrial ruin. This is a poem set mid-collapse.

The presence of the lover introduces intimacy, but without comfort. Even love feels imperiled, subject to the same decay that overtakes belief and architecture. The final gesture toward Jacob and Rachel evokes a deep unease. The road offers no salvation. To flee may mean safety, or it may mean death. The grief here is anticipatory and the fear is that we are already too late.

Touchpoints and Lineage

The poem stands alongside a lineage of devastated lyric: Czesław Miłosz, Paul Celan, Yehuda Amichai. Its tone recalls Carolyn Forché at her most restrained, or Jorie Graham's mystical urgency grounded in historical fact. There is also kinship with the poetry of exile, in theme and orientation. This is the voice of someone writing from within the event.

Scripture enters as presence, its ground unsteady. The echo of Genesis gestures toward faith without securing it, raising the question of whether any sacred story can survive repetition. The biblical language arrives scorched, untrustworthy and haunting. This is also a poem of diasporic pressure where memory is the residue of what is broken beyond repair.

Musicality: Post-Rock Elegy / Dustbowl Blues

The sound carries the weight of post-rock elegy. Long tonal movements, minimal percussion, a slow layering of emotional tension. The pacing recalls the quieter tracks from Mogwai or Explosions in the Sky, music that builds through accumulation.

Underneath, a thread of Dustbowl blues runs through the tone, flat, stripped, witness-heavy. Like field recordings from a collapsed landscape. The rhythm holds and carries a dry, restrained grief. The music stays inside the loss.

Visual Art: Neo-Expressionist Allegory / Post-War Figurative Abstraction

Visually, the piece recalls the allegorical intensity of Anselm Kiefer. There is rust, ash, monument, ruin, and also distance. The residue of images arrives scorched, their meaning fractured, their timeline uncertain.

The figural presence in the poem, the speaker, the lover, echoes Leon Golub's haunted bodies: fragmented, unsanctified, and vividly human. Rendered in strain. The poem's visual logic avoids narrative depiction. It presents a landscape after violence, where everything remains touched by what has occurred, even if the moment itself is no longer visible.

In that sense, the poem is a painting of war's continuation through memory. A field marked by grief but unwilling to monumentalize. The lyric voice stands inside that wreckage, remaining present with what cannot be undone.

Poem 27: Cliffard Gawthorp's Trade

Function in the Collection

Cliffard Gawthorp's Trade returns the poetry collection to a world of grit, ritual, and skilled labor. Positioned after *After the Fall of the First World*, it reframes collapse as physical inevitability, worn into the body, carried in the lungs. The poem honors a single life shaped by work and burn: Cliffard Gawthorp, whose trade, toughness, and care become a kind of elegy.

It grounds the reader again in the tangible. The metaphysical dissolves into steel and smoke, repetition and fatigue. The poem also continues the collection's attention to inheritance as gesture: the passing of cigarettes, the visualizing of a weld, the pride in something built to last. It serves as a reminder that the epic often lives inside the ordinary, and that sacrifice sometimes looks like habit.

Structural Role

Formally compact, the poem works in stanzas that land with the weight of breath, short and deliberate. The rhythm holds a conversational gravity, firm, unsentimental, edged with wear. Rather than expand outward, the structure turns inward: from remembered image to repeated action, from mythic gesture to a final offering.

Placed immediately after a poem of spiritual collapse, *Cliffard Gawthorp's Trade* shifts the gaze to a single man's endurance. The structure echoes that pivot. There is no revelation, only recurrence. The poem enacts what it describes: care through repetition, weight through rhythm. The structural logic reflects the ethic of the trade itself, each part precise, functional, held together bead by bead.

Interpretive Reading

At its center stands Gawthorp, held in balance between pride and exhaustion. He lives through what he touches: the torch, the bead, the Marlboros. Mortality moves beside him, steady and unadorned. His insight arrives in gestures: the chosen brand, the brief lesson passed to a younger worker, the quiet wink that joins irony to allegiance.

The cigarette is more than a vice; it's a ritual. When he says Camel Filters are "second best," the joke works both ways. Everyone on the site gets it and the laugh that covers what can't be said. It's half about sex, half about dying young, all about pretending neither matters.

The poem doesn't reduce Gawthorp to a type. It watches him. It records without correcting. The steadiness of that gaze mirrors his own: care as endurance, craft as witness. The poem trusts the ordinary act, the bead, the burn, the smoke, to carry its moral weight.

Touchpoints and Lineage

This poem draws from a lineage of American poets who dignify labor without embellishment, Philip Levine, B.H. Fairchild, and Larry Levis in particular. Each line carries weight, unadorned. It also echoes the quiet sorrow of James Wright, and the restrained clarity of Raymond Carver.

In Gawthorp, there are shades of Hayden's winter father, seen at last, but here the figure stands plainly in view, offering his Camel Filters as both relic and rite. There's no sentimentality. The poem's respect lies in its exactness.

Musicality: Narrative Folk / Field Recording Americana

The pacing follows the logic of breath and ritual. Its sound belongs in the lineage of narrative folk, plainspoken, melodic, and closely tied to work. The tone evokes the stripped-down presence of John Prine or Gillian Welch, where the story carries the rhythm.

Beneath this is a deeper undercurrent: the ambient honesty of field recordings, where a voice in a room holds the weight of history. The poem's tempo reflects this: steady, physical, and worn.

Visual Art: American Regionalism / Grit Realism

Visually, the piece belongs to the world of American Regionalism, but one stripped of romanticism. The eye moves across surfaces: metal, smoke, cracked fingertips. It shares terrain with Thomas Hart Benton and the WPA murals yet shifts their register from heroic to human.

There is no symbolic elevation. The work is the meaning, where every detail is rendered with exactitude, like a Walker Evans photograph, bare, composed, and honest. The poem trusts this mode. It stays close to what can be seen, and in doing so, honors what is disappearing without spectacle or nostalgia.

Poem 28: False Suns

Function in the Collection

False Suns returns the collection to a nocturnal field illuminated by modern glow and memory's residue. It extends the quiet attention of *Cliffard Gawthorp's Trade*, shifting from the bodily rhythm of labor to a more atmospheric form of apprenticeship. The transmission here is presence rather than skill, a shared walk, a forest, silos, an elder whose seeing becomes instruction.

The world they traverse shimmers between rural familiarity and estranged light, where guidance lingers though faith has dimmed. The poem broadens the collection's meditation on reverence and endurance, portraying inheritance as an act of sustained looking. Within the sequence, it serves as an elegy of continuation: for a teacher, for the craft of seeing, for meaning's quiet persistence after its source recedes.

Structural Role

Placed after a grounded portrait of industrial craft, this poem rises into a more atmospheric terrain. Its long, enjambed lines guide the reader through a slow unfolding, paced like a night walk across ground both known and changed. The structure follows a rhythm of climb and suspension: the scaling of a silo, the drift of fog, the widening glow of distant towns.

The form mirrors the experience it holds. Each line lengthens perception, creating movement through duration rather than conclusion. Companionship becomes the poem's organizing gesture, the old man shaping the moment through presence alone. The spatial logic carries that ethic forward, shaping ascent as awareness, and leaving revelation in the quiet continuation of light.

Interpretive Reading

At its core, the poem holds a moment of shared witness. The speaker and the older man move through a landscape humming with residual significance. Churches still glow. Silos still stand. The town names still hold their shape. Yet the meaning has shifted; what persists is a kind of vigil. The old man's seeing teaches the speaker how to remain within what is fading.

The "false suns" gesture toward a larger inheritance: a light that continues after its source has dimmed. The poem senses how knowledge, like illumination, can survive detachment from certainty. The Methodist church still lights the dark, though its glow feels more like care than conviction. The silos wait, the names ring faintly, each holding the memory of work and watchfulness.

In the poem's final movement, the old man imagines staying atop the silo through October, waiting for weather or for crows. The vision is plain, without ceremony, yet it carries quiet devotion. His presence lingers as method, how to look, how to endure. The poem becomes its own continuation of that lesson, each false sun a reflection of the light he left behind.

Touchpoints and Lineage

This poem shares ground with writers who have treated the Midwestern landscape as both moral and metaphysical field. Larry Levis, in his late visionary mode, offers a tonal echo, while Rodney Jones and James Galvin remain close in their capacity to drift through rural time without sentimentality.

George Oppen's material precision hums beneath the surface, the fencepost, the silo, the quality of light, while Marilynne Robinson's *Gilead* forms a literary neighbor, its quiet faith reshaped here into endurance. The poem's reverence leans toward fatigue, yet what endures is a disciplined attention. It trusts the world by continuing to see it, even as its meanings shift.

As an elegy, it joins a lineage of witness rather than praise. The false suns glow with a thinning hope, a faint brightness drawing down with him, still enough to see by.

Musicality: Ambient Folk / Post-Rural Hymn

The piece moves with the stillness of ambient folk, low register, reverent pacing, quiet instrumentation. Its sonic atmosphere recalls artists like Sufjan Stevens in his most rural modes or Mount Eerie at his most elemental.

Beneath this is the trace of a post-rural hymn: something once sacred, now filtered through electric hum. The rhythm walks rather than sings. Its pulse is soft and sustained, shaped by drizzle and distance rather than chorus or climax.

Visual Art: Apocalyptic Sublime / Postmodern Iconoclasm

Visually, the poem dwells in the uneasy light of overexposure. The landscape glows with meaning that flickers and fades. The false suns burn with echo. Their beauty is haunting, their presence ambiguous.

The visual lineage blends the sublime intensity of John Martin's celestial dramas with the destabilized surfaces of Sigmar Polke or Raymond Pettibon. Halos flare without source. Icons tremble. Light stutters across cloud cover, unclear in origin, uncertain in effect.

The poem inhabits a world lit by afterglow. What remains of the old man is absorbed into reflection, light bending off steel, echoing through cloud. The landscape itself performs remembrance, continuing what he once saw.

Poem 29: On a Bridge Over the Oka

Function in the Collection

This poem widens the collection's geographic and tonal horizon. Set above the Oka River near Nizhni Novgorod, Russia, it anchors the reader in a suspended moment: a taxi driver changing a flat tire while trolleybuses cross an aging bridge. The scene is literal, not symbolic, a precise rendering of a world in slow erosion.

It extends the manuscript's thread of artificial illumination, shifting from mythic or personal radiance to the hum of infrastructure. The poem registers light as exhaustion rather than revelation: the headlamps, the flickering interiors of the trolleybus, the sheen of oil spreading on the water. It marks a tonal pivot from communal memory in *False Suns* to solitary endurance within structural fatigue. What is described is the anticipation of collapse, the pressure that gathers in advance.

Structural Role

On a Bridge Over the Oka unfolds through four-line stanzas, each carrying the measured balance of a bridge span. The structure feels deliberate, weight-bearing, composed for endurance. Line by line, the poem builds its rhythm through even distribution rather than ascent, its tone steady, its motion horizontal. The pacing mirrors the physicality of infrastructure and the quiet transfer of pressure through steel and air.

Each stanza functions as a chamber of attention, holding observation under strain. Enjambment operates like the bridge's own joints, distributing weight rather than releasing it. The symmetry produces a sense of containment, a composure that borders on fatigue. Movement occurs laterally, through accumulation and recurrence, held in pressure rather than release. The poem's architecture becomes its subject: weight sustained, duration held in equilibrium.

Interpretive Reading

At its center stands a man alone on a mid-century bridge, changing a tire on his Volga taxi as traffic trembles by. He leaves the engine running, the headlamps bright, and trusts his tools to keep him safe. He knows the bridge's age, the fatigue in its steel, the rumors of failure, but he works anyway. He smokes a Yugoslavian cigarette, tastes its bitterness, and considers the errands that follow: bread, peanut butter, Pepsi.

The trolleybus passengers blur into a single collective face, expressionless, waiting for passage. One figure stands slightly apart, as if already living in what comes next. His gesture of crossing himself with Mary and Gabriel closes the poem with quiet reverence, faith as habit rather than plea. Beauty enters through endurance: the rainbow of petrol stretched across the water, the unbroken act of looking.

The poem honors what persists within fatigue. There is no spectacle, no ironic distance. It records awareness within the hum of decay.

Touchpoints and Lineage

On a Bridge Over the Oka joins the lineage of post-Soviet and post-industrial poetics, attentive to labor, wary of transcendence. Its stillness recalls Brodsky's spatial patience, Simic's detached observation, and Zagajewski's later, disciplined empathy. Structurally, it aligns with the documentary mode, where poem becomes record and awareness replaces resolution.

Its imagery resists metaphor. The rainbow sheen is oil, not symbol. The trolleybus is public transport, heavy with ordinary lives. The bridge functions as a figure of endurance only because it continues to hold. The poem listens for that tension and the vibration of weight over compromised ground.

Musicality: Eastern Classical / Post-War Minimalism

The sonic field recalls the austerity of Eastern classical forms, Shostakovich's preludes, Pärt's tintinnabuli, or the nocturnes written between wars. The rhythm moves through long rests and low resonance. Sound gathers in duration, a single tone held through dusk.

Visual Art: Social Realism / Melancholic Impressionism

Visually, the piece inhabits a palette of industrial fatigue. Its composition recalls the fidelity of social realism:

muted light, worn surfaces, human scale against structure. Yet a softer wash overlays the realism, a haze of melancholy closer to late Valentin Serov or Isaak Brodsky's sketches. The tone privileges atmosphere over contour. Light lingers rather than falls, detail fades into air. The figure remains small, centered by stillness.

Poem 30: Americus, for Ferlinghetti

Function in the Collection

Americus, for Ferlinghetti gathers the fatigue running through the poetry collection and concentrates it into a single, scorched address. Set against the slow ache of *On a Bridge Over the Oka*, it moves back into American territory with a tone that is wide-eyed, raw, and unsheltered. Its civic scale is matched by its emotional wear; this is a poem written from within the long aftermath.

The title places it in conversation with Ferlinghetti, whose civic poetics once blended resistance, joy, and surreal astonishment. Here, that inheritance is acknowledged and carried forward, but through a lens altered by decades of attrition. The speaker remains present, still attentive, but with no illusions of arrival. The poem becomes a gathering point for the poetry collection's larger tensions: ethical exhaustion, global simultaneity, the frayed continuity of witness.

Structural Role

Positioned at the poetry collection's later half, the poem acts as a reckoning. It draws together threads of observation, disillusionment, and persistence. Where earlier poems hover in metaphysical or psychological ambiguity, this one speaks outward, naming what surrounds and presses in.

Its rhythm alternates between clipped phrases and longer collapses, moving like a tired procession. The repeated phrase "everyone in the world" gives it a chant-like gravity, a rhythm pulled from the street or the broadcast. The structure expands and contracts, beginning with restless motion, jets, highways, heat, and settling into a fatigued stillness where even desire turns hollow.

Interpretive Reading

Americus, for Ferlinghetti opens with the image of motion. The speaker doesn't interpret these scenes. They receive them. Planes carve the sky, highways radiate heat, and bodies move. The world arrives as simultaneity: beauty, fatigue, desire, dislocation. The line "everyone in the world" repeats like an atmospheric pressure system.

Pleasure appears first, touch, glow, imagined fulfillment, but doesn't hold. The more the speaker names, the more the energy turns. The fullness grows dense, then volatile. "So that you are full and happy, / and want to kill." The line doesn't accuse. It tracks a transformation: how saturation destabilizes, how abundance breeds fracture.

The jets that first passed high in the sky return, lower now, slower, with their bellies open. The shift is structural. The fantasy of global motion has condensed into force. The overhead presence is no longer benign. The planes hang above upturned faces just before the killing begins.

The speaker never leaves the ground. Even the poem's earliest line, "The highways are a current / of the earth's bones," plants the frame deep beneath all motion. The jets dominate the sky, but what they orbit is older: the fight for matter, for minerals, for energy pulled from the earth's interior. The real subject of the poem is extraction.

By the final lines, the poem has traced a loop, from desire to violence, from surface to depth, from saturation to detonation. No rhetoric guides it. The sequence speaks for itself. The speaker remains inside this pressure, neither elevated nor immune.

Touchpoints and Lineage

The poem enters a lineage shaped by civic attention and poetic endurance. It follows Ferlinghetti in its outward regard, attentive to the public reach of language. The tonal register bears traces of Adrienne Rich's late-era clarity, the cracked civic lyricism of Brenda Hillman, and the post-industrial testimony of Mark Nowak.

One line carries the poem's memorial burden directly: "The heart of city lights is overcome." It is a farewell. The phrase recalls Ferlinghetti's *Coney Island of the Mind*, City Lights Bookstore, and the poetic publicness he helped build. Its use here is elegiac, acknowledging a civic imagination dimming under the weight of global saturation and ethical exhaustion.

There's also kinship with post-9/11 documentary lyric voices that emerged after spectacle and wrote from within its detritus. But *Americus, for Ferlinghetti* doesn't document aftermath. It holds in the present and names what still flickers.

The poem's power comes from how little it dramatizes. It stands as witness. The names, the lights, the bodies, it records what remains visible after illumination has failed.

Musicality: Beat Jazz / Spoken Blues

The rhythm rises from Beat-inflected phrasing: swung, guttural, and loose at the edges. There's a tonal grit reminiscent of Charles Mingus or the fractured improvisation of Ornette Coleman, carried in the phrasing like a second instrument.

Beneath this runs a current of spoken blues, Gil Scott-Heron in tone, grounded in endurance. The voice leans into repetition as a kind of scaffolding. The cadence stays close to the body. It carries the poem like a backbeat that keeps time through pressure.

Visual Art: West Coast Assemblage / Neo-Expressionist Muralism

Visually, the piece moves like assemblage: layered, unrestored, politically weathered. Its aesthetic recalls the West Coast materiality of George Herms or Bruce Conner, scraps, fragments, residue assembled into presence without smoothing the seams.

Overlaying this is the scale and urgency of neo-expressionist muralism. The visual field feels marked by gesture, accumulation, and haste. Each image lands like a torn scrap: a jet, a stretch of highway, a face lit from above. The composition never resolves into narrative. *Americus, for Ferlinghetti* gathers what still adheres to the nation.

Poem 31: Human Waste Dump

Function in the Collection

Human Waste Dump plunges into grotesque immediacy. It is short, furious, and deliberately unrefined. Positioned here, it acts like a punk interlude in a symphonic sequence, a primal scream interrupting the collection's composed lyricism.

It brings rupture and reflection, and the voice of moral fatigue gives way to disgust, stripped bare. The poem accuses but includes the speaker within the indictment. The "we" of the closing line remains unsettled, righteous, complicit, implicated in both harm and recognition. That instability threads back into the collection's tension between perceptive presence and entanglement.

Read immediately after *Americus, for Ferlinghetti Human Waste Dump* becomes more than rupture. It becomes consequence. If the prior poem holds a gaze on planetary saturation, jets overhead, desire inverted, faces turned upward, this one answers from inside the machinery that created that condition. The civic distance collapses into physical consequence. It is the voice of those who ordered the bombing, after impact.

The moral distance collapses. The speaker speaks from what remains. Speech has curdled and consumption has turned toxic. The poem becomes empire's physiological recoil, where no ethics are claimed, only exposure. Whatever was felt in *Americus, for Ferlinghetti*, ache, fatigue, awareness, arrives here as aftertaste.

Structural Role

Human Waste Dump cracks open the collection's steady lyric flow with a compact jolt. After the spiritual and geopolitical scope of *Americus, for Ferlinghetti*, the poem drops the reader into the raw mechanics of the body. It shifts tone and scale in a single gesture. Its placement resembles a guttural solo within a composed suite, disruptive, unvarnished, unavoidable.

Formally, the poem moves with jagged enjambments and rapid-fire pacing. The opening lines gag on imagery of gas and bile. The second half tightens into a chant, "We take... We are... We will..." a liturgy turned grotesque. The stanza does not release and there is no compositional breath. The reader is pressed into a single, suffocating field.

While earlier poems reach toward history or memory, this one tunnels into filth, offering no abstraction.

Interpretive Reading

This poem stages a confrontation with consumption, language, and collective behavior. It opens in the body and refuses to leave. The imagery is intestinal, goo, regurgitation, bile, and the progression turns that mess into indictment. What we take in, what we imitate, what we discard: these are not separable acts. They belong to a single system of waste.

The poem's "we" is corrosive, animate, and still conscious. It chews, degrades, and buzzes with awareness. The syntax stutters. Even thought seems contaminated. The poem suggests that the very conditions of language and social attention have become unstable.

The final line, "We will destroy you," remains suspended. It could be an external threat, an internal confession, or a recursive attack from the collective onto itself. Its ambiguity undoes any moral foothold. The poem hates what it is made of and refuses to climb out.

Touchpoints and Lineage

This poem draws from the tradition of anti-aesthetic rupture: Antonin Artaud's theatre of violation, Kathy Acker's grotesque disassemblies, Diane di Prima's rage fugues, and the early convulsions of Ginsberg's *Howl*. It resonates with post-industrial poets like Ariana Reines and CAConrad, who insist the body remain present even when it fails to cohere.

Its voice shares tonal ground with performance poetry and noise-based composition. It is meant to be survived more than admired. Structurally, it mirrors the psalm:

repetition, cadence, call. But the form has been stripped of devotion and filled with damage. The "we" becomes a swarm of accusation and confession, without relief.

Within the poetry collection, this is a necessary rupture. Where other poems bend toward grace or restraint, this one burns through. Nothing purifies until it has passed through the rot. This is the exposed nerve.

Musicality: Industrial Noise / Protest Folk

The piece runs on industrial abrasion. Its rhythm echoes the clang of early Einstürzende Neubauten or Throbbing Gristle, mechanical, percussive, corrosive. Each phrase hits like metal striking metal, repetition without relief.

Beneath that violence, there's a trace of protest folk, almost inaudible. Like a rusted guitar or a drowned voice still trying to carry a tune. If it sings, it sings to no one. But it sings anyway. The cadence stays close to the body, as if keeping time is the only way not to fall apart.

Visual Art: Eco-Gothic Realism / Post-Industrial Witness

Human Waste Dump inhabits the visual territory of ecological exposure. Its imagery aligns with the large-format photography of Edward Burtynsky or the surreal contamination of Alexis Rockman. These works show what systems leave behind, poison, sediment, wreckage, rendered in exact detail.

The aesthetic is clinical. Each image arrives like a specimen: bile, buzz, rot, declaration. The effect is one of haunted intimacy. Like a botanical plate of decay drawn in watercolor, or a medical etching of the body's failure. The poem catalogues its disgust.

Poem 32: Poet Compares Their Work to That of a Terrorist

Function in the Collection

This poem marks one of the collection's most decisive shifts. The voice no longer observes, interprets, or resists. Meaning is no longer negotiated. It is enacted through procedure. Where the previous poem erupts, this one executes.

Following *Human Waste Dump*, *Poet Compares Their Work to That of a Terrorist* narrows the field of consequence. What was previously rendered as a collective engine now appears through localized action. Instruction replaces reflection. The speaker moves through assigned steps and arrives at outcome. Harm enters not through spectacle, but through routine.

Together with *Americus, for Ferlinghetti* and *Human Waste Dump*, this poem completes a descent into structural participation. *Americus* surveys the system. *Human Waste Dump* renders it as a cycle of consumption. *Poet Compares Their Work to That of a Terrorist* speaks from within the mechanism itself. The earlier poems maintain distance. Here, the poem operates inside the process.

Structural Role

The poem occupies a pivotal position in the late collection, where composure shifts into participation. Collective reckoning gives way to procedural alignment. The speaker appears as one element within a larger mechanism: functional, replaceable, defined by sequence rather than reflection.

The form enacts this structure. Four-line stanzas with alternating indentation mirror hierarchical motion: statement followed by response, command followed by echo. Each unit balances authority and compliance. The indented lines register as lowered position, not diminished voice. The final single line isolates the speaker as residue once the sequence has completed.

Spatial movement remains procedural. The crate, the small room, the bar function as stations rather than settings. Enjambment pulls sentences forward across stanza breaks, maintaining continuity of action. The rhythm accumulates through repetition, carrying the reader through and leaving only the condition that remains after execution.

Interpretive Reading

Poet Compares Their Work to That of a Terrorist constructs a mirror between poetic labor and sanctioned harm. The speaker follows instruction, carries out each task, and dissolves into aftermath. Their obedience follows from fear, the pressure that governs institutions, art, and public life. The man with the stub finger becomes an emblem of control: the one who decides what can be said, which gestures are permitted, which silence will be rewarded.

Through this architecture, the poem critiques poetry as a civic practice shaped by the same forces that sustain social order. It exposes how art systems, like power systems, depend on managed fear. The plan, the partner, the act of forgetting, each mirrors cultural procedure: the negotiation of safety, belonging, and compliance. To "forget the entirety of the plan" is to relinquish conscience for acceptance, to perform endurance as virtue.

The poem's procedural tone reproduces the cadence of institutional speech. The poet becomes indistinguishable from the worker, the worker from the citizen. Each participates, unwilling yet compliant, in a choreography of caution.

The final line, "We haven't been anywhere else for a long, long time," extends the frame outward. It moves between the speaker's confinement and a society shaped by fear posing as responsibility.

Touchpoints and Lineage

The poem extends from political surrealist and procedural traditions. It shares the institutional unease of Kafka, the moral dislocation of Coetzee and Herta Müller, and the declarative force of Carolyn Forché's *The Colonel*, where violence appears through routine rather than spectacle. Its gravity is not expressive but structural.

It also resonates with post-9/11 and Iraq-era writing, where harm operates through protocol, repetition, and record. The poet functions. Language performs duty inside power.

Musicality: Post-Punk Dissonance / Spoken Performance Art

The rhythm moves with the tension of post-punk: staccato, angular, stripped of ornament. Its cadence recalls Gang of Four or early Wire, where pulse replaces melody. Each pause lands with percussive restraint, every phrase bearing the weight of documentation.

The tonal field also parallels performance art: Laurie Anderson's measured narration, Henry Rollins' compressed intensity. The sound is built from pressure, repetition, and withheld release, its energy accumulating through discipline rather than flourish.

Visual Art: Neo-Expressionism / Figurative Confrontation

Visually, the piece aligns with the raw surface of neo-expressionism. Its imagery recalls Leon Golub's distressed figures and the scorched clarity of Goya's *Disasters of War*. The aesthetic is scraped, flattened, held at the threshold of legibility.

The poem's form resembles a slab, scarred, dense and resisting beauty. Its ethical force echoes Arnulf Rainer's overpainted photographs and Wesley Kimler's visceral figuration. These works sustain confrontation rather than representation. The poem inhabits that same field, holding the reader within the charged surface where consequence and awareness converge.

Poem 33: Dirt

Function in the Collection

Dirt marks one of the most unflinching turns in the collection's final arc, arriving as both culmination and collapse. Following *Poet Compares Their Work to That of a Terrorist*, it moves beyond moral implication into a mythic register where authorship becomes structural rather than personal. The voice that speaks is less an individual agent than an embodied force, describing how worlds are shaped through repetition rather than choice.

Placed here, *Dirt* functions as a dark creation myth, gathering the collection's strands of war, masculinity, motherhood, and language into a single, procedural vision. What earlier poems witness, react to, or internalize, this poem renders inevitable. The system no longer pressures the speaker. It speaks for itself.

Across the preceding sequence, the collection shifts from civic exposure to allegorical rendering to psychological absorption. *Americus, for Ferlinghetti* surveys the larger cultural machinery. *Human Waste Dump* renders that machinery as an engine of consumption and waste. *Poet Compares Their Work to That of a Terrorist* shows how fear reshapes the speaker from the inside. *Dirt* no longer reacts to the system. It describes how the system reproduces itself.

Structural Role

Within the architecture of the collection, *Dirt* functions as a point where description gives way to decree. The poem no longer observes systems of harm or dramatizes their effects. It speaks from within them. The voice assumes an operative authority, issuing statements that behave less like reflection and more like instruction.

The poem's short, declarative movements resemble commands rather than images. Each stanza establishes a condition, assigns a role, or enacts a transformation. Space becomes procedural: womb, home, battlefield. These are not settings but chambers of function. The language itself becomes the mechanism through which consequence is carried forward.

Interpretive Reading

Dirt unfolds as a corrupted genesis. A woman appears already shaped by vigilance. A child enters a structure where nurture merges with preparation for disappearance. The voice that assigns these conditions does not argue or explain. It declares.

Creation here is procedural. Names become destinies. Spaces become functions. "War" is not an event but a condition into which bodies are placed. The language does not persuade. It arranges.

The calm delivery intensifies the devastation. Authority moves through syntax. Harm travels through certainty. The voice does not reflect on violence. It installs it.

In the final gesture, the child is returned to the system that produced him. Consumption replaces care. Generation folds into erasure. What remains is not shock but recognition: this is how the structure sustains itself.

Touchpoints and Lineage

The poem aligns with a lineage that reduces myth to its structural core. Its diction echoes the authority of biblical and legal language, Genesis, Job, Ecclesiastes, where utterance establishes reality through decree rather than reflection. Language operates as placement.

In modern terms, *Dirt* shares ground with the procedural gravity of George Oppen and Charles Reznikoff, where the voice does not interpret experience but arranges it, letting structure carry consequence. Meaning arrives through compression, not explanation.

Musicality: Acoustic Blues / Lo-Fi Americana

The rhythm moves like slow blues, earth-toned, deliberate, and continuous. Each phrase carries the drag of soil and the hum of endurance. The cadence resembles lo-fi Americana: rough, grounded, unornamented. The poem accumulates rather than resolves, every sentence settling into silence as if returning to ground.

Visual Art: Earth Art / Material Minimalism

Visually, *Dirt* mirrors the ethos of Earth Art and Material Minimalism. It behaves like shaped matter, scored, placed, and left to weather. The aesthetic recalls Smithson's entropic geometries, Mendieta's ritual imprints, and Eva Hesse's weighted forms. Each gesture carries pressure without decoration.

Poem 34: Three-Legged Nag

Function in the Collection

Three-Legged Nag does not extend the sequence that precedes it. It redirects the collection's momentum into a new mode of reflection. After the procedural, allegorical, and mythic pressures of the prior poems, this piece opens a different register: solitary, unsettled, and resistant to explanation.

Placed late in the collection, the poem carries the weight of what has already unfolded. It does not respond to the system so much as move beyond it. The speaker is no longer shaped by command, fear, or institutional force, but by endurance. What remains is a journey without instruction, a burden without clarification, and a landscape that offers no resolution.

In this way, *Three-Legged Nag* functions as a late bridge within the collection. It gathers the ethical gravity of the earlier arc and redirects it toward a quieter, more uncertain terrain. The poem does not restore order or deliver meaning. It prepares the ground for what follows by establishing a condition of sustained attention without authority.

Structural Role

Placed near the end of the collection, this poem shifts from symbolic escalation to sustained, private movement. The scope narrows to a single speaker and a burden that remains physically present throughout. The settings change, yard, road, river, but the action stays consistent: forward motion under strain.

The form is spare and sequential. Short, declarative lines establish weight and direction. Early stanzas emphasize environment and physical detail, dew, ticks, rot. As the nag resists, the pacing fractures. Control gives way to exertion. The poem accelerates toward a final obstruction, a burning river that halts progress without offering closure. The structure holds tension through continuation rather than resolution.

Interpretive Reading

This is a parable of sacred burden. The nag might be poetry, conscience, memory, prophecy. It does not speak. The speaker tries to ride it, guide it, then contemplates killing it. The animal refuses all roles. It endures. Its refusal to move mirrors the speaker's deeper crisis: a confrontation with meaning that no longer arrives through action, but through resistance.

The poem alludes to Balaam's donkey, a biblical beast who sees the divine when its rider cannot. The speaker wrestles with doubt: Is this burden a punishment? A message? A god in disguise?

The poem's most powerful question arrives at the end. If the speaker tries to strangle the nag, will it finally speak? Will it reveal what it knows? Or has the test always been endurance?

Three-Legged Nag isn't symbolic in the traditional sense. It doesn't present a key. It withholds: the allegory is damaged, tired, unsanctified, and that damage is the point. The poem leaves the speaker, and the reader, in a state of unresolved struggle with something too broken to carry and too sacred to abandon.

Touchpoints and Lineage

This poem draws from the tradition of spiritual allegory, particularly biblical and post-biblical literature where beasts carry messages and trials arrive without context. It recalls *The Book of Numbers*, Rilke's *The Man Watching*, and elements of Cormac McCarthy's *The Crossing*, where moral trial replaces revelation.

Its visual field echoes the expressive realism of James Wright or Franz Wright, but with the distortion of late Philip Guston: figures bent under symbolic weight, moving through grotesque yet intimate terrain. There's also kinship with outsider artists like Martín Ramírez or Judith Scott, where repetition and burden form meaning slowly, through insistence rather than explanation.

Musicality: Junkyard Ragtime / Broken Ballad

Three-Legged Nag lurches like junkyard ragtime, rhythmic, unstable, mournful. It shares musical DNA with Tom Waits or Captain Beefheart, where melody is fragmented but persistent. Beneath that surface lies a broken ballad: tired, limping, unresolved. The rhythm doesn't drive. It drags. The song doesn't uplift; it mutters, and what emerges is grit.

Visual Art: Outsider Expressionism / Visionary Figuration

The imagery suggests Outsider Expressionism: crude forms, broken symmetry, but charged with moral presence. The nag could be carved from burned wood, sewn from scraps, or molded from earth. The aesthetic shares lineage with Judith Scott's wrapped forms, Martín Ramírez's repeated corridors, or Dubuffet's childlike urgency. The poem's visual register is handmade, and resistant to polish.

Poem 35: The Devourer

This poem marks a rupture in the collection's late sequence. Where *Three-Legged Nag* moved through silence and burden, *The Devourer* arrives as eruption: accusatory, elemental, and unrelenting. The tone shifts from endurance to exposure. What was carried is now confronted.

Positioned here, the poem breaks the quiet labor of the preceding work with a force that names what had only been endured. The language turns sharp, intimate, and consuming. Care becomes pressure. Closeness becomes threat.

This shift accelerates the collection from reflection into reckoning. The figure of the devourer does not resolve earlier tensions, it intensifies them. Its presence recasts prior moments of failed protection, inverted nurture, and moral fatigue as part of a larger pattern now brought into the open.

Structural Role

Placed deep in the final quarter, *The Devourer* transforms the collection's composure into reckoning, building on what was first ruptured in *Don't Tell Me You*

Haven't Thought This Before. Where earlier poems sustained ambiguity or held perception at a contemplative distance, this one speaks from inside the storm. Its presence signals a structural shift from the poetics of observation to the poetics of survival. The speaker no longer hovers near implication. They enter the force field.

Formally, the poem resists continuity. It proceeds by accumulation. The lines are jagged, breathless, and immediate. Images surface abruptly, bound by tonal force rather than sequence. The pacing lurches and seizes, as if meaning itself were arriving faster than it can be organized. This refusal of cohesion enacts the poem's pressure: to let pain speak without mitigation.

Interpretive Reading

The Devourer transforms the unsettling history of violated care into fable. Its origins lie in real stories, nurses who poisoned those they tended, swindlers who preyed upon the frail, but the poem resists mere documentation. Instead, it elevates those events into an archetype of moral inversion: the healer as predator, the caregiver as thief.

The figure addressed recalls the shadows cast by both the falsely accused and the truly culpable, names like Filipina Narciso, Leonora Perez, and Jane Toppan, women through whom society's fears about power, gender, and trust have long circulated. The poem gathers those echoes into a single, composite presence: a devourer of faith, of inheritance, of intimacy itself.

Each epithet, "spirit cannibal," "zombie soul," "hair-trigger of destruction," functions less as accusation than as spell, language spoken to hold a force at bay. The voice carries both rage and caution, the understanding that evil often appears in the shape of care.

In the closing vision, a creature of light whose brilliance lures and consumes, the poem becomes a moral warning. Its radiance is predatory. What gleams here is the peril of misplaced trust, and the need for vigilance in the face of what dazzles.

In the architecture of the collection, *The Devourer* answers an earlier eruption, *Don't Tell Me You Haven't Thought This Before*. That poem voiced the fantasy of violence. This one embodies its arrival. Where the earlier piece sanctified anger as survival, *The Devourer* reveals its cost, the point where imagined retribution takes form. Read together, they trace a descent from thought to manifestation, from fury as protection to fury as contagion.

Touchpoints and Lineage

This poem belongs to the lineage of poetic confrontation, driven by moral clarity rather than self-exposure. It recalls the psychic voltage of Sylvia Plath's *Lesbos*, the accusatory precision of Ai's monologues, and the mythic inversions of Louise Glück's *The Wild Iris*. Yet its structure is more fractured, more elemental. It draws from the Symbolist and surrealist inheritance, where form bends to psychic pressure instead of narrative logic.

The voice also resonates with prophetic traditions, Jeremiah, Nahum, Ezekiel, where the vision carries fury without comfort. The address is personal, but its moral field is collective. The poem speaks from a place where betrayal of care becomes a civic and spiritual wound. In its unrelenting tone, it stands beside Antonin Artaud's letters and Clarice Lispector's mystical fragments, works that burn through coherence to reach a deeper form of witness.

Musicality: Gothic Drone / Ritual Percussion

The musical register of *The Devourer* belongs to the slow, immersive gravity of gothic drone, music where tone outweighs melody, and repetition becomes a form of spiritual pressure. Think of Dead Can Dance, Swans, or the layered density of ambient dirges. Rhythm here is less about beat than about psychic interval, like a ritual drum barely audible behind a wall. The poem's breath catches and stutters. There is no buildup, only engulfment.

Visual Art: Neo-Expressionism / Apocalyptic Allegory

Visually, the piece shares a lineage with large-scale allegorical work from the neo-expressionist tradition, particularly pieces that stage psychic trauma without resolving it into symbol. The figure of the devourer may be imagined through the scarred surfaces of Anselm Kiefer, the animalistic scale of Wesley Kimler's canvases, or the contorted figuration of late Philip Guston. These are fields of ethical pressure.

There is also sculptural presence here, akin to Louise Bourgeois's spider forms, protective in appearance, consuming in function. The visual texture of the poem feels clawed, gouged, fused from refuse and gold.

Poem 36: Scarecrows

Function in the Collection

Scarecrows extends the collection's attention from individual reckoning into collective habit. Following the intensity of *The Devourer*, the poem settles into a scene where something deeply unfamiliar has already been folded into ordinary life.

What stands in the field appears as practice rather than protest. The men enact a custom that requires no explanation within the world they inhabit. Meaning arrives through repetition, inheritance, and shared acceptance. What once may have begun as intention now circulates as expectation. In this way, *Scarecrows* sharpens a central pressure of the collection: that choice becomes difficult to locate once a practice is established.

Structural Role

Scarecrows unfolds as a downward-moving utterance shaped across three compact stanzas. Each stanza accrues weight through enjambment rather than propulsion, extending phrases across lines in a way that slows motion and emphasizes continuity over event.

The first two stanzas are driven by descriptive accumulation. Clauses stack without resolution, creating lateral movement that mirrors the figures' sustained exposure in the field. Line breaks delay closure, holding attention within an ongoing present rather than directing it toward outcome.

The final stanza tightens both syntax and pacing. Shorter lines and reduced enjambment compress the poem's motion, bringing it to rest without conclusion. The poem does not culminate so much as settle. Its ending functions as a structural deceleration rather than a turn.

Interpretive Reading

The title names what the figures resemble from a distance. Upright shapes in a field. Arms held open. A posture familiar enough to pass without inquiry. The word *scarecrows* allows the scene to remain unexamined.

Closer attention alters that ease. These are men. They go out into the field dressed as they have always dressed, moving through ground they know by habit and touch.

They stand upright and remain exposed. Arms extend toward the flatland they have worked and watched for years. Labor does not end so much as change form.

These men carry a form of enlightenment shaped through endurance, injury, care, and time. It taught them how to live and how to remain. It did not resolve the larger field that surrounds their lives. The flatland opens without boundary. Scale exceeds measure. Standing becomes a way of meeting that expanse directly, like being on open water or under a moonless, cloudless sky, where orientation loosens and scale no longer answers back.

They know what follows. Petrification belongs to the practice. Still, they proceed. Only afterward do the daughters enter the frame. Before passing, the men instruct them to leave the bodies where they stand so their shadows may fall back onto the ground.

What unfolds does not interrupt the life around it. The ritual persists within a world that otherwise appears legible. Roads remain. Buildings stand. Other customs continue. Within the field, a different order holds. *Scarecrows* marks a point where choice becomes difficult to separate from practice, carried forward without explanation.

Touchpoints and Lineage

Scarecrows aligns more closely with the deadpan surrealism of James Tate than with pastoral tradition. Its power comes from the quiet presentation of something fundamentally strange, delivered without explanation or dramatic emphasis. The tone recalls the way Tate allows the uncanny to settle into ordinary scenes, where the bizarre is treated as a fact of daily life rather than a disruption.

There is also a cinematic kinship with Quentin Tarantino's method of placing unsettling material inside casual, familiar settings. The poem does not heighten its strangeness through spectacle. It normalizes it. The figures in the field are not framed as symbols or warnings. They are simply there.

Musicality: Dark Folk / Ambient Minimalism

The sonic atmosphere of *Scarecrows* is sparse and unsettled. While its rural quiet recalls the restraint of Nick Drake, the emotional temperature is flatter, less mournful than strangely composed. The deeper influence lies in ambient minimalism, Harold Budd, Stars of the Lid, where sound drifts without narrative or release. The music here does not guide feeling. It simply remains.

Visual Art: Symbolist Figuration / Rural Surrealism

The visual logic of *Scarecrows* aligns with José Guadalupe Posada's skeletal figures performing ordinary tasks. Like Posada's calaveras, the bodies in the field are not treated as spectacles of death but as part of daily life. They stand, endure, and serve a function. The unease comes from how calmly this is accepted. Nothing in the landscape resists their presence.

The strangeness of the poem lies in how calmly this practice is held. Nothing in the landscape reacts. The fields remain open. The sky stays wide. The bodies stay where they are. In this sense, the atmosphere aligns with Andrew Wyeth's rural stillness, where the ordinary becomes unsettling only when one looks long enough. What appears familiar is quietly impossible.

Poem 37: The Perennials

Function in the Collection

The Perennials is an act of gentle reentry. After the estrangement of *Scarecrows*, this poem turns back toward a world shaped by tending, memory, and loss. It returns to rural space as field condition, material, inherited, and altered. Its gestures feel modest, but they hold. The structures are failing, yet life persists. A house sloughs its siding, daffodil blooms, a hand remembers the feel of wool.

Positioned late in the poetry collection, the poem offers a tonal rebalancing. It attends to what has endured. Its attention is precise, steady, and quietly held. *The Perennials* begins a movement away from rupture toward perceptual grace.

Structural Role

This poem initiates the final arc of the collection, an arc defined by return. The affect is elegiac, but the structure is observational. The speaker and their companion arrive with food, with memory, with presence.

Formally, the poem unfolds in long, breath-aware lines, with a pacing that echoes the slow yield of seasonal change. Enjambments are fluid, tonal shifts gradual. The poem's structure mimics the work of tending: noticing, returning, repeating. Its scale is intimate, and its tempo stretches time rather than marking it.

Interpretive Reading

This is a poem about presence under conditions of loss. The farmhouse still stands, the sheep are gone, and still, the cats eat. The earth remembers.

The act of bringing food becomes a form of care. These domestic rituals, feeding, observing, walking, compose a form of stewardship that resists sentimentality. They register decay without disavowal. The return of the peacock, improbable and unsignaled, holds the poem open. His voice punctures the soft light of memory with something stranger, wilder, more exalted.

In this way, the poem proposes a theology of recurrence as practice. What blooms and what returns remain legible through cycles of ruin and care.

Touchpoints and Lineage

The Perennials shares compositional ground with post-pastoral poets like James Galvin, Louise Glück, and Larry Levis. It echoes Glück's interest in seasonal perception, Galvin's attention to rural architecture, and Levis's ability to tether memory to landscape without requiring resolution. Its lineage also includes the quiet endurance of Jack Gilbert's later work, where affection and loss are spoken in the same breath.

The poem remains within the American pastoral field, but it resists closure, redemption, or elegy. It belongs to a poetics of attention and it simply names what continues.

Musicality: Chamber Folk / Neo-Classical Pastoral

The musical sensibility here draws from chamber folk and neo-classical pastoral: sparse, acoustic, and durational. Its phrasing evokes the softness of early Iron & Wine or the intimate austerity of Nick Drake. Beneath that is a tonal bed reminiscent of Ólafur Arnalds or Max Richter, where strings hold and repeat, offering quiet momentum without climax. The poem's rhythm is seasonal rather than linear. Its sonic world feels carried by breath and light.

Visual Art: Botanical Illustration / Serial Minimalism

Visually, the piece resonates with botanical illustration and serial minimalism, forms that work through repetition, patience, and calibrated restraint. Its perennials are archival. Like Ellsworth Kelly's plant drawings or Vija Celmins's meditative surface renderings, the visual field is organized by recurrence and attention.

There is also kinship with Agnes Martin and Michelle Stuart, artists whose serial works offer spiritual rhythm without spectacle. The garden here is diagrammed rather than imagined, felt rather than adorned. The image world is exacting, minimal, and quietly sacred.

The visual atmosphere is one of mapped return: the geometry of seasons. The peacock at the close, luminous and improbable, refracts that geometry. He arrives strange, gorgeous and ungoverned.

Poem 38: The Multitude of Opalescent Grackles

Function in the Collection

The Multitude of Opalescent Grackles appears as a luminous compression, a short, charged meditation arriving near the end of the poetry collection. Its scale is miniature, but its force is vivid. Where *The Perennials* moves through memory and care, this poem delivers a sudden tilt toward animal witness and corporeal legacy.

The poem binds the human and the more-than-human into a shared field of instinct, residue, and continuation. Here, death is no longer abstract or symbolic. It is a site of instruction, first in stone, then in swarm. The poem holds neither lament nor consolation. It names what stains, what survives, and what multiplies.

Structural Role

This poem functions as a concentrated sequence of descent and transfer. Its four stanzas move through distinct registers of continuity: stone, mind, body, and matter. The opening frame situates the dead in fixed form, statues and sculpted eyes standing guard. The second stanza turns inward, where memory becomes voice and inscription. The third projects forward through inheritance, the body reproduced in children and carried through time. The final stanza returns to the material world, where birds stain the ground with a juice that resembles blood.

Rather than building toward climax, the poem proceeds by quiet conversion. Each stanza lowers the field of attention, shifting presence from monument to thought, from lineage to residue. The structure is spare and ritual-like, its movement steady rather than dramatic. What remains is circulation: memory carried forward through endurance.

Interpretive Reading

The poem stages a dialogue between human legacy and animal instinct. The dead offer guidance. Their stone faces appear weary, alert, almost animate. Their message is simple: leave something behind. Whether in gesture, bloodline, or language, continue. The answer is embodied and carried.

The grackles, when they arrive, perform the message. Their movement forms a theology of function. They swarm, feed, and scatter. Their presence fills the air with sound and the ground with color. The juice they spill resembles blood, and the effect is carnal and vivid: stain without martyrdom, life without translation.

Touchpoints and Lineage

The Multitude of Opalescent Grackles traces a compositional lineage to poets who treat animal life as a force rather than a symbol: Charles Wright's lyric decay and the dark ecology of Jorie Graham's later work. It shares Mary Ruefle's tonal clarity and Brigit Pegeen Kelly's mythic fauna, particularly her refusal of animal transparency. The poem enters a tradition where nature is participatory, where birds carry forms of knowledge the human barely registers.

There is no myth of return here, no elevation through suffering. What persists is density, presence, and motion. The poem aligns with a lyric tradition that holds the sacred inside the ordinary and finds its most haunting images in the overlap between human meaning and animal continuance.

Musicality: Avant-Garde Jazz / Electroacoustic Swarm

The sonic atmosphere of *The Multitude of Opalescent Grackles* emerges from collision and syncopation. Its movement resembles the scatter of avant-garde jazz, fluid, frenetic, radiant in its disarray. Tonal comparisons include Ornette Coleman's bright ruptures or the erratic grace of Sun Ra's ensemble pieces, where rhythm fractures into momentum.

Beneath this is a murmur of processed sound, where field noise and tonal shimmer blend into an electroacoustic swarm. Think Matmos, Ben Frost, or early Tim Hecker, composers who layer signal and silence into structures that feel both technical and feral. The poem's rhythm contracts, expands, glints, and dissipates.

Visual Art: Iridescent Realism / Swarm Composition

Visually, the piece operates within a kinetic field, closer to swarm choreography than static image. The grackles shimmer with metallic color and mechanical motion. Their iridescence echoes the layered realism of Walton Ford, where animals are rendered with anatomical intensity and historical residue. Their movement recalls the aerial scatter of Cai Guo-Qiang's explosive drawings, marks created through detonation and held together only by trajectory.

The poem's attention to glint and multiplicity also finds kinship with James Prosek's fauna, where precision accumulates into excess. What emerges is a radiant disorder: purposeful, dense, and unreadable in motive. The composition holds through saturation rather than design.

Poem 39: Ode to a Roadkill

Function in the Collection

Ode to a Roadkill offers one of the collection's sharpest tonal reversals, brief, brutal, and strangely elegiac. Its voice enters with a deadpan lyricism that skirts satire without collapsing into it. Positioned after the spectral scale of *The Multitude of Opalescent Grackles*, this poem drops the register and scale, returning the reader to a single body, a patch of road, and a speaker reckoning with estrangement that feels both petty and cosmic. The gesture is deflating, but not dismissive. The address to the raccoon is specific, while the condition it exposes is systemic: alienation rendered ordinary.

Structural Role

This poem serves as a necessary contraction, tightening the aperture after the broader philosophical and visual sweep of surrounding poems. It narrows both field and tone, enacting a local brutality that refuses elevation. The form is split: declarative strophes hold one line of address, while parentheticals interrupt with fragments of sky, planet, and urban glow. That split creates a jittered, halting rhythm, pulling the poem between bodily witness and metaphysical drift. The movement stalls and returns, tracking the speaker's oscillation between intimacy and detachment.

Interpretive Reading

The raccoon is both encountered and addressed, a fellow occupant of the same damaged terrain. Its body, destroyed by traffic, draws forth a monologue that sounds like elegy until it turns. The speaker recalls the animal's minor infractions, knocked-over cans, interrupted sleep, and places them beside its dismemberment. That juxtaposition is neither fair nor comic. It's reflexive. Two forms of life sharing the same space, subject to the same pressures, one more vulnerable to the road's indifference.

The parentheticals widen the frame without offering relief. Jupiter, snow-filled clouds, distant light. The same sky hangs over both raccoon and speaker, suggesting not transcendence but proximity. The animal species has likely occupied this terrain longer than the houses, the cans, the cars. The human voice registers this but does not resolve it.

The raccoon remains in the ditch. The speaker remains unsure what any of it means. The final line, "On purpose. Perhaps," delivers the only overt inflection, but even that turns away from certainty. The death is ambiguous. The motive is unknowable. What endures is the shared exposure: two lives under the same night, one erased, one still looking.

Touchpoints and Lineage

Ode to a Roadkill draws from a plainspoken, observational lineage where address replaces abstraction and attention carries the weight of meaning. Its structure recalls Ted Berrigan's conversational directness, where tone remains casual even as the subject turns severe. The poem speaks outward, naming what it sees without interpretive cushioning.

There is also kinship with the American anti-pastoral, where nature is shaped by human routine rather than reverence. But unlike poems that convert violence into metaphor or reflection, this one stays with the body. The road is not symbolic. The animal is not a mirror. The act is not redeemed. The poem witnesses and stops.

Musicality: Heartland Rock / American Alternative

The tonal register of *Ode to a Roadkill* moves within the restrained, observational mode of American alternative and heartland rock. Its rhythm is steady, unembellished, and grounded in ordinary scenes of loss. Musically, it carries kinship with R.E.M.'s "Cuyahoga," where ecological damage and quiet mourning unfold without spectacle, through plainspoken witnessing rather than emotional release.

There is also resonance with the somber clarity of Johnny Cash's late recordings and the stripped-down gravity of 16 Horsepower, where lamentation is carried in simple phrasing and unadorned tone. The poem leans toward the death-ballad tradition, not through ceremony, but through aftermath. This is a minor requiem, heard after the impact, when only the scene remains.

Visual Art: Anatomical Realism / Morbid Romanticism

Visually, the piece recalls anatomical drawing and morbid romanticism. The raccoon is rendered in fur, gut, and position. This restraint aligns with the brutal intimacy of Lucian Freud's figuration, where flesh is observed without embellishment, and with the cataloguing spirit of Mark Dion's taxonomic work, which presents natural remnants as specimens within failed systems of order.

There is kinship, too, with Géricault's severed studies or Otto Dix's battlefield detritus, works that hold their subjects in view until attention becomes its own act. The poem positions the raccoon's death without ceremony. The road is the frame, and the body becomes part of the ordinary landscape.

Poem 40: Consequences of an Old Lady and Her Dog

Function in the Collection

Consequences of an Old Lady and Her Dog narrows the poetry collection's attention to a single domestic pressure point, a neighborly resentment rendered with psychic precision. It arrives in the final arc, where spiritual aftermath and spectral return give way to intimate reckoning. Where earlier poems stretch toward cosmology, memory, or grotesque humor, this one enters the moral weather of a fence line, a gesture held too long. Its setting is small, but the domestic scale acts as a chamber, holding a cruelty that once flickered as thought and now echoes in absence.

This poem exposes the minor violences that live just beneath civility. It does so to stay with the trace of harm once imagined and now half-remembered. The poem holds its tension without release. No one speaks. No one is redeemed.

Structural Role

Placed after the cosmic unrest of *The Multitude of Opalescent Grackles* and the bleak comedy of *Ode to a Roadkill*, this poem contracts the collection's scope. The field narrows from sky and road to lawn and church pew. The emotional register tightens with it. The poem moves from public and environmental witness into a private, interior reckoning shaped by proximity and irritation.

Formally, the poem unfolds in uneven stanza blocks. Short lines and abrupt stanza breaks regulate pacing, creating a stop-start movement that mirrors the speaker's shifting attention. The structure alternates between observation, imagined action, and aftermath, allowing each mode to stand on its own. The final stanza returns the speaker to physical presence, where the residue of the earlier thoughts lingers quietly.

Interpretive Reading

The voice begins from irritation. The speaker recounts the routines of an aging neighbor, mowing beyond the boundary, leaving dog waste, asserting presence in quiet ways that become intolerable. The irritation calcifies into desire, and then into fantasy. A wish forms, with a kind of rehearsed geometry: harm displaced, then directed. The speaker imagines killing the dog. The imagined act is less about the animal than what it represents: control, defiance, tether.

What follows is recoil. The neighbor disappears. The dog is no longer seen. Time passes. The speaker recalls the wish with a physical response, the heat of shame, unclaimed. The moment lingers. Its residue is a kind of psychic bruise.

The power of the poem lies in its refusal to indict or forgive. It documents a flicker of malice and the trace it leaves behind. No judgment lands. The speaker remains aware and the silence thickens.

Touchpoints and Lineage

This poem enters the lineage of unspectacular confession, where the speaker offers no virtue, only presence. Its tonal ancestry includes the psychological focus of Elizabeth Bishop's *Crusoe in England*, the suburban menace of Amy Hempel, and the ethical friction in Louise Glück's late short poems. There is also kinship with the clipped clarity of Rae Armantrout, though here the structure steadies rather than fragments.

The poem shares a temperament with quiet realist fiction, Raymond Carver's unresolved domestic spaces, Mary Gaitskill's emotional opacity. But this is lyric, and the force comes from containment.

Musicality: Lo-Fi Waltz / Domestic Dissonance

The piece moves in the rhythm of a lo-fi waltz, off-center, resistant to crescendo. Its musical analogues include the understated eeriness of early Magnetic Fields, or the domestic tension in Erik Satie's *Gymnopédies*, slowed further. There's a kind of music-box energy here, ornamental on the surface, dissonant in the mechanism.

Visual Art: Psychological Realism / Muted Surrealism

The poem occupies a visual plane where realism bends under emotional weight. Its world could be painted by Luc Tuymans, faded light, ambiguous gestures, flattened affect. The lawn, the leash, the old woman's figure, each could be rendered in a palette of grays and acidic greens, framed as if through memory.

There is also resonance with the domestic surrealism of Dorothea Tanning's interior rooms, where the familiar begins to unmoor. The leash becomes a tether between control and dependence. The dog becomes a proxy. The space remains quiet, but the tension accumulates.

Poem 41: Fathom

Function in the Collection

Fathom enters late in the poetry collection as a moment of elemental surrender. It follows a long sequence of rupture, exposure, and corrosion across psychic, civic, and ecological registers. This poem offers no restoration, but it alters the atmosphere. Where earlier poems confront damage through witness, impulse, or reckoning, *Fathom* loosens those frames. Marsh, water, breath, and body converge in a space without edges. The reader is asked to descend.

Structural Role

Positioned near the close of the collection, *Fathom* functions as a slowing threshold. The poem redirects momentum away from rupture and toward submersion, where sensation replaces action and depth replaces distance.

Formally, the poem unfolds as a field shaped by regular tercets rather than continuous flow. Lineation delays breath, suspends phrasing, and regulates the pace of reading to mirror the pressure of water. Rather than driving sequence, the structure accumulates atmosphere. The surface dissolves early, and the poem remains in saturation.

Interpretive Reading

Fathom enacts a descent into the elemental, where perception and body enter a shared field. The marsh becomes medium, a living body through which attention passes. The speaker's invitation, "take my lake heart through your fingers," turns intimacy into immersion. Touch becomes a way of entering rather than possessing.

The poem's force resides in its restraint. There is no narrative progression, only deepening. Breathing "with the bluegill" aligns the human body with the water's rhythm, a shared system of endurance. The gesture remains grounded in matter rather than transcendence. Meaning emerges through saturation, through staying within what presses and holds.

Touchpoints and Lineage

Fathom draws from a lineage of elemental lyricism where perception is physical and attention is immersive. Its movement echoes the submerged prayer of Merwin, the river-grounded precision of Niedecker, and H.D.'s fusion of body and tide. These influences appear not as quotation but as current.

There is also an affinity with Mary Biddinger, whose immersive lyric practice allows environment and body to meet without hierarchy or resolution. The poem carries tradition as undertow rather than statement. Its voice advances through pressure, sound, and texture, testing how lyric attention operates when experience outweighs explanation.

Musicality: Ambient Submersion / Tidal Hymn

The sonic field unfolds slowly, vowel-rich and resonant. It evokes the ambient submersion of Julianna Barwick, the tidal drag of William Basinski, and the dissolving loops of Loscil. Each phrase extends rather than divides; rhythm becomes suspension. The music gathers pressure instead of motion. Breath thickens, cadence lengthens, and sound inhabits the body as vibration.

Visual Art: Subaqueous Color Field / Elemental Minimalism

Visually, *Fathom* inhabits the realm of submerged color field painting, where depth replaces perspective. It recalls Rothko filtered through water, Helen Frankenthaler's soaked pigments, or Gerhard Richter's seascapes blurred into memory. The palette moves through fog-gray, reed-green, and inked blue, tones that suggest absorption rather than light.

No figure anchors the field. Depth emerges through density. Like Roni Horn's glass works or Per Kirkeby's layered surfaces, the image invites descent. The structure mirrors the emotional register, a slow fall through translucence.

Poem 42: Jubilee

Function in the Collection

Jubilee enters near the collection's close as a tonal widening, a moment of astonishment shaped by presence. Composed as a gesture of celebration and gratitude, it carries the cadence of offering. The poem provides counterweight to the collection's earlier violences and fractures through its act of memory and return. Where much of the book traverses collapse, *Jubilee* pauses within continuity.

Its setting, a house near a ravine with trees overhead, anchors the gaze in rootedness and inheritance. The poem enacts recognition. It looks back without retreating, standing fully inside what endures.

Structural Role

Placed near the collection's close, *Jubilee* functions as a tonal and thematic aperture. It opens the sequence outward, shifting its energy from reckoning toward recognition. Where earlier poems trace rupture, displacement, and ethical disquiet, this one steadies the gaze. The poem grants the speaker footing, a way to remain within memory without being consumed by it.

Formally, the poem unfolds in long, breath-held lines that rise and settle. Syntax extends across time, allowing perception to accumulate. The rhythm holds, slow and suspended, shaped by reverence rather than urgency. Each image, rain-soaked roof, stone lion, carved initials, gathers toward a presence that is both ordinary and sacred. The poem's upward motion is tempered by gravity; it rises with the understanding that what lifts must also remain rooted.

Interpretive Reading

Jubilee turns remembrance into architecture. The poem revisits a childhood house at the edge of a ravine and finds in its details, chipmunk paths, initials carved into bark, a language of inheritance. Each image gathers its symbolism from the world it inhabits. The edge becomes both boundary and revelation. It is the place where memory touches what continues.

The poem's title opens a larger frame. In scripture, the Jubilee Year is one of release, of debts forgiven and land returned. Here, that idea translates into emotional and generational terms. The speaker releases possession, holding memory as something communal and unfinished. The house, the ravine, the tree: each carries its own continuity, its own measure of return.

The final image, those carved initials lifted by the tree's growth, becomes emblematic of the poem's symbolic order. What began as a private mark rises into air, a visible testament to time's expansion. The carving remains as a scar, a quiet witness in the beech. In that gesture, *Jubilee* closes its long arc of the familial and elemental, turning inheritance into renewal.

Touchpoints and Lineage

The poem draws from traditions of lyric witness and contemplative lineage. Its tonal restraint and attention to memory suggest kinship with Li-Young Lee or Robert Hass, especially in their layering of natural image with personal inheritance. There is also something of Seamus Heaney in the way place becomes portal. James Wright's reverent Midwestern gaze flickers here.

Musicality: New Orleans Funeral March / Deconstructed Gospel

Jubilee moves like there's gospel in the phrasing, but bent, unraveled, stripped of certainty. Think of Tom Waits in his quieter moods, or Meshell Ndegeocello channeling sacred music through distortion. It walks forward like a second line played at half-speed, lifting joy from loss without denying the weight.

Visual Art: Social Abstraction / Festive Realism

Visually, the piece evokes a vibrant field under pressure, color pushed through exhaustion. The street scenes of Jacob Lawrence, the heat and blur of Beauford Delaney, the joyful restraint of Alma Thomas. The image is of a celebration held together by memory and paint. Streamers still hang, but the sky has dimmed. The poem suggests a mural after a parade, banners faded, confetti wet, but beauty still visible in the remnants.

Poem 43: To A Young Malcolm X

Function in the Collection

To A Young Malcolm X is both a rupture and a reckoning. It speaks to the younger Malcolm, volatile and clear-eyed, rather than the mythic figure sanctified by history. Addressing that version, the poem reveals the speaker's interior combustion: a conflict forged in shame, history, and the unbearable mechanics of power. What emerges is a confrontation staged from inside the architecture of whiteness.

Within the collection's broader arc, *To A Young Malcolm X* forces what had remained submerged to rise. Earlier poems approach collapse through place, ecology, or estranged intimacy. This one refuses metaphor. It addresses race directly, but without appeal or absolution. The poem holds the speaker inside the very structure they cannot dismantle. In doing so, it recasts the collection's descent beyond the civic and emotional, into the historical and embodied.

Structural Role

Placed near the close of the poetry collection, *To A Young Malcolm X* functions as a psychic break. The collection has already moved through violence, disorientation, and collapse. This poem inhabits those conditions. Its address is raw, unguarded, and destabilizing. By speaking to Malcolm before the icon was shaped, the speaker dislodges themselves from inherited roles, while also revealing how deeply those roles persist. The poem alters the tonal register of the final arc. It injects volatility into composure, requiring the reader to hold that dissonance without reprieve.

Formally, the poem fractures its own rhythm. Sentences stall and lurch. Line breaks arrive mid-thought. There is no scene, no setting, only a charged interior field. The structure performs the very collapse the speaker cannot narrate cleanly. Its form breaks open as the content refuses coherence. The voice strips itself of metaphor, authority, and protection. This disintegration is intentional. The poem composes the conditions of its own erosion.

Interpretive Reading

The Borges epigraph aims inward. It names the wound without seeking closure. "Your seed had come to nothing" is judgment. The speaker carries that judgment like a scar, revealing the shape of inheritance. The address to Malcolm is not conciliatory. It rises from a refusal to occupy any of the available roles: sympathizer, confessor, ally. The poem recognizes each of these as untenable. Instead, it stages a rejection of the structures that made Malcolm necessary.

This is a poem of loathing, of the roles handed down, and the scripts made compulsory. The speaker recognizes whiteness as a role given rather than chosen and wants out. The gesture is clear: take it. But the structure won't allow release. Power adheres. Race holds. The speaker fractures, and what remains is a dog in shadow, low, unspeaking, outside the frame. The closing image is absurd, gentle, and devastating. A hand touches fur. No absolution follows, just contact.

Touchpoints and Lineage

The poem enters a rare tradition of works that turn whiteness inside out. James Baldwin's critique of white innocence echoes through the speaker's awareness of history's weight. So does the spiritual blade of Borges, whose epigraph carves the poem's tonal boundary. There are traces of Robert Lowell and Philip Larkin, but this piece offers no claim to control or literary mastery. It spirals instead. Its compositional kin lie with Lucille Clifton and Jericho Brown, in the capacity to hold rage and tenderness without flinching.

The poem interrogates race to survive its pressure. It is a failure to escape and composes within that failure a form of witness.

Musicality: Spoken Word Protest / Free Jazz Disruption

The piece pulses with the cadence of protest, but inward, inverted. Its rhythms resemble spoken word stripped of crowd and stage. There is syncopation, but no performance. Beneath the phrasing runs the tonal volatility of free jazz: Ornette Coleman, Matana Roberts, Charles Mingus. Structures form, collapse, and re-emerge. The poem agitates rather than resolves.

Visual Art: Political Portraiture / Iconoclastic Expressionism

The visual analogue is a wall where scorched slogans lie beneath new paint, their shapes and pigments rising through the surface in rough relief. The brushwork recalls Leon Golub, figures scarred into visibility, power made flesh. There are echoes of Jean-Michel Basquiat in the layering of symbol, text, and fracture. The image is destabilized, incomplete, bearing the marks of its own revision.

Rather than sanctify Malcolm, the poem renders him untouchable, too early, too wild, too true to be claimed. The speaker, by contrast, dissolves. The portrait is of someone undone in the act of looking.

Poem 44: After a Year of Flooding

Function in the Collection

After a Year of Flooding speaks for what endures only in trace, the world altered and the presence that once moved through its fields. The poem extends and completes earlier threads in the collection concerned with natural cycles, time, and the futility of dominion. Appearing late in the sequence, it bridges the intimate gesture of throwing a stone with the planetary scale of melting ice and receding seas. The aperture widens, yet the poem remains grounded in touch, sound, and material image. Within the book's larger arc, it quiets the register, returning to meditation and to the elemental persistence of what endures.

Structural Role

Positioned near the end of the collection, *After a Year of Flooding* functions as tonal descent, a quieting and sedimentation. It follows poems that name lineage, rupture, and historical urgency, allowing those energies to pass into a broader register where scale exceeds human passion. The speaker recedes, absorbed into geologic and environmental rhythm. What had been charged with inheritance and demand settles into elemental continuity.

Structurally, the poem returns the sequence to ground: water, field, bone, echo. Its placement allows it to serve as both elegy and mirror for the vanishings threaded through the book. The poem does not dispute what comes before it. It carries those intensities forward into a field where they no longer seek outcome. The gaze steadies. Attention remains. Disappearance is accepted as condition rather than defeat.

Formally, the poem moves through slow, deliberate lines that mirror the drag of silted water, the incremental motion of glacial time. Line breaks arrive mid-thought, creating the sensation of drift rather than propulsion. Rhythm loosens and widens. Spacing and breath reinforce erosion's pace, presence dissolving into field, sound into stalk. The restraint carries its power. The poem widens, then disappears.

Interpretive Reading

After a Year of Flooding unfolds in two temporal registers. One is the present: a speaker alone, throwing a stone and walking through a flooded field in winter. The other lies far beyond us, when our era has hardened to fossil and the world continues. What seems fixed becomes residue, and someone after us bends to the ground in the same gesture of looking and living. The speaker attends to geologic, ecological, and historical layers, registering time's accumulation rather than its loss.

The poem's core images, deer tracks fossilized, a man's bones murmuring within rock, refuses sentimentality. Human presence becomes mineral, reduced to the same record as mosquito and shell. This reduction conveys austere beauty and the serenity of scale. The closing image, stalks rattling across a frozen floodplain, sounds like a river still moving beneath ice, suggesting that life, and the sound of life, continue after us.

Against this expanse, the passions of the current age appear as momentary weather. What feels urgent now will one day be sediment, trace, or echo. The gaze that sees our smallness also affirms our participation in the larger field. The speaker accepts the vast continuum of time and allows the reader to feel both humbled and steadied within it.

Touchpoints and Lineage

The poem echoes the spirit of W.S. Merwin and Louise Glück, poets who have written about time, landscape, and extinction without dramatization. It also carries a trace of Seamus Heaney's reverence for what the earth records, the faith that matter itself holds memory.

Philosophically, the poem draws from deep-time thinking, an archaeological consciousness in which human presence is a flicker within a vast continuum. In this sense, it belongs to a lineage of post-human lyric, where attention replaces lament, and observation becomes a form of care. The poem studies our residue with composure.

Within the collection, *After a Year of Flooding* serves as a grave song, quiet, patient, and enduring. It listens rather than declares. The sound that returns is elemental: the wind through stalks, the earth remembering what once passed over it.

Musicality: Slowcore / Drowned Hymn

After a Year of Flooding moves like a slowcore ballad, minimal, spacious, emotionally heavy. Think Low, Red House Painters, or the glacial phrasing of Jessica Pratt.

Each line wades through water, slowed by memory and silt. Beneath the language is the ghost of a drowned hymn, a song of faith altered by ruin. The repetition is liturgical but waterlogged. This is music that holds sorrow without dramatizing it, letting silence do most of the speaking.

Visual Art: Post-Minimalist Landscape / Environmental Lamentation

The visual analogue is found in post-minimalist land art and the abstract residue of environmental trauma. The poem aligns with the work of artists like Ana Mendieta or Richard Long, where marks left on earth, water, and memory suggest both impermanence and wound. The flood here is aftermath: the silted, saturated quiet after the disaster has passed through.

It evokes a landscape installation half-erased by weather. There's a sense of quiet subsidence, forms blurred by time, surfaces water-logged and sun-bleached. Agnes Denes' *Wheatfield – A Confrontation* comes to mind, but inverted: a slow relinquishing.

The poem's vision aligns with artists who let time shape their materials, Sugimoto's patient light, Celmins's slow surfaces, Horn's shifting ice. The field holds its form through weather and wear. Stone, stalk, and water keep recording change, carrying memory forward grain by grain. What emerges is the world remade through persistence.

Poem 45: Humdrum

Function in the Collection

Humdrum studies interior erosion through the lens of daily repetition. Among the most dissociative pieces in the collection, the poem locates the speaker inside a landscape of observational fatigue, psychic static, and absurdity.

Positioned near the book's end, it serves as a murmuring counterpoint to the elegiac and spiritual tones around it. Rather than lifting upward, it drifts. Rather than resolving, it lingers in disintegration. The voice is dry, self-aware, almost comic in its depletion. Within the larger arc, *Humdrum* shows that some forms of survival occur beneath clarity, beneath transcendence.

Structural Role

Placed late in the sequence, *Humdrum* acts as a chamber of dissociation, a pause that neither uplifts nor collapses, a stalled interior monologue without promise of arc. It follows poems shaped by elegy or endurance but refuses both. The poem recognizes that certain psychic states are not passages but climates that saturate. The reader is asked to stay inside that weather, to feel the dull ache of continuation. Structurally, *Humdrum* absorbs the collection's momentum into suspension. Its role is to sustain the murk, to let the haze accumulate, to test how long language can drift before it stops meaning altogether.

Formally, the poem mirrors this condition through deliberate instability. Lines break unevenly, syntax frays, tenses blur. Diction slides between the domestic and the surreal, the tedious and the strange. The pacing mimics a restless but spent consciousness, flat, looping, and self-observing. Fragmentation here is lived condition. The poem holds just enough structure to keep dissolution audible.

Interpretive Reading

The speaker arrives unmoored. Isolation defines the field, stripped of romance or tragedy. The world drones forward, flat and continuous. Time sheds its outline; days lose identity. "Did I wake up on the 17th?" replaces narrative with fog. Thought drifts until it finds no boundary. "It takes hours of drinking to unravel a thought" becomes almost a confession and a description. The poem's language loops through absurdity and fatigue, a horsehair rope binding fingers, police cruisers circling the neighborhood, beetles ticking along the ceiling.

Even within disintegration, perception endures. The speaker continues to register the ordinary: insects, animals, the low pulse of streets, the texture of confinement. This is attention stripped to its frame, a consciousness that persists when meaning thins. The poem carries that endurance as its core gesture, observing what remains when coherence recedes.

The closing image widens slightly. "Outside the night / stretches things with its hands." The movement feels hallucinatory yet calm, as if the world itself keeps shifting the furniture of thought. Night rearranges, time adjusts, and the speaker remains within that motion, dimly aware, and quietly present. The poem ends there, suspended in the hum it names, still vibrating with life.

Touchpoints and Lineage

Humdrum shares its tonal lineage with Frank Stanford's *The Battlefield Where the Moon Says I Love You* and the quiet psychosis of Russell Edson's prose. It inherits their inward sprawl and dry surrealism, where consciousness loops through monotony until it becomes landscape. Beneath that lineage runs the influence of Ted Berrigan's *American Express*, whose drifting monologue and fractured time anticipate this poem's suspended interior. From Berrigan, *Humdrum* borrows a sense of living inside syntax itself, where thought keeps speaking long after intention has gone quiet.

There is also kinship with Beckett, a matter of stance rather than style. The poem accepts futility as atmosphere. Among contemporary voices, it resonates with Ariana Reines and Matthew Zapruder, poets of ambient dread and interior static, though *Humdrum* leans toward stillness rather than proclamation.

Its compositional act is endurance. The poem makes no argument for its importance. It records duration: the long, dim stretches between events that shape a life by accumulation rather than clarity. In the context of the collection, *Humdrum* is one of its bleakest, most unguarded rooms, where consciousness stays on simply because it hasn't found a reason to stop.

Musicality: Post-Punk Deadpan / Minimal Synth Pulse

The piece moves with the dry insistence of early New Order, steady, unornamented, propelled by rhythm more than emotion. Its phrasing carries the clipped precision of post-punk minimalism, where detachment becomes its own form of expression. Each line clicks forward like a sequencer loop, the sound of persistence measured against fatigue.

Beneath the surface hum runs a low, melodic undercurrent, something wounded but still functioning. The rhythm neither rises nor resolves; it sustains. The poem breathes in repetition, holding tension through duration rather than crescendo.

In this field of muted percussion and static air, *Humdrum* listens rather than speaks. The language may flatten, but the pulse continues, quiet and exact. It evokes the strange intimacy of music that endures its own exhaustion, a human signal carried through machinery.

Visual Art: Conceptual Banality / Deadpan Realism

Visually, the poem aligns with artists like John Baldessari and Ed Ruscha, whose work isolates the mundane until it begins to vibrate with unintended meaning.

It also recalls the still geometry of Stephen Shore's strip-mall photographs and the temporal marking of On Kawara's date paintings, where time layers itself as record. In that lineage, the poem's interior landscape, a ceiling, a rope, a flicker of night, becomes a kind of conceptual tableau: plain, persistent, slightly surreal.

In this register, *Humdrum* reads less as void than as study: a portrait of consciousness enduring its own monotony. The flatness is deliberate, but never vacant. Beneath the surface hums an intelligence that keeps noticing, even when meaning slips. What emerges is a quiet realism of drift.

Poem 46: Network

Function in the Collection

After the psychic confinement of *Humdrum*, *Network* expands outward, reestablishing connection through simultaneity rather than identity or story. It attends to a wide field of relations: a cardinal, a pine, a monarch swarm, a sleepless man, the fractal arms of sycamores. Each image exists in motion, held briefly within a shared current.

Network marks the collection's reentry into relation through pattern and resonance. Meaning arises through coexistence and the poem affirms that perception itself can be connective tissue, that awareness, distributed and unfinished, remains a form of wholeness.

Structural Role

As the antepenultimate piece in the sequence, *Network* creates a clearing. It follows several poems shaped by interior pressure and perceptual stall. Rather than resolving that tension, it opens a broader range of response. The poetry collection has passed through exhaustion, violence, mourning, and drift. *Network* gathers those threads into a wider spatial logic. It repositions experience within a frame shaped by co-presence and quiet structure. This shift widens the field and restores perceptual balance. The final movement of the book depends on this clearing.

Formally, the poem behaves like a loose circuit. Image and insight emerge in pulses, connected by drift rather than design. Syntax stretches or snaps depending on where the pressure sits. Enjambments lift the rhythm forward, then drop it back into stillness. The pacing follows attention rather than outcome. Lineation varies with thought, allowing space where it's needed and compression where it holds. The form mirrors the poem's thesis: structure arises through relation.

Interpretive Reading

Network traces the hidden infrastructure of relation, not the internet or the natural web alone, but the living circuitry of words, memory, and perception. Each image, a cardinal's flight, a pine on the ridgeline, a sleepless man shifting a bottle from window to window, exists as part of one linguistic and sensory field. The poem understands connection as movement through language: each phrase touches another, each image carries a current.

The sleepless man becomes the poem's hinge. His repeated stories hold as acts of survival rather than failures of memory. Through speech he maintains orientation, keeping himself tethered to the world. The speaker's silence, their decision to listen without interruption, extends the network outward. The poem reveals that communication itself, however fractured, is the structure that holds.

The poem's motion, its drift from forest to city, from insect to star, mirrors the way words pass between minds, carrying presence across distance. Language here behaves like weather: diffuse, shared, shaping and shaped by what it crosses.

In its closing image, the sycamores rise into a lattice of reflection and echo. Their branching pattern is also the pattern of thought, repetition, variation, continuation. The poem ends with a recognition: language is the medium of connection, and the network we inhabit is made, line by line, from the stories we keep repeating to survive.

Touchpoints and Lineage

Network aligns with a tradition of lyrical phenomenology, poets like Jorie Graham, Robert Hass, and Mei-mei Berssenbrugge, who shape thought as sensory pattern. Its impulse toward simultaneity gestures back to Whitman, though without assertion or self-centering. The tone remains composed, exploratory, and restrained.

Its spatial openness recalls the field poetics of Charles Olson and the generative listening of John Cage, yet the poem stays warmer. It keeps hold of the human while moving within broader networks of perception. Visual analogues include the patterned luminosity of Agnes Martin or the quiet repetitions of Vija Celmins, artists who translate attention into form.

Within the poetry collection, this is the poem of reentry. Toward a frame where contradiction can breathe, unforced.

After dispersion and collapse, *Network* rebuilds a structure capable of holding attention. Its gesture is simple and sustaining: to stay open, to listen, to remain within the living field.

Musicality: Post-Punk Ambient / Glitch Minimalism

The rhythm fuses the clarity of post-punk ambient with the interference of glitch. Lines move like soft pulses disrupted by static, fragments stitched through pressure and drift. Each phrase enters as signal, partial and human. Beneath the surface, a low hum persists, patient and unresolved.

The atmosphere recalls *Your Silent Face*-era New Order, Oval's fractured warmth, or Burial's nocturnal reverb, music where precision meets disarray. The pacing feels analog, metered but unstable, alive but unsynchronized. Within that pulse, language behaves like tone: repetition as current, silence as measure. The music doesn't close; it hovers continuous, luminous, and unfinished.

Visual Art: Systems Aesthetics / Data Abstraction

The visual logic of *Network* draws from Systems Art, where relation itself becomes structure. Its lineage includes Hans Haacke's ecological networks and Mark Lombardi's diagrammed histories, artworks that reveal consequence through connection. The poem moves within that same discipline of pattern and correspondence, translating observation into quiet architecture.

Each image functions as a node in a living diagram: the cardinal's flight, the shifting bottle, the canopy of sycamores. The composition recalls a graphite map or a layered drawing by Julie Mehretu, where pattern gathers through intersection and shared motion.

Like Sarah Sze's suspended installations, *Network* turns material into movement and movement into map. What endures is passage, the way perception travels through the work. The poem holds that motion in balance, a pattern still forming in light.

Poem 47: Tomorrow Is a Long Time

Function in the Collection

Tomorrow Is a Long Time closes the sequence of solitary, first-person lyrics and opens the threshold for the book's final expansion. It gathers what remains of attachment, love thinned by distance, devotion lingering without address. The speaker sits within a narrowing radius: a stump, a yard, five cigarettes, the hum of approaching night.

Yet the world continues to sound. Thunder rolls in drizzle, a train passes through the dark, and dogs bark somewhere beyond the house. Each sound moves farther from the body, widening the field even as the speaker stays still. These layered echoes, domestic, mechanical, elemental, form the poem's horizon of presence. From this low ache, the book's last widening begins.

Structural Role

As the penultimate poem in the collection, *Tomorrow Is a Long Time* serves as hinge and quiet aperture. Its architecture depends on counterpoint: a still voice surrounded by a world in motion. While the speaker withdraws, trains pass and thunder rolls. The poem listens rather than speaks, shaping structure through what continues outside the self.

Lineation follows that listening. Indented stanzas act like auditory drift, each line a pulse, an echo, a pause between external sounds. Syntax loosens, but the composition holds: duration becomes the governing rhythm. The world's persistence frames the speaker's composure and the poem's restraint holds open the field that *Upland*, will later inhabit.

Interpretive Reading

The poem carries a sorrow that never rises into spectacle. Grief disperses across ordinary gestures, rain, trains, barking, the missing keys, without ever forming a single scene. The speaker inhabits the still point while everything else drifts outward. Everywhere in the poem is elsewhere.

The deepest ache gathers around the absence of return: *"you love, / you aren't coming home / tonight."* The line holds both tenderness and removal. Love is spoken into air already leaving. The word *tonight* softens what it cannot disguise: that the absence is forever. Syntax loosens, punctuation fades, and the voice drifts into suspension. The recognition of distance becomes the atmosphere itself.

Trains carry objects into other geographies. Dogs call across the dark, their echoes teaching distance. The speaker does not follow. Stillness becomes composure, a kind of grace after motion.

The title, drawn from Bob Dylan's *Tomorrow Is a Long Time*, places this stillness within a lineage of longing. Yet where the song yearns toward reunion, this poem stands at the edge after hope. The melody remains only as echo, absorbed into the soundscape of an evening that keeps on happening.

From this quiet perimeter, the frame widens. The lyric self has reached its farthest radius. Beyond this point, voice yields to field.

Touchpoints and Lineage

Tomorrow Is a Long Time stands within the lineage of late W.S. Merwin's restraint and Larry Levis's tender desolation, where syntax carries emotion by what it withholds. Its emotional clarity recalls Raymond Carver's quiet domestic scenes, moments where loneliness becomes atmosphere rather than theme.

The echo of Dylan remains like a trace melody, a folk cadence carried into language. Yet the poem's inheritance is literary before musical: it joins a long conversation on solitude and endurance, on how the smallest gestures can hold the weight of absence.

Within the collection, this is the closing of the intimate register, the final lyric spoken from within the human radius before the book opens to the larger field beyond the self.

Musicality: Folk Reverie / Alt-Country Lament

Tomorrow Is a Long Time is written in the shape of a song. Its rhythm follows the open-handed cadence of an acoustic ballad, unhurried, plaintive, and circular. The voice moves like a guitar fingerpicking through dusk light, each phrase resolving just enough to begin again.

The tonal ancestry becomes legible: Dylan's early laments, the weary warmth of Townes Van Zandt, the quiet ache of Gillian Welch or Iron & Wine. This is music made from the ordinary, rain, trains, distance, the sound of someone gone, and its simplicity is its strength.

Each line feels sung rather than spoken. Syntax becomes breath; repetition becomes measure. The world around the speaker keeps time: thunder, dogs, and passing locomotives forming the percussion of absence. The song carries love's residue forward, where endurance becomes its form. This is the poem's truest register, the voice, the chord, and the held note of someone still singing after the door has closed.

Visual Art: Contemporary Realism / Rural Minimalism

The visual logic of the poem rests in patient observation. Its world unfolds like a small painting held at dusk, where light lingers without emphasis. The atmosphere recalls the work of Rackstraw Downes, whose landscapes attend to space, distance, and modest human presence without drama. Each object is given its place. The field feels spare, but not empty.

There is also a secondary kinship with Andrew Wyeth's quiet rural scenes, where stillness carries emotional weight and the ordinary becomes charged through restraint. The palette leans toward gray-green, rust, and soft cream, the tones of late evening when definition gives way to atmosphere.

Silence is not absence here. It carries weather, distance, and breath. Compositionally, the frame remains still. Sound becomes texture. Distance becomes shape.

Poem 48: Upland

Function in the Collection

Upland closes the collection in illumination and hum. It doesn't turn the lights out or turn off the mic as perhaps a final poem should. The title gestures upward toward elevation, but the ascent is partial, and what rises is a shift in bearing rather than relief. The poem gathers everything that has come before, flood, loss, love, sound, and places it within one enduring register: the persistence of what we inhabit, even as we try to leave it behind.

If *Tomorrow Is a Long Time* ends in the solitude of one voice listening outward, *Upland* answers from the shared distance of "we." It speaks from within the field rather than above it, where leaving and remaining fold into the same motion.

The poem's closing radiance, television light and highway sound, does not resolve the collection. It steadies it. What persists is not departure, but the quiet continuity of signal across distance.

Structural Role

Upland arrives through accumulation rather than resolution. Its structure relies on extended, staggered couplets that move in slow, deliberate units, each line carrying the weight of inventory, memory, and refusal. The poem does not build toward revelation. It gathers objects, places, and residues until the field feels saturated.

The consistent indentation creates a visual rhythm of approach and withdrawal. Each thought advances, then hesitates. This pattern mirrors the poem's thematic motion: the impulse to leave followed by attachment to what remains. Syntax stays plain and procedural, driven by repetition and restraint rather than lyric escalation.

The shift from "I" to "we" expands the voice from private reflection into shared condition. What once felt singular becomes collective. The poem's final turn does not open outward. It returns to sound, distance, and continuity, echoing the collection's earliest gestures while grounding them in lived, physical space.

Rather than offering closure, *Upland* settles the collection into a sustained field of presence. The light remains on. The sound continues. What endures is the hum of what we inhabit, carried forward without instruction.

Interpretive Reading

Upland completes the collection's long gesture of approach and return. The poem inhabits a geography both physical and interior: a gas-station town where departure has been rehearsed so often it becomes ritual. Every object, the dog's leash, the sweating plaster walls, the glow of television screens, belongs to a human field of repetition. Escape is enacted but never achieved. Going becomes another form of staying.

The voice recognizes the boundary that has always encircled the book. The world we've made is the same world we try to flee. *Skyscraper* found that truth in steel and signal; *Upland* finds it in dust and memory. Both stand beneath the same reflected light. The prayer that once rose skyward now returns as screen-glow and interstate hum, transmissions of our own making that illuminate and confine us at once.

And yet the poem listens. In its composure there is quiet mercy. The sound of the road and the flicker of unseen rooms remain, not as answers, but as signs of endurance.

To stay within what we have built is still to look outward. Even containment carries light.

The final image, that field between here and the sound, does not close the book so much as hold it open. Voices and echoes continue to move through it. What the poems trace is not escape, but attention itself, a way of standing inside the circle we make.

Touchpoints and Lineage

The poem stands in lineage with the late work of Larry Levis and Philip Levine, poets of industrial afterlife, of memory shaped by terrain and labor. It also echoes the grounded voices of Brian Turner and Larry Smith, who write the after-conditions of place and body with quiet precision and dignity.

There is a deeper echo within the word upland itself, a term that gestures toward refuge, toward the high ground of spirit and endurance. Yet the ascent moves without promise of redemption. Each rise echoes the same arc: a departure that curves toward return, carried by persistence. Like Lot's wife, we try not to look back, though the body remembers. The land remembers too. The landscape holds our turning.

Musicality: Appalachian Drone / Sacred Minimalism

Upland moves with the tonal gravity of Appalachian drone, steady, grounded, shaped by repetition rather than melody. Its rhythm recalls the weathered quiet of mountain folk hymns, sung without adornment. The pace feels slow enough to match the movement of water under ice.

There is also a kinship with sacred minimalism, composers like Arvo Pärt or Morton Feldman, where stillness becomes structure. The music does not build. Each phrase enters with weight, and each silence carries tone.

Visual Art: Spiritual Landscape / Tonal Abstraction

The visual register of *Upland* shifts toward spiritual landscape. The landscape rises through tone and presence, its height carried by atmosphere rather than detail. The image holds more atmosphere than scene, where memory becomes visible through restraint.

The aesthetic recalls the tonal fields of Agnes Pelton or the horizon works of Wolfgang Laib, where color and light serve as quiet forms of belief. Etel Adnan's landscapes also come into view, paintings that reduce form to essence without losing warmth or depth.

...

The upland is not a destination but a state of attention. It holds like breath rather than ground. The space remains spare, never empty, carrying what lingers without speaking.

The collection closes in light and low sound. Windows glow. Fields hold their quiet. What remains is the human condition of waiting inside what endures, unsure of what has been lost, unsure of what will come, unable to step outside the hum.

Break in the Frame

When I first began writing poems, I thought the work was to turn the ordinary into the extraordinary, to take the world as it was and lift it somehow into meaning. That was an early misunderstanding. The work was to bring the extraordinary back down to the human, to sit with what had already arrived and learn to listen to it without trying to improve it.

Every act of making still begins in astonishment. Something appears, unbidden, precise, alive, and for a moment I stand inside its brightness. It feels like grace, but what follows is the reckoning: the light fades, and I am left with what it showed me. That is where the real work begins.

I have learned to stay within that doubleness, to let the prism turn both ways, toward illumination and toward the shadow it casts. The poem, the song, the brushstroke, each is a way of holding that uncertain radiance long enough for it to take a shape that endures.

I have lived in these poems the way a painting, a photograph, or a broadside might live on my wall. I have been in conversation with them, embarrassed by them, proud of them, angry at them, irritated at them for not being more social. I created them, but in almost all cases where they came from is not entirely evident. What I never wanted them to do was preach at me or tell me something definitive. I am more comfortable in unknowing, in the suspension mid-bridge between here and the sound of a groaning interstate.

I have always been aware of the distance between polite society and the reality beneath it. Literary theory would call this deconstruction, but even as a third grader in Detroit I was already living it. I could not understand why I was not allowed to see an R-rated movie when the world around me was R-rated or worse. That was my first education in contradiction, the quiet recognition that what is said aloud and what is true rarely occupy the same space. It is a lesson that returns again and again. We speak of fairness, of justice, of order, but the truth moves elsewhere, quiet, invisible, and beyond what the world can make right.

Endurance and Estrangement

Situated at the intersection of lyric tradition, philosophical disquiet, musical structure, and visual intensity, *Between Here and the Sound of a Groaning Interstate* moves across multiple artistic lineages without settling into any single tradition or school. What emerges is a poetics of lyric refusal and estrangement, a formally attentive body of work shaped by influence yet composed with deliberate distance from inherited frames.

The literary ancestry of the collection is rich and layered. Echoes of twentieth-century lyric traditions, especially those shaped by labor, locality, and spiritual fatigue, resonate throughout. The poems attend closely to those below the line of sight, workers, wanderers, and figures caught in the machinery of modern life. Rather than reaching for moral uplift or formal closure, the work remains rooted in an unresolved present shaped by opacity and drift. Transcendence yields to the quiet dignity of sustained attention.

This compositional stance holds intimacy without disclosure. The speakers circle sites of memory, loss, and pressure with minimal gesture, allowing atmosphere to take precedence over epiphany. Tonal gravity replaces narrative drive. Refusal replaces revelation.

Structurally, many of the poems carry the imprint of compression and fragmentation. Breath-driven lines, material precision, and philosophical severity shape the collection's movement. There is a kinship with traditions that favor irony over system and symbolic tension over resolution. These poems move through the residue of myth, prayer, and celestial figures, tracing belief in its faded form where structure has collapsed but presence endures. Attention rests on what persists after coherence dissolves, fragments, gestures, echoes.

The collection's estranged lyricism also draws from experimental modes that question stable meaning. Rather than dismantling form, the poems lean into fractured syntax, disrupted cataloging, and atmospheric uncertainty. The language remains ethically alert, practicing refusal in the face of simplification.

A quieter thread of civic poetics runs through the work, especially in poems that attend to violence, infrastructure, and elegy. These pieces carry a commitment to public presence shaped less by persuasion than by listening. They remain aware of the world beyond the page, even as they resist direct address.

If the literary inheritance of the collection is multifaceted, its musical lineage moves just as deeply. These poems do not reference music as subject. They embody it as structure. Rhythm and tonal motion guide each piece through pattern rather than narrative sequence.

Across the collection, one hears the pulse of roots-based traditions, where repetition bears weight. Refrain becomes endurance, ambiguity holds, and presence remains, without spectacle.

A throughline also emerges in the work's alignment with minimalist composition. Many poems take the form of sonic loops, repetitions with difference, small evolutions that shift emotional ground without fanfare. In these pieces, stillness takes on weight.

Later poems adopt more fractured textures. Disjunction, error, and sonic erosion enter the field. Language begins to behave like signal interference. Musicality hums inside the syntax, shaping emotional architecture.

Elsewhere, a quieter mode prevails. Emotional force is carried through patience rather than amplification. The voice lowers rather than rises.

The visual aesthetic that undergirds the collection aligns closely with its musical and literary counterparts. It favors intensity over polish, and rawness over finish. Many poems evoke sacred minimalism, apocalyptic abstraction, or expressive distortion. Their surfaces feel shaped by ruin, memory, and myth. These works appear salvaged rather than composed.

Other poems draw from more intuitive, unvarnished traditions. Their imagery arrives through urgency rather than refinement. Figures feel carved by persistence. Ornament gives way to necessity.

Even the collection's composure finds visual kinship in pared-down surfaces where stillness becomes a field of inquiry. Silence operates as atmosphere. Texture becomes a mode of thought.

This lineage does not illustrate the poems. It mirrors their ethic. The visual energy does not clarify or reinforce. It vibrates alongside the text like a second signal. Meaning gathers in the interference.

Taken together, the literary, musical, and visual systems shaping this collection serve as scaffolding. Their influence moves beneath the surface, guiding structure without demanding attention. The result is a body of work composed through listening and looking, carried by humility and formal precision.

A distinction of *Between Here and the Sound of a Groaning Interstate* does not rest on novelty of theme or innovation of form. Its strength lies in the steadiness of its refusal. The poems decline climax, revelation, and payoff. Their motion is circular. Their inquiry remains open.

These poems do not reach toward transcendence. They remain inside the moment itself, its texture, its friction, and its quiet refusal to resolve. Their movement is inward. Their logic is atmospheric.

Rather than build toward revelation, the collection stays close to the threshold of experience. The poems hover, precisely and with care, inside moments already vanishing. They hold presence through progression.

When the speaker suggests that "the other side is never a surprise," the tone does not collapse into defeat. It sharpens into protective clarity. The poems understand what repetition brings, erosion, return, forgetting. And so, the speaker lingers, if only for a breath, where something real once touched the surface.

These poems resist the arc of closure. Inside that holding space, we encounter the rattle of a rail line through dusk, the flash of a possum's teeth, the moment a voice fails to finish its sentence. These fragments do not announce themselves. They persist quietly, held in the poem's frame.

To shape a poem around such a moment is to affirm its weight, even in brevity. It asks only presence. It carries forward no answer, only the moment itself.

This is precision. A form of trust that honors both the poem's integrity and the reader's capacity to remain inside its tension without needing rescue.

PART TWO

Threshold

Fear shapes the margins of poetic practice, and in the early twenty-first century it shapes the center as well. The constraints poets face now move through subtler channels: visibility, moral alignment, and cultural legibility. These forces are ambient and anticipatory. They shape what is withheld as much as what appears, influencing how a poem takes form and whether it appears at all.

Within this climate, fear functions as structure rather than mood. It gathers through political division, identity demand, economic fragility, diminished arts education, and the algorithmic management of attention. These pressures create a field condition in which the poem is expected to declare itself in legible terms or risk vanishing. Ambiguity appears evasive. Reserve becomes suspect.

These pressures do not announce themselves as prohibition. They move instead through expectation. A poem begins to sense what it will be asked to clarify before it has settled into what it needs to hold. The pressure arrives through imagined reception and anticipated judgment rather than decree. What once belonged to craft is increasingly interpreted as posture.

Technology sharpens these pressures. Systems trained to generate verse according to selected literary values now claim to rival non-expert writers. Whatever the merit, the consequence is real. Poetry increasingly moves through mechanisms that reward fluency, sentiment, and consensus over form, friction, or ambiguity.

Within such conditions, the question is no longer only how a poem is written, or how it will be read. A more basic question emerges first, and often without ceremony:

whether to write a poem at all, or even to bother reading one.

Fear and Artistic Risk

A poem cannot endure if it seeks protection before it risks being made. Art has always required exposure, yet the nature of that risk shifts with each era. Today poetry circulates within a culture uneasy with uncertainty. Pressure comes from politics, economics, algorithms, and spectacle. It arrives through the etiquette of outrage. These forces generate distortion and a slow attrition.

The central danger now is unreadability. A poem that resists ideological coherence, tribal allegiance, or the therapeutic expectation of disclosure risks disappearance. The poet becomes illegible to systems that prize legibility above all else.

This tension is not entirely new. The lyric has long kept a necessary distance from the dominant tone of its time. It resists promotion, instruction, and conclusion. For this composure, poetry has often drawn suspicion from authority, orthodoxy, and movements invested in purity. Its reluctance to be used makes it vulnerable.

That vulnerability has changed form. Punishment appears less as censorship and more as self-censorship. The poet hesitates with full knowledge of craft and full awareness of consequence. Ambiguity is framed as evasion. Irony is framed as cruelty. Lyric strangeness carries the suspicion of moral failure. The poem enters the world already bent by precaution.

Even stillness can attract suspicion. A poet at work resembles a watcher in a field, alert to what appears and attentive without claim. In a culture that mistrusts distance, even this gaze seems suspect. To observe without declaring motive invites misreading. The one who listens, who looks with care, becomes mistaken for someone who withholds, or worse.

This inversion defines the moment. Attention becomes suspect. Composure is mistaken for privilege. Contemplation is taken as concealment. The act of looking without declaring intent absorbs meanings projected onto it.

We live in a climate where accusation can precede understanding. Misreading is no longer an accident. It is often a ritual. A person may be charged with harm through projection, held responsible for what another imagines they said or for how their presence unsettles certainty. Around this ritual gather the vultures of conviction, ready to feed on ambiguity as if it were weakness.

For poets, this is a perilous condition. The lyric depends on ambiguity, on the space between intent and interpretation. When that distance collapses and every phrase is treated as confession or offense, poetry itself becomes suspect. When a poem rushes to declare its position, it loses its capacity to see. It reflects rather than perceives.

Fear as a Field Condition

Not all fear raises its voice. Some enters through etiquette. It rarely appears as repression and more often moves through taste, tone, and civility: a glance in a workshop, a note in the margins, a quiet decision to leave a line unwritten, or a whispered conversation about a poet's malfeasance.

The poetic field now runs less on decree than on anticipation. Its influence is subtle and felt through expectation. A phrase may be shaped by the imagined reception of its motive. The pressure arrives before the line is written.

This is not simply ideological. It reflects a puritan instinct reborn within a culture that once prized freedom. The result is a choreography of compliance. Urgency becomes softened for approval. Vulnerability is polished to charm. Honesty is shaped to avoid offense.

Poems emerge bearing that pressure. They arrive already explained, buffered by context, careful in tone. Expression carries its own disclaimer. The line bends toward defense. The vision waits for permission.

Fear also alters what enters the poem. Not only what is withheld, but what is added. Lines arrive carrying gestures meant to reassure, to signal awareness, to establish relevance before perception has settled. Clarifications appear where ambiguity once stood. A tone of preemption settles in, as if the poem must prove its awareness before it can proceed. Even work grounded in attentiveness may feel pressure to introduce a corrective note, not because the poem requires it, but because the field does.

Within such conditions, dissonance is difficult to sustain. The space where complexity might breathe is narrow. Clarity presses toward premature resolution, and suggestion loses room to remain intact. Art begins to resemble the prescribed forms through which publication and signaling now occur. Some work appears not to matter only because the conditions of attention required to recognize its weight have thinned.

Fear in this register shapes the atmosphere of praise and neglect. It guides tone more than subject. Its power lies in subtlety, until something stands unmoved within it.

The Poems Abandon Righteousness

To witness without declaring becomes a form of composure. The poems in this book relinquish righteousness understood as the pressure to establish moral position in advance of perception. They move through violence, estrangement, absurdity, memory, and love as atmospheres the language must cross, without converting those passages into proof of virtue or alignment. The speaker stands within the world rather than above or beneath it.

The lyric voice meets brutality and injustice without rising above them. The poem offers no corrective frame and no claim of moral exemption. It remains inside the wound and continues to listen, allowing what is encountered to retain its weight without translation into stance.

Even at its most mythic or intimate, the work resists sanctification. It withholds gestures meant to reassure, clarify motive, or signal ethical correctness. Difficulty is neither dramatized nor resolved. The poems stay with what they hold long enough for perception to register, without forcing closure or redemption.

In a culture drawn toward moral display, this posture reads as refusal. The poems step aside from the demand to demonstrate goodness or relevance and accept the risks that follow, including misreading or neglect. Their refusal is compositional rather than declarative, shaped by what is left unadded rather than by what is announced.

To abandon righteousness in this sense is not to abandon ethics. It is to refuse the instrumental use of poetry as evidence of virtue and to keep lyric attention from collapsing into declaration.

On Misreading and Control

Fear belongs to the conditions of reception, not to the act of making. These poems did not originate in anticipation of judgment or consequence. They arrived with their own internal demand, carrying forms and voices that did not seek permission or protection. Any unease attached to them emerged afterward, as recognition, and did not guide their composition. What follows concerns not how the work was made, but what happens once work of this kind enters circulation.

Once a poem enters the world, meanings begin to gather around it that were never operative during its making. Reading does not remain neutral. Silence is interpreted as omission. Distance is read as intent. Attention without declaration becomes suspect. What appears as composure from within the work is often received as withholding, or worse. Control does not arrive as censorship. It arrives when interpretation hardens into verdict.

Misreading, in this sense, is not a failure of understanding. It is a defensive act. When a poem renders a structure visible without providing justification, explanation, or moral alignment, as several of the poems in this collection do, it is often reassigned a role it did not claim as a way of neutralizing what it has exposed. Description is taken as advocacy. Exposure is treated as complicity. Withdrawal is framed as evasion. Through this reassignment, what the poem has unsettled is returned to legibility.

This process operates most forcefully where fear already governs the field. Work that refuses to declare its innocence or announce its position in advance becomes especially available for projection. Diagnosis is mistaken for endorsement. Intensity is confused with intent. The poem is no longer encountered on its own terms but is pressed into service as evidence for or against a claim it never made.

In such conditions, control appears less as an external force than as a shared reflex. Reading becomes anticipatory. Judgment precedes attention. The interval between perception and response collapses. What cannot be resolved quickly is treated as dangerous. What does not reassure is assumed to conceal.

Work of this kind does not evade this process. It does not argue against misreading or attempt to outpace it. It proceeds without appeal, remaining accountable to what insisted on being said. Misreading follows as consequence, not as correction. What is constrained is not meaning itself, but the work's capacity to remain unresolved in public.

This is the cost of refusing alignment in climates that demand it. The poem is not silenced. It is contained. Its disturbance is absorbed into familiar categories. Control succeeds not by forbidding speech, but by deciding in advance what such speech will be taken to mean.

Certainty as Narcotic

For years in Chicago, a man stood at the corner of State and Madison with a microphone and a stack of pamphlets. His voice never wavered. He preached condemnation in a steady cadence. Everyone was guilty for one reason or another. He was not trying to persuade. He was issuing verdicts.

I passed him countless times. He seemed like part of the street's fabric, no more disruptive than pigeons under the tracks or the buskers at dusk. Now his voice feels strangely familiar. What once seemed fringe has become ambient. We are all preachers now on platforms, in commentary, and in daily life. Certainty has become a narcotic.

It works like any quick sedative. It numbs doubt and intensifies conviction. It flattens complexity. It shifts perception toward division and trains us to perform knowledge rather than pursue it. It narrows attention until we forget that we once moved through the world with greater range.

Cormac McCarthy's Judge in *Blood Meridian* embodies this theology of domination. To name is to own, he insists. Ambiguity is weakness. Authority leans on mastery rather than attunement. Within this logic, the lyric becomes illegible. There is no room for doubt or for a poetics grounded in uncertainty.

Even science, once the modern cathedral of certainty, now reveals its fractures. The systems that once held the cosmos in order flicker with contradiction.

This poetics refuses both the corner and the public square, turning its energy toward listening rather than declaiming. It attends to what appears before it settles into name. Ambiguity becomes fidelity to complexity. It becomes rigor shaped by restraint.

A poem that preaches resembles a pamphlet. A poem that listens refuses the anesthetic. It remains inside the unresolved and the real. It understands that meaning precedes language and cannot be contained without loss.

The Poetics of Refusal

In this book, refusal operates as a compositional method rather than a position. It shapes what the poem will serve by establishing limits that preserve the conditions under which perception can occur before alignment, explanation, or extraction.

Refusal begins as a decision about limits. It governs how language is shaped under pressure, determining which demands the poem will carry forward and which it will leave outside its structure. Encounter remains encounter, ambiguity remains active, and difficulty retains its density rather than being translated into stance, virtue, injury, or claim. These limits arise from the poem's internal requirement to remain answerable to what it perceives.

These limits function compositionally. They shape how pressure is held, how ambiguity remains suspended, and how meaning gathers over time. Refusal works through form, pacing, compression, and omission. What is present is shaped by what has been deliberately left out.

This method sustains the interval in which attention remains active. Perception gathers before posture arrives. The poem remains open to interpretation without being delivered into judgment-ready form.

Refusal also governs the poem's handling of intensity. When the work moves through violence, injustice, or extremity, it sustains presence rather than display. Harm retains its weight. Difficulty remains unresolved long enough to be felt. The poem carries what it encounters forward without converting intensity into performance.

Within contemporary conditions where visibility, identity signaling, and fluency function as currencies of recognition, refusal establishes a different orientation. The work remains guided by internal pressure rather than by reception. It proceeds according to its own duration, shaping meaning through attention rather than appeal.

Work shaped in this way may be received as evasive, withholding, or irrelevant. Refusal accepts that exposure. It proceeds in fidelity to what insists on being written and allows reception to follow in its own time.

By limiting what the poem will serve, it sustains the conditions in which attention remains active rather than instrumentalized. Composure becomes structural. Meaning is allowed to move without being compelled to arrive.

Against the Charge of Silence

Lyric work articulates through form. Poems shaped through interiority, restraint, or indirection carry meaning through arrangement and pacing, allowing relation to accumulate pressure over time. What registers is structure in motion rather than declared position.

This method is not unique to poetry. A painter makes parallel decisions through composition: what to include, what to omit, where to place weight, how color and negative space interact. A musician works similarly, not only through lyric but through rhythm, harmony, instrumentation, and silence. Meaning emerges from relation and timing rather than declaration. In these arts, articulation does not announce itself. It is carried by structure.

Lyric poems generate meaning through arrangement. Pattern, rhythm, and duration organize experience as it unfolds. A lyric moment holds tension through construction, allowing relation to carry meaning. Clarity emerges from within the moment itself, shaped by form as it comes into contact with attention.

Work composed in this way places its intelligence in structure. Cadence, pacing, epigraph, title, and sequence perform labor that cannot be paraphrased without loss. A line gains weight through placement. Pressure accumulates through adjacency, delay, and return.

Several poems in this collection work in registers that require this mode of attention. Violence, inheritance, power, and moral recursion appear not as themes to be summarized but as conditions rendered visible through form. The work brings these forces into view by staging them, allowing the reader to encounter their motion rather than receive their conclusion.

Meaning develops through sustained attention rather than instruction. Judgment does not arrive pre-packaged. The poem creates a site where encounter precedes position and where perception gathers before response.

Such work carries density rather than volume. What registers as quiet often reflects compression. What appears indirect often reflects layered construction. The poem holds multiple pressures in play, allowing contradiction and resonance to remain active within the frame.

The ethic at work here resides in method. Refusal operates as compositional discipline, shaping what the poem will carry and how it will carry it. Form governs meaning's emergence, preserving complexity through structure rather than explication.

Within this practice, articulation resides in construction. Meaning becomes audible through how the work is made. By arranging its materials and allowing their relations to be felt, the poem speaks. Attention completes the circuit. Art does its thinking in placement, pressure, and duration rather than announcement.

Supposed Sons

My inheritance runs through two lines. One passes through an early American township founder in the North. The other runs through an enslaved woman in Virginia whose child remained unfree in law, though not in practice.

In 1802, my fifth great-grandfather Simeon Prior left Massachusetts for the Western Reserve of Ohio. A blacksmith and Revolutionary War veteran, he traveled with his wife Katharine and their ten children into the frontier and helped establish what became Northampton Township. He served as trustee and road supervisor and formed part of the civic frame that anchored the young state. One of his grandsons later died fighting for the Union. This was the version of ancestry I knew. It was northern, civic, and free.

Another branch carried a quieter record. Peggy Robertson, my fourth great-grandmother, appears in an 1827 will. She is never named as a wife, yet the will identifies her son, Thomas Pendelton Wilkinson, as a supposed son of the testator. The language is deliberate. Peggy is named. Thomas is qualified.

Such arrangements were not uncommon in Virginia in the years before Nat Turner's rebellion. Paternity could be acknowledged without being declared. Law supplied one language. Daily life required another.

Thomas was both enslaved and the biological child of the man who enslaved him. Mother and son lived inside that contradiction.

Virginia law was explicit. A child born to an enslaved woman inherited her status. Thomas should have remained enslaved for life. No petition for freedom exists. No record of sale, punishment, or flight appears. Instead, he lived in Virginia, married, raised a family, worked land, and moved through the world as a free man whose status remained unspoken. The family crossed out of bondage through ambiguity sustained by silence rather than decree.

Legal freedom arrived with the next generation. Thomas's son, William Dudley Wilkinson, was born in Virginia to a white mother. Under the law, her status determined his. He was free at birth, the first in his paternal line to enter the world without legal bondage.

He later served in the Confederate army and lived as a white man. By then race had been absorbed into convenience. DNA reaches back through that convenience to Peggy, whose name survives only through the law.

The story extends beyond the family. It shows how slavery could loosen through neglect rather than justice, how biological paternity could remain unspoken even as inheritance flowed, how freedom might arrive through maternal status while the paternal line remained marked, and how passing could follow momentum rather than deliberate choice.

Two Black individuals moved with the family to West Virginia after the war and were buried in the same cemetery. Their presence suggests connection. The record offers no certainty. Silence holds.

No one appealed to the courts. No one contested the law. Freedom arrived through tolerance of ambiguity rather than the recognition of rights. That is part of the American story. Bondage dissolving without acknowledgment and absorbed into continuity.

The plantation became a family farm. The enslaved became heirs. Freedom entered the lineage without ceremony. Silence protected as much as it concealed.

William Dudley Wilkinson, free by birth and descendant of enslaved kin, wore a Confederate uniform. The reasons remain unknown. Fear, obligation, belief, or the need to keep older truths submerged. He was not buried with Confederate honors. That absence carries weight.

The Civil War ended slavery in law, yet many newly freed Americans entered a world shaped by segregation, disenfranchisement, and exclusion. My line crossed just before those barriers rose again.

This recognition occurred while I was already working under similar pressures. While articulating a poetics shaped by refusal, attention, and endurance under constraint, I was also engaged in genealogical research I had pursued for decades. These activities were not paired by design. What surprised me was the moment they converged. A long-standing puzzle in my family's history resolved itself while I was thinking through the mechanics of refusal as a compositional stance. The discovery did not generate the poetics. It clarified it. I recognized the same structure operating in a different field more than two hundred years ago, under conditions far more consequential than art.

The silence my ancestors lived within functioned as endurance, a refusal shaped by necessity rather than declaration. It held without explanation. In an age when naming could end a life, silence became shelter.

This history shows what refusal can do under pressure. Poetry works under pressure too, though of a different order.

Olympus Is Empty

For generations poets wrote into lineage. Influence moved across time, sometimes in harmony and sometimes through resistance. There were mentors to learn from and elders to challenge. Pantheons existed even for the poets who questioned them. That structure has changed. The pantheon has quieted. Olympus is empty.

Contemporary poets often emerge without anointed elders. Many voices rise, yet few remain central. Recognition moves through visibility and momentum rather than sustained engagement. Culture favors emergence over endurance. Profile grows faster than poetics. This condition is not unique to poetry. Across fields, recognition accelerates. What endures often does so quietly. By the time argument arrives, its work is already done.

This is no plea for return. Many old hierarchies needed to fall. Their absence creates a different kind of space. Without shared lineage, poets reach outward toward older structures, deeper rhythms, and quieter currents.

The risk is not disorder. It is isolation. Each poet builds a scaffold or drifts.

Structure has not disappeared. It no longer arrives by inheritance. It must be found or remembered. It appears through attention rather than authority, through compositional ethic rather than succession. Listening replaces proclamation. Duration replaces ascent. What remains follows what endures after succession has fallen away.

The lineage here feels closer to jazz than dynasty. There are echoes and intervals. Riffs rise and recede. Influence moves without claim or inheritance. There is an ethic in that posture. An ethic of restraint and regard. An ethic of continuing without needing to be next.

The silence at the summit is a condition. Olympus is empty, its poets scattered everywhere, while recognition now rises through momentum rather than stillness or weight. In its place are pockets of resonance. Singular books. Individual voices. Accounts carried through time. And sometimes a reader who pauses long enough to receive what is offered.

If succession has ended, something else remains.

The Law of Moral Recursion

Any moral system shaped through fear of erasure, whether through death, domination, or historical return, will, without proportional restraint, begin to recreate the conditions of the harm it fears.

Every community carries a memory of threat. When that memory becomes its organizing force, fear hardens into virtue and survival gathers the weight of righteousness. A group seeking safety elevates its wound into a moral framework. Vigilance becomes proof of goodness, suspicion proof of loyalty. In time, the very defenses built to prevent oppression start to resemble the structure of oppression itself. The wound becomes creed and the creed repeats the wound's motion.

Proportion, conscious limits, humility, and the willingness to recognize oneself in the adversary can slow the loop. Without these measures, the moral system turns inward. The persecuted slides into the posture of persecutor. The reformer assumes the role of inquisitor. The savior crosses into destruction. Each shift appears justified by the intensity of fear.

The law shows itself through several corollaries.

Reflective violence. Acts of protection, when unrestrained, begin to resemble the threat they oppose.

Diminishing empathy. The louder a group insists upon its innocence, the less able it becomes to perceive another's.

Historical echo. Each generation believes it is repairing the past, though many restage it with altered symbols.

Magnified recursion. The cost of recursion grows with power. When fear of erasure concentrates within a leader, a state, or an ideology that holds total authority, the loop intensifies. Defensive myth settles into bureaucracy, propaganda, and organized cruelty. The mechanism that draws small communities toward insularity draws empires toward atrocity. The distinction lies in scale rather than kind.

The escape clause. Proportion invites balance under pressure. It is not neutrality; it is the discipline to remember without reenacting. It asks for defense without dehumanization and conviction without purity. A moral system capable of that balance survives its own history rather than repeating it.

The fragility of proportion. Proportion runs against instinct. Human attention leans toward threat rather than restraint. Empathy takes energy. Doubt resembles betrayal.

Delay reads as weakness. In crisis, the structures that protect proportion, including law, deliberation, and due process, erode first. Reaction fills the space they once held.

To name moral recursion is sometimes mistaken for evasion, as if acknowledging a shared motion were an abdication of responsibility. Naming the motion does not absolve responsibility. The law does not flatten difference. It describes the gravity that draws all moral systems, even the just ones, toward repetition when proportion thins.

The American principle that a person is innocent until proven guilty was built as civic proportion. It offers a pause between accusation and punishment. It encloses humility within law by admitting how certainty distorts judgment. When that restraint dissolves and accusation becomes verdict, outrage replaces evidence. A republic enters the same recursive pattern it condemns. The courtroom becomes a crowd. The institution meant to guard against injustice becomes its stage.

Proportion finds no permanent home. Each generation must sustain it through the discomfort of doubt. When that discipline weakens, fear resumes command and the law of moral recursion continues its motion, quietly and steadily, like gravity.

Where Machiavelli traced the movement of power, Hobbes framed fear within political order, Nietzsche revealed the psychology of resentment, and Arendt described the drift toward bureaucratic harm, this poetics, shaped through years of civic, academic, and artistic attention, attempts to trace the moral law that drifts beneath them.

PART THREE

Held Voltage

There are moments when attention becomes a threshold. These poems emerged from that posture, revised over years, shaped with care, carried forward through listening more than assertion. They feel overheard or returned from a distance, guided into form by presence rather than force.

This sensibility threads through many arts. Eddie Van Halen spoke of music arriving through him. Merwin let punctuation fall away so breath could carry the line. Painters and musicians describe similar arrivals, when the work develops its own rhythm and asks only that the artist stay close enough to receive it.

Through quiet attention, a trace enters the poems: a shift in weather, a memory near the edge of recall, a presence felt before it is named. Ego loosens its grip long enough for the current to move. From that movement flow formal decisions, a held tone, a structure without spectacle, a rhythm close to breath.

From this interior ground, stylistic bearings gather naturally. They accumulate through long listening, repeated drafting, and the endurance of pressure. What takes form is a poetics shaped by lucidity and inward motion, by a tension that does not search for release.

The speakers absorb more than they announce. Their stance remains steady, alert, and receptive. They inhabit the charged space between emergence and retreat, letting the current settle without dispersal. Energy circulates through them, shaping the line, its silences, and the field the poem enters.

At the center of the work lies a voltage held in place. The pressure stays concentrated. The charge gathers in the language and holds there by design. Composure becomes the vessel for that force, and the held tension becomes an ethic.

Stylistic Bearings

The poetic style of *Between Here and the Sound of a Groaning Interstate* resists a single lineage. Its influences move across literary, regional, and spiritual terrains, yet the work stays concentrated rather than fragmented. Across the collection, certain bearings settle into view, steadying the poems even as they move through ambiguity, estrangement, and restraint. These bearings create a field where emotional resonance and structural clarity share the same frame.

One bearing is a surrealism rooted in the material world. The poems follow dream logic, yet their strangeness rises through bodies, objects, weather, and gesture. The surreal extends the real rather than departing from it.

Another presence comes from biblical and apocalyptic undertones. The poems advance no doctrine, yet they echo sacred cadence. Certain pieces carry the tonal residue of scripture pared to its essentials, reverence, hunger, ache. What enters the line comes less from belief than from inheritance.

A further lineage gathers from Midwestern and industrial elegy. Infrastructure marks the landscape: interstates, culverts, riverbanks altered by work, runoff, and residue. This terrain becomes a register of memory and consequence.

Alongside these bearings is a plainspoken strangeness. The poems state their oddities without emphasis. A man drives with the bust of a dead friend beside him; the detail stands untouched, which gives it shape. The surreal arrives as lived fact rather than ornament.

Absurdity carries a seam of sorrow. Humor sharpens at the edges. The grotesque intensifies the emotional field rather than distorting it.

Throughout the book, the voice shifts as witness, outsider, and inheritor. It stays close to the scenes it encounters while leaving space for what cannot be fully articulated. The speaker stands at a threshold, near enough to register intensity, composed enough to keep the frame open.

Together, these bearings shape the tonal landscape of the collection. The poems stand in their tension, surreal and real, sacred and ordinary, intimate and estranged, each element holding with the others without settling into unity.

Thematic Currents

Across the collection, certain tensions return as conditions the poems learn to inhabit.

Estrangement moves through much of the work. Whether in the fractured self, the altered city, the shifting family, or the dream-logic of interior life, the poems linger in scenes where nearness offers no promise of intimacy.

Beside it stands witness. The poems speak through presence rather than display. Violence, grief, and the grotesque register through composure. Stillness replaces amplification. This becomes an ethic of regard, attention held with care and shaped rather than extracted. The natural world enters through the same posture, encountered as presence rather than emblem.

Failure circulates as another current. It appears as the faltering of connection, form, and certainty, less collapse than drift. The poems approach thresholds and then turn toward silence or distortion. Revelation loosens into endurance. Even change arrives unfinished, more motion than arrival.

A final tension moves between reverence and disbelief. Biblical echoes, prayer-like syntax, and spiritual longing rise beside anatomical absurdity, dark humor, and doubt. The sacred and the senseless share the same frame without seeking alignment.

These currents form atmospheric fields, conditions the poems accept and remain inside. They offer ways of carrying pressure without dispersal.

Where these atmospheres set the tonal ground, the compositional forces show how the poems hold their shape.

Compositional Forces in the Work

Across the collection, five compositional forces shape how the poems carry tension and move through pressure. Each marks a way the work gathers and sustains presence.

Preservation stands first. The poems keep hold of what flickers or drifts. This is attention under pressure. "The other side is never a surprise," one poem says. Nothing lasts, yet the gaze stays steady.

Witness follows. These poems endure through presence rather than persuasion. The speaker absorbs charge without dispersal. Even the most surreal pieces sharpen toward emotional precision. They listen. They take in. They hold voltage without spectacle.

Estrangement acts as structural shift. The poems move through disrupted grammar and spatial dislocation as form responds to pressure. The surreal and the exact meet here, creating a field where the unsayable remains perceptible.

Rhythmic intelligence shapes the architecture. The poems move by pulse rather than argument. Rhythm carries tension. Line breaks and pacing seek balance rather than conclusion. The reader travels through changes in pressure instead of narrative turns.

Ethical refusal grounds the work. Emotion lives within composure. The poems remain present without heightening their own pain. Clarity rises through what the language chooses not to perform. Refusal becomes care, holding what cannot be restored.

Together, these forces create a compositional field defined by refusal. The poems hold more than they release. Their strength gathers through endurance, through the ability to keep tension intact.

Beneath this structure moves a deeper pressure, who speaks, how the voice forms, and what the poem allows it to carry.

On Persona and Poetic Masking

In this collection, the voices are shaped by the poet but speak through character and mask. This distinction, once assumed, has grown faint in a culture drawn to biography. The line between speaker and self, between poetic utterance and personal fact, thins. What earlier generations understood as mask is now often read as confession.

As that boundary narrows, the field of expression narrows with it. Persona becomes harder to sustain when readers expect the voice to align with the poet's visible identity. The imaginative act, stepping into another register of experience, faces scrutiny. The poem is nudged toward declaration: I lived this. I own this.

Yet poetry has long moved beyond autobiography. Even the confessional poets shaped selves for the sake of form. Lowell altered family history. Plath turned memory into myth. Sexton built voices that exceeded her own. Their personae created conditions for truth rather than diversions from it.

Persona, in this sense, becomes a form of freedom. It opens a space where knowledge arrives indirectly, through image or drift. It creates a vessel capable of carrying what the unguarded self might strain to hold.

The speakers here emerge as configurations of voice, fragments, apertures, witnesses. Some draw on lived experience; others arise through imagination. Their ambiguity is deliberate. It widens the field.

Masking also protects the poem. It keeps the work from being treated as credential or proof. It resists the expectation that identity must verify the art. It grants the poem its own terrain. The voices shift, contradict, vanish, and reappear. They move as art rather than affidavit. They let truth arrive sideways and expand what the poem can carry.

Identity and Its Shadows

If persona opens the field, identity complicates it. Identity is real and formative, yet on the page it holds only part of the story. What matters is how the voice moves and what it risks by appearing.

Identity acts as both recognition and demand. It shapes belonging across politics, faith, sexuality, and community. It guides how we read, whom we trust, and what we reveal. In this atmosphere, identity becomes a sorting mechanism, a way to map intention in a culture uneasy with ambiguity.

Poetry moves within these pressures. Institutions often treat identity as both entry point and credential. The impulse behind this attention carries real weight, yet it can narrow the interpretive frame. When identity becomes the primary lens, the poem risks being treated as emblem rather than art. It is pushed toward stance, explanation, and purpose. Ambiguity grows suspect. Opacity gathers unease.

Yet poetry has long worked through partial presence, through echoes and shadows, through the distance between what appears and what stays withheld. Enduring poems loosen identity rather than fix it. They shift the self enough for something more porous to take shape.

The speakers in the poems remain present without anchoring themselves to a single frame. They move between intimacy and drift. What they carry aligns with experience yet exceeds it. Their authority rises from tone, structure, and attention rather than biography.

The poems offer no single thread of identity to follow. Their openness invites multiple approaches shaped by contradiction, distance, and change. The self appears less as subject than as signal.

Identity here neither governs nor disappears. It flickers. It leans in and recedes. It stays part of the field without determining it. The voice keeps moving.

Estrangement and Participation

Poetry moves along a quiet line between distance and closeness. One side inclines toward estrangement, a voice that observes from a slight remove, attentive without assumption. The other leans toward participation, rooted, exposed, and present. Most poems drift between these postures. They shift as the moment shifts.

Closeness often reads as confirmation. The poet is urged toward revelation, toward testimony. Yet distance holds its own fidelity. Estrangement allows perception to rest on what is present without enclosing it. The refusal to over-identify becomes a form of regard.

In this collection, the voice often stays near the edge of the scene. It holds close enough to register charge yet leaves space around what it encounters. It lingers. It listens. Tone rises from that patience.

This restraint carries emotional weight. It shapes an ethic of attention, presence without claim. The poems remain beside what they meet, letting their texture stay visible. Composure creates room rather than filling it.

Estrangement and participation become dynamic movements. The voice leans in, then loosens. Understanding remains provisional. The world keeps part of its strangeness.

Presence settles lightly here. It stays steady, aware of its limits. In that balance, a different nearness becomes possible, one shaped by listening rather than possession.

On Semantic Freedom

When personae widen the field of expression and identity shapes the air a poem enters, language becomes the remaining terrain, a place where meaning can stay fluid, unsettled, and whole. Poetry trusts this terrain. Meaning shifts, gathers, recedes, returns. Language moves through surprise and drift rather than clarity alone. Misreading becomes part of the encounter, a sign that meaning lives through motion rather than closure.

Semantic freedom, the freedom for language to take its time, has grown scarce. That pressure reaches poetry, yet the art draws much of its force from delay, from images that sound before they settle, from rhythms that carry thought beyond argument.

These poems trust that meaning can emerge through pattern and pressure rather than directive speech. Their clarity grows through rhythm, repetition, and drift, recognizing that some truths approach obliquely, like sound heard before its source is known.

This stance is also an ethic. It grants readers room to return, to re-hear, to move without instruction. It assumes attention precedes understanding and that understanding can shift. Semantic freedom preserves a shared space where interpretation remains open.

Language carries its own life. To attend to that life is to treat mystery as presence and quiet as knowledge.

Charles Bernstein's *A Poetics* seeks release through fracture, through a burst that breaks the frame. This work moves differently. Its release comes through pressure and refusal, through listening beneath the surface until something steadier begins to sound. Both motions widen the field.

Meaning, when it approaches, moves like angled light under a closed door, enough to illuminate without declaring the room's shape. In that light, poet, reader, and poem remain free.

Here the lyric meets what it encounters and leaves it open. It stays near what gathers, the way weather crosses a field without deciding its form. Presence rises from attention carried long enough for something interior to surface, then continues.

PART FOUR

Opening Note

Before the lyric was framed as private voice, it moved through rhythm and structure. This part of the book listens for those architectures as they move through the poems, shaping experience across time.

Where earlier sections attend to attention and refusal, this section turns to sonic pressure, musical drift, and hidden structural weight. It listens for rhythm, recurrence, and tonal shape as they operate in the poems, a poetics composed through movement and held together by returning pressure, memory, and tone.

reVerse and the Architecture of Musical Poetics

In 2004, when the music industry was hemorrhaging and poetry drifted between academic seclusion and performative spectacle, an independent poetry and music CD quietly emerged from Chicago. Titled *reVerse*, the project arrived without fanfare. It was not commissioned, crowdfunded, or engineered for visibility. It was built.

There was nothing quite like it at the time. *reVerse* felt less like a mixtape and more like a civic signal, an audio cross-section of how poetry might sound in a city if the city were listening. The project moved freely across forms.

Some poems were sung, others spoken, others set into electronic sound or left to stand in silence. Music carried language. Language moved through music. Voice became the medium, and the city its resonance chamber. The tonal range stretched from gospel cadence to lo-fi grit, from atmospheric drift to deliberate quiet.

Its creation reflected its ethos. Clarke, a poet with a background in arts administration and civic poetics, missed the hybrid recordings he once found on late-1980s Sire Records samplers like *Just Say Mao*. Those compilations, Depeche Mode next to Ice-T next to The Throwing Muses next to Lou Reed, offered collisions that felt generative. Clarke wanted the same for poetry. But here, poetry was no visitor. It was the medium.

Asked why *reVerse* mattered, Clarke answered plainly. "There isn't that much out there that combines poetry and music with respect for the art form of poetry," he told *Litkicks* in 2004. "Most of the stuff out there is either self-indulgent or poorly recorded and produced." *reVerse* took the opposite tack: careful attention, high production values, no fetishizing of form. If a track worked, it stayed. If it didn't, it was cut. "We listened to the tracks over and over and found stuff we hated or were bugged by and fixed or replaced those things in other sessions."

But *reVerse* is more than a recording. It is a method. Clarke's advice to young poets was simple: host your own readings, on rooftops or in garages. Use whatever you have, even your phone. Read aloud until you are hearing the poem, not your own voice. That ethic runs through the album's sequencing. *reVerse* does not perform poetry for approval. It experiments for insight. Even its strangest tracks feel curated by ear.

Directed and produced by Clarke, *reVerse* brought together fourteen poets and musicians into a structured listening experience that resisted genre. It was not jazz-poetry nostalgia. It did not rely on beat-driven pastiche. It was quieter and more deliberate: a civic structure composed of voice, instrumentation, licensing agreements, and financial risk.

The work began in 2001. Clarke recalled, "I decided to create a poetry and music compilation CD that was artistic, enjoyable, high quality, and ultimately very listenable." As director of the Poetry Center, he also sought a structure that would let supporters tie personal artistic projects to a civic mission, particularly the poets-in-residence program.

By 2002, Clarke had secured funding from Chicago philanthropist John Dangora, a long-time backer of Clarke's civic work. He and co-producer Richard Fammerée began curating a lineup that crossed style and generation, aiming to feature both established and emerging artists.

Recording began in June 2003 at Soma Electronic Music Studios. Mikael Jorgensen, then a local engineer and newly joined to Wilco, handled engineering, contributed keyboards, and helped shape the first eleven tracks. They recorded late into the night for four straight days. Clarke called it "exhausting but exhilarating."

The fall session was delayed. One key slot remained: an established musician with a poetic bent. Billy Corgan had initially agreed, but as October passed and the Cubs surged, the poem never came. In December, Corgan withdrew, citing a new book contract.

Clarke and Fammerée regrouped. They wrote letters. They faxed. They waited. Eventually they reached Alexi Murdoch through CD Baby and Lou Reed through Ram Devineni of *Rattapallax*. Both agreed.

In April 2004, Reed recorded a reading from his adaptation of *The Raven*. On July 2, the final session took place. With Jorgensen on tour, Tim Iseler engineered. Mastering followed. The album was printed in October.

reVerse, released in 2004, occupies a rare place as a public-facing literary audio object conceived at album scale. Emerging during a brief period when poetry and music were beginning to coalesce in new ways, the project did not adapt poems into songs. Instead, it assembled spoken text, sound, and silence through sampling and sequence, treating the album itself as the primary compositional unit. Meaning accrues through placement, recurrence, and drift, rather than performance alone.

Its reception reached beyond niche audiences. Spins on Chicago and Minnesota public radio, ads in *The New Yorker*, *Village Voice*, and *Poetry Daily*, and press across literary and music platforms confirmed it as a serious audio object. At a time when poetry largely lived behind podiums, *reVerse* offered a different model: listening as civic act, shaped through music and held by formal care.

Some saw *reVerse* as an heir to the Beats. And in certain ways, it was. Clarke shared their belief in poetry as sound and their urge to bring poems into public life. But where the Beats leaned into performance, Clarke leaned into design. His poetics emphasized structure: curated, durable, quiet.

Rather than howl, he wired the room. *reVerse* included Lawrence Ferlinghetti, recorded from the back room of City Lights. His presence functioned less as endorsement than as continuity. Ferlinghetti had always been more civic than confessional. He became a hinge between generations; a voice of public poetics rooted in risk and regard.

The album itself moved like a poem. It opened with Li-Young Lee's soft invocation, ambient and spare. Clarke's *Skyscraper (delux)* combined city field recordings, his own keyboard, and Jorgensen's ambient textures. The track list folded from gospel to spoken word to ambient drift. It closed with Lou Reed reciting "The City and the Sea" a cappella. No remix. No overdub. Just voice and void.

The project was organized around its architecture. Clarke paid all costs upfront. Artists were positioned to be compensated first if any profit emerged. Any proceeds beyond were designated for Chicago Public Schools through the Poetry Center's Hands On Stanzas program. When sales fell short, Clarke absorbed the loss.

reVerse functioned as practice rather than display. Its structure mirrored its ethics. The album assembled spoken text, sound, and silence into a composed sequence, shaped by listening and recurrence. It did not announce a musical poetics so much as enact one. What the album made audible was already present: a poetics carried through attention, repetition, and the formal pressure of sound.

The album was modestly received but recognized. About.com ranked it the number four poetry CD of 2004 in a list curated by Bob Holman, who later mailed Clarke a handwritten postcard of thanks. *Poetry Flash*, *Newcity*, *Chicago Reader*, WBEZ, and WGN Radio all covered it. Ads ran in *Pitchfork*, *The New Yorker*, *Village Voice*, and *Poetry Daily*, funded not by grants but by Clarke's credit card.

Caryn Thurman, writing for *Litkicks*, framed *reVerse* within a moment shaped by Saul Williams, García Márquez screen adaptations, and Billy Corgan's brief literary pivot. She called it "a unique blend" that dared "to blur the lines of music, poetry and activism."

Clarke also uploaded *reVerse* to streaming platforms before streaming mattered. Long before poetry playlists or Spotify's spoken-word category, *reVerse* appeared on

Apple Music. It remains there, a civic signal in archival form.

What *reVerse* built was not simply a CD, but a civic poetics rendered in sound. The project gathered artists from across the country into a shared frame. Voices arrived from Chicago, New York, San Francisco, and Los Angeles, drawn together by tone, purpose, and compositional care. It was built like a poem. It functioned like a bridge. It endures like a song, still audible beneath the noise.

Flip Sides

Think of this sequence more like a curated run of singles, ten poem pairings spread across the collection, each with an A-side and a B-side. The A-side draws you in. The B-side deepens, complicates, or flips the signal.

The format may feel analog, but that's the point. Vinyl's resurgence isn't just about sound, it's about structure, patience, and the surprise that lives on the flip. You don't stream a B-side. You discover it. You drop the needle. You turn the thing over.

These ten pairings hum through the book. Each A-side offers a clean hit, a lyric surface, a formal stance. Each B-side complicates what came before. Together, they sketch a kind of counter-arc. Something slow, durable, and meant to be reentered.

1. Skyscraper / Upland

Two tracks on the same frequency. *Skyscraper* shoots its prayer through glass and circuitry, only to have the signal bounce right back. *Upland* stands inside that echo, the hum, the afterglow, the persistence of what we build. One sends; one receives. Together they close the loop.

2. Americus, for Ferlinghetti / To a Young Malcolm X

Two letters, two inheritances. *Americus, for Ferlinghetti* writes to the wide-open street; *To a Young Malcolm X* speaks from the quiet room after the march. One's elegy, one's invocation. Both ask what it means to step into a voice that was already burning before you arrived.

3. Humdrum / Network

Everyday unraveling and the pattern underneath. *Humdrum* drifts through blurred days and frayed nights; *Network* plugs the silence into current and finds a pulse. One crumbles; the other hums.

4. The Devourer / Don't Tell Me You Haven't Thought This Before

Two takes on appetite. *The Devourer* goes in teeth-first, swallowing what it can't name. *Don't Tell Me You Haven't Thought This Before* looks the same hunger in the eye and says it out loud. One eats; the other indicts.

5. This Charming Man / My Friend and His Wife

Front and back of the American mask. *This Charming Man* wears the tarnish of fame; *My Friend and His Wife* catches the fallout in kitchen light. Fame fades. Love cracks. Traffic keeps passing on the street.

6. Tomorrow Is a Long Time / Waiting for Daylight

Late-night transmissions. *Tomorrow Is a Long Time* listens through distance; *Waiting for Daylight* waits without promise. One holds the ache; the other the air after it.

7. The Humming Bridge / Cliffard Gawthorp's Trade

Work songs in minor key. *The Humming Bridge* opens with vibration, a tone passed down through hands and metal. *Cliffard Gawthorp's Trade* answers in sparks and welding flash. One hears the chord; the other forges it.

8. Orion / The Possum

One looks up; the other keeps to the ground. *Orion* drives through the constellations, restless for a sign. *The Possum* slips through the dark edges of town, ordinary and indestructible. One scans the heavens for meaning; the other rummages under the porch and finds it anyway.

9. Bridgebuilder / Jubilee

Two gestures of faith. *Bridgebuilder* builds knowing the bridge will rust and fall, hands working anyway. *Jubilee* looks back through family and forest, seeing the same truth in smaller continuities, the initials in bark, the chipmunk's path, the quiet persistence of care. One makes what will not last; the other finds meaning in what remains.

10. Desire / Mercury Fish

Two temperature tests. *Desire* burns hot, the body lit from within. *Mercury Fish* drifts cool through poisoned water, beautiful and wrong. One feeds on want; the other glows with its residue. The record ends where it began.

The Rhythmic Contour

This is a macro view of the collection's rhythmic arc across six compositional phases: Tension → Drift → Collapse → Compression → Suspension → Open.

The poems in *Between Here and the Sound of a Groaning Interstate* move by rhythm and tonal pressure, unfolding through recurrence rather than sequence. Their structure behaves like a waveform, shaped less by narrative order than by shifts in pressure and release. This interval listens for that internal architecture: how intensity builds, disperses, withdraws, and reshapes itself across the six-part cadence.

Structure moves beyond scaffold. It becomes a shape sensed through rhythm, tone, and musical pressure. A fuller rendering of this contour appears later in the visual waveform at the back of the book (page 393). The collection holds itself together through contour rather than plot: tension rising, loosening, breaking apart, gathering again, settling into stillness, then opening into air.

Tension (Poems 1–10)

A field of pressure forms. Surfaces stay composed while emotion coils underneath. The line holds breath. Syntax tightens. Violence lingers near the frame. Refusal stiffens the field. Everything feels wound, charged, waiting.

Drift (Poems 11–20)

The thread loosens and tone begins to slant. Spatial dislocation sets in as surreal imagery and ambient movement take over. Lines lengthen, logic bends, and sound travels sideways across the page. What stays withheld gathers force until drift itself becomes atmosphere.

Collapse (Poems 21–28)

Grief and absurdity rupture the restraint that shaped the earlier arc. Syntax fractures and sentences scatter. The line struggles to hold its shape as tonal cohesion erodes. Meaning sinks into the background, leaving resonance in its place. Each poem becomes a thin container for what outruns articulation.

Compression (Poems 29–36)

Form gathers itself and pressure returns shaped by what the poems have carried. The line draws close at first, trimmed and concentrated, as memory arrives in brief flashes like struck notes. Within this tightening, a brief spaciousness appears as the tonal field opens. After this interlude, containment forms again. Rhythm grows denser and sound lowers into a deeper register. The field settles into something weighted and steady, a descent that holds the sequence in place. Cadence slows, and this renewed density carries the pressure forward.

Suspension (Poems 37–44)

The voice holds its position. These poems live at the edge of thresholds where time elongates and motion thins. The line steadies. Sound lingers. Stillness acquires its own form. The poems seek balance rather than forward motion. Suspension becomes duration, a held note extended past measure.

Open (Poems 45–48)

Pressure eases into expansion. Silence returns with less weight. Syntax lightens. Familiar images reappear with more air around them. The line stretches. Structure lifts. What remains is an opening, spacious and continuous.

The Rhythmic Behavior

What emerges when we shift from the six-part arc of the collection to its inner movement is a field of rhythmic behavior rather than a fixed structural shape. *Between Here and the Sound of a Groaning Interstate*, when listened to closely, reveals a dynamic interplay of pressure and breath, density and release. Each poem functions as a tonal unit, a rhythmic measure within a larger score. When traced across the full collection, these measures form a waveform: undulating, asymmetrical, alive. The waveform extends beyond sound. It carries into visual density, pacing, and emotional pressure. The rhythmic behavior of the collection appears near the book's end in the second-to-last figure (page 394).

This rhythmic behavior serves as compositional force. The collection unfolds through modulated shifts in sonic density, emotional tempo, and formal compression rather than through narrative escalation or thematic accumulation. Instead of building toward climax, the work circulates intensity. Pressure rises, dissipates, and gathers again. These fluctuations follow an iterative logic.

Near the midpoint of the collection, intensity compounds. A cluster of poems gathers tonal weight and syntactic pressure, tightening the field through accumulation. Their force develops through vocal density and compositional concentration as much as through expansion. Where one piece may settle into place as a hinge within this movement, the surrounding works reinforce the strain through brevity and impact. The effect is architectural. Energy circulates inside the sequence rather than escaping it.

This passage of the book produces a heightened zone of rhythmic stress. Breath shortens. Phrases arrive with less air around them. Recurrence begins to operate as gravity. What had moved episodically now behaves as system.

After this crest, the sequence alters its posture. The poems open laterally. Space returns, though it carries residue. These works function as buffers or antechambers where charge redistributes across quieter surfaces. The temperature lowers without dispersing. What remains continues to vibrate beneath the language.

Later in the collection, rhythmic pressure gathers again, now turned inward. The force here is not expansive but torsional, drawing the lyric into density. Cadence contracts. Syntax begins to shear. The tonal field grows heavier, more interior, as if the poems have entered weather rather than event.

These pieces deepen rather than climb. Their motion is horizontal, subterranean, and resonant below articulation. Sound becomes structure. Meaning follows pressure.

This rhythmic behavior reinforces the ethical posture of the collection. The poems resist the lure of catharsis. Even at their most charged, they temper eruption through composure. Anger rises briefly, then settles into quiet. Grotesque moments enter without amplification and are met with steadiness. The pacing argues for tonal complexity rather than for intensity alone. Pressure meets breath. Force meets stillness. Rhythm and ethics merge as compositional restraint becomes a deliberate refusal to turn suffering into spectacle.

To say that the collection moves more like an album than an argument serves as structural recognition. Its rhythmic contour shapes progression independent of narrative or theme. Modulation drives the work. High-intensity sequences alternate with lower-pressure interludes, forming a waveform of linguistic density and affective tempo that carries the reader across the book's tonal and emotional terrain.

When rendered visually, the rhythmic arc resembles dynamic systems: the textured contour of a radio signal, the modulated amplitude of a wave moving through resistance. These forms echo deeper structural affinities. The poems behave like signal systems in motion. Pulse. Variation. Return. The collection follows recursive asymmetry rather than conventional arc. This rhythmic structure enacts a poetics that resists closure. Its movement aligns more with adaptation than with linear or cyclical pattern.

Within this framework, rhythm becomes a field of relational energies. Though the poems were not written with Henri Lefebvre's Rhythmanalysis in mind, his later work listens for meaning in layered temporalities of experience. Breath, stress patterns, line breaks, pacing, and cultural expectations create overlapping rhythms. These layers interfere with one another, and that interference becomes a measure of the human condition: indeterminate, unstable, felt.

The rhythmic structure offers a parallel reading that attends to how the poems behave across time. This behavior is discontinuous, responsive, and compositional. The collection sends out tonal and structural signals without assurance of reception, launching them into a cultural atmosphere shaped by noise, distortion, and delay. Signals that return arrive altered by their passage: refracted, partial, and still marked by poetic intention sustained across an unsettled field.

Mapped more granularly for tempo, the perceptible speed, density, and urgency of each poem contributes to an internal pulse structure that supports the larger waveform. High-tempo poems cluster mid-collection, generating sustained sequences of pressure. Low-tempo pieces create stillness at the margins. Medium-tempo works serve as chambers of transition, absorbing tonal shifts and anchoring change. This distribution modulates energy without narrative propulsion. Each poem acts as a pulse, contracting or expanding, and together they maintain rhythmic coherence.

Mapped for architectural tension, through average line length and variability within the poem, the collection reveals a similar waveform. Formal expansion and contraction mirror the tempo arcs. Extended lines coincide with low-tempo stillness. Abrupt shifts and length disparities signal high-pressure zones. This structural rhythm reinforces the recursive pacing and affirms rhythm as central compositional logic.

To make this rhythm visible, the collection was read as a field of measurable pulses. Each poem was read across four dimensions: tempo, compression, sonic texture, and average rhythmic intensity. These interpretive scores were applied consistently to surface structural patterns that thematic reading alone might miss. The resulting waveform reflects rhythmic behavior across time.

This is the rhythm of transmission. What returns arrives marked by its passage: refracted, partial, and shaped by intention carried through a structurally unsettled field. Each reading becomes a pulse, erupting, dissipating, then held in the distance between here and the sound of a groaning interstate.

Though tempo and architectural tension ease in the final poems, the arc resolves at a higher register. Its lift emerges through composure rather than propulsion.

Reverberation

The poems in *Between Here and the Sound of a Groaning Interstate* engage music through compositional logic rather than direct reference. Their kinship with musical practice arises through pacing, suspension, repetition, and delay. Even when a poem's title echoes a song, such as *This Charming Man* or *Tomorrow Is a Long Time*, the relationship remains structural. The work listens for the architectures that sound makes as it moves.

This orientation aligns with the six-part rhythmic waveform: tension, drift, collapse, compression, suspension, open. The sequence unfolds through tonal modulation rather than narrative progression or autobiographical revelation. What gathers on the page is pressure shaped through shifting density, carried forward by rhythm.

The musical parallels draw from traditions that privilege duration, restraint, and clarity of form. Sustained tones, spare harmonies, and devotional intensity shape these affinities. Extended repetitions and layered crescendos demonstrate how energy deepens through patience and how form extends through quiet force.

The poems move through resolution, pause within it, and circle back again. This motion turns attention toward tension as an abiding compositional field. Lineation settles into rhythm. Syntax carries breath. Memory returns in patterns rather than declarations, the way a phrase resurfaces in a score.

To describe these poems as musical gestures is to describe how they are built. Like a phrase sustained across measures in a minimalist composition, each poem holds pressure as it moves forward. The work relies on a shared logic of construction, where duration becomes an ethical stance and resonance shapes the frame.

Reverberation and imitation part ways here. The poems draw energy from musical practice while remaining grounded in their own forms. Their gravity lives in tone rather than symbol. Rhythm settles quietly into its measure, a field attentive to its own unfolding.

In listening, these poems discover structures that hold pressure with clarity, shaping a space where sound and silence return to each other.

PART FIVE

The Weather Makers

Certain works alter the conditions around them. They change the air a reader moves through. In music, a single track can set the weather for an entire album. In a gallery, one painting can recalibrate how the room is felt. In novels, a chapter can evoke a storm, shifting the emotional climate of everything that follows. Poetry has always possessed this same atmospheric force.

Aesthetic theory has long returned to this problem. As Gernot Böhme argues in *Atmosphere as a Fundamental Concept of a New Aesthetics*, atmosphere occupies an indeterminate space between object and subject. It cannot be located solely in the work nor solely in the perceiver. It fills space. It arrives before interpretation. Gaston Bachelard, writing from a different register in *The Poetics of Space*, describes how poems and images evoke inhabited states rather than represent them, shaping how we dwell inside imagined worlds.

What these thinkers describe abstractly is now encountered daily. Readers and listeners recognize that certain works do more than stand on their own. They exert influence outward, governing pacing, attention, and emotional pressure across a larger field. In a culture of excess circulation, with albums, playlists, exhibitions, feeds, and shelves all competing at once, this atmospheric effect is no longer rare. It is the one song on an album that changes everything, or the new skyscraper in a skyline that quietly uplifts or oppresses, altering how all that follows is received.

The poems gathered here are chosen deliberately. They are named and traced because they exerted sustained atmospheric force during the making and rereading of the book. This is not a claim of inherent status, nor a declaration of fixed hierarchy. It is an act of attention. To follow atmosphere at all requires choosing a path through it, entering where pressure feels concentrated, and staying long enough to register its effects.

These pieces, *Mary's Field*, *This Charming Man*, *After the Fall of the First World*, *Cliffard Gawthorp's Trade*, *Dirt*, *The Perennials*, *Ode to a Roadkill*, and *After a Year of Flooding* are distinguished by how they hold space through tonal saturation and sustained intensity. Their placement marks moments of absorption, where pacing decelerates, imagery deepens, and attention extends across the reading experience.

Some of these poems introduce new atmospheric registers, while others serve as thresholds where tonal pressure shifts. Their placement corresponds with moments of absorption, where pacing slows, imagery thickens, and attention stretches across time. Rather than interrupting momentum, they reshape its conditions, altering how the surrounding poems are felt.

Close attention clarifies this role. These poems align with moments where pace loosens or gathers and tonal pressure shifts. Their architecture resembles an adagio bridge or an ambient swell inside a faster score. Their pacing carries tension through extension. Time adjusts around them, allowing time to be felt as altered presence.

This architectural function reflects a deeper compositional ethic. These poems ask for attention without seeking control. Their energy stays close to the body, felt in breath, throat, and the aftermath of reading.

Together, these poems recalibrate the poetry collection's pacing and tonal density. Their placement corresponds with internal shifts where rhythm slows, imagery deepens, and presence turns durational. Rather than pause momentum, they reshape its conditions, altering how subsequent poems are registered and absorbed.

To follow how atmosphere moves through the book, each poem was read through a shared set of compositional cues, including its sense of space, image density, temporal stretch, pacing, and tonal pressure. These qualities were considered not as fixed properties, but as ways poems shape the conditions of reading around them. By tracing how these forces rise, linger, and recede across the sequence, broader patterns of atmospheric influence became visible. The chart reflects this process of attention: a way of noticing how certain poems do not simply appear, but alter the weather of what follows. A visual rendering of this atmospheric contour appears in the waveform at the back of the book (page 395).

Poem 2: *Mary's Field*

A sacred, rain-soaked field becomes an inhabitable spiritual environment. The shrine, water, mud, and ritual language create a sustained atmospheric presence that lingers beyond the poem itself.

Poem 9: *This Charming Man*

Cultural myth, death, place, and memory form a dense emotional climate. The poem doesn't just narrate, it *holds* the reader inside a charged, mournful field.

Poem 25: *After the Fall of the First World*

History, ruins, faith, and storms merge into a devastated but resonant environment. The poem sustains tonal pressure through shared dread and fragile hope.

Poem 26: *Cliffard Gawthorp's Trade*

Smoke, welding, cigarettes, and labor form a thick industrial atmosphere. The poem's slow pacing and material density create a working-class weather system.

Poem 33: *Dirt*

War, motherhood, violence, and consumption saturate the emotional air. The poem's heaviness doesn't lift, it settles and stays.

Poem 38: *The Perennials*

Generational decay, animals, seasons, and long memory create a durational field. Time stretches across decades, and the atmosphere becomes almost geological.

Poem 41: *Ode to a Roadkill*

Blood, winter, light, and aftermath form a quiet but saturated environment. The poem holds grief in the air rather than resolving it.

Poem 44: *After a Year of Flooding*

Fossils, future worlds, forest husks, and frozen fields generate a deep, lingering calm. The atmosphere feels vast, slow, and sustaining.

Together, these eight poems form part of the collection's internal architecture, shaping how momentum gathers and silence expands. Their presence shapes how momentum gathers, how silence expands, and how attention shifts. Each introduces a subtle recalibration. They deepen the current that moves through the book.

They affirm a central principle of the work's poetics: intensity can arrive through presence, through tonal concentration, and through atmosphere sustained across time. These poems carry energy through resonance and duration. They shape intensity through attention. In doing so, they expand the frequency range of the collection and extend its tonal reach.

A reader may find other Weather Makers in the collection. These eight mark one path through the field, yet the book offers many places where tone gathers, where the air inside a poem shifts, where pacing settles into a deeper register. Another reader may feel the atmosphere change in different corners of the book. That variation belongs to the work. It keeps the field open and allows each reader to sense their own pattern of weather across the poems.

PART SIX

A Quiet Intervention

Rhythm gives the poems their frame, and certain pieces shift the weather inside it. What holds the collection together through these movements gathers more quietly. It rises through presence sustained across time, through attention that stays with the world.

Endurance enters through this kind of patience. It grows in the spaces where expression softens and listening carries the weight. In those slower intervals, life around the poems leans toward life within them.

The lyric, in this register, moves through steadiness. It remains close to experience through time spent, through care held after a moment has passed. It allows the poems to open and return, to hold their field alive.

Some forms of attention move before language, enacted through care, through composure, and through the quiet refusal to look away. What follows begins in labor, in the work that allows art to take shape. The ethic it reflects moves alongside the poems. There is a kind of work that asks only to be done well.

For a time, Clarke worked within a humane society as a sworn officer and executive. The role was not a poetic one, yet its demands moved close to the poems. It required steady attention to the cast-off, the injured, the voiceless, and those who care for them. Animals arrived in pain or silence, and their needs had to be read.

Here the poetics return through stance alone. Quiet withholding, humility, and the refusal to dramatize suffering arise from an ethical posture rather than a stylistic preference.

During that time, Clarke supported an unusual artistic gesture within the shelter by editing and publishing a cartoon book created by nationally syndicated artist Jenny Campbell, who has long served as the humane society's cartoonist-in-residence. The work is gentle and precise. It carries sorrow and absurdity in the same breath. Like the poems, it creates space for what cannot be argued, only shaped.

This becomes a throughline. The instincts that guide the poems, restraint, space-making, compassion without sentiment, also guide the daily work.

Animals communicate through posture, breath, and movement. Their signals are clear when attended to. The poems listen in a similar register. Without interpretation. Without summary. Presence held long enough for something to emerge. Witness holds close to what cannot name itself.

From a distance, the poet and the officer may seem divided. Yet the stance is shared. What first appears separate begins to echo across the work.

The Long Account

Some voices flare and vanish. Others settle like residue. They hold the aftermath, the slow drift of experience that gathers in layers and carries its own weight. This is the long account. It accumulates through presence. It listens for what persists after the moment has passed.

Between Here and the Sound of a Groaning Interstate moves in this register. Its force builds through recurrence and tonal pressure. Fields, engines, weather, memory, the half-life of belief all emerge without emphasis. They arrive the way traces do, through quiet return. The poems record in this slower way.

The poems track tonal impacts, small shifts that remain long after their cause recedes. They stay close to what might otherwise disperse.

This attention moves alongside archival work, fieldwork, and the practice of listening for patterns across time. The stance remains steady rather than reactive. It watches for changes in pressure, for the subtle rearrangements that shape experience beneath the level of event. The poems follow this instinct.

Autobiography enters the collection quietly. The speaker stands near the work but never at its center. What holds attention is what was noticed, what stayed, what returned in sound or image. The lyric stance offers a form of shelter, a structure that holds what the moment cannot contain. It creates space where experience can rest without explanation.

This is composure as presence. It extends through tone. It remains through rhythm. The poems gather their strength gradually, through sediment rather than statement. Their impulse is to carry, to hold, to keep what might fall away.

The poems deepen through accumulation. They open room for what remains unsettled to retain its shape. The gesture becomes a form of care; regard carried across time.

To keep the long account is to remain. Through attention. Through rhythm that continues after the poem quiets. What follows is a drift, a resonance carried by the space the poem makes for it.

The Work of a Poet

Before I ever placed a poem in public space, I submitted them quietly and steadily, often without result and sometimes with success. In 1993, I served as poetry editor of *Oxford Magazine* at Miami University. Around that time, I began sending my own work to journals across the country. Most were rejected. A few returned with handwritten notes. Some were accepted. I kept sending the same poems out.

This was not strategy. When I began submitting, I was still a student. By 1995, I had entered nonprofit work. But the discipline stayed with me. I sent out poems I believed were complete. The labor lived in the writing and in the steady willingness to offer it to the world. And then I stopped submitting.

I did not stop writing. But I stopped mailing envelopes, logging responses, and waiting. Over time, the act of submitting began to feel compulsive, a cycle of rejection and occasional acceptance that no longer shaped the work. So I let that part of the practice fall away.

During my time as Executive Director of the Poetry Center of Chicago, I submitted almost nothing, aside from one contest at a friend's urging. But I picked the work up in another form. I began placing poems, written by others, into civic space. I curated broadsides and readings, and commissioned visual collaborations. Poetry entered the city, the schools, the walls of gallery halls and classrooms.

That was the turn. What began as editorial instinct became public poetics. The poems in this book, and the essays that accompany them, arise from that shift. They belong less to the marketplace than to the street, the wall, the held breath of a room where something is being made visible.

Few people knew how seriously I took my own poetry. Mark Strand was one of them. He read the collection in its early form, and I still have his edits. Once, in front of others, he called me a "real poet." Coming from him, the gesture carried its own quiet resonance.

Selected Submissions and Acceptances

Between 1993 and 1997, I submitted poems to more than sixty literary magazines. The record from that time reflects the rhythm expected of poets who try to place their work in the world. The overall acceptance rate from this period was 13.4 percent.

Several pieces found homes. *Scarecrows* and *The Humming Bridge* were taken by *Riverrun*. *The Possum* and *Love Poem (#102)*, now *First Psalm*, appeared in *Black River Review*. *Mary's Field* landed at *Indiana Review*. *Tomorrow is a Long Time* and *Upland* were accepted by *Poet Lore*.

Many others circulated through the usual rounds. *The New Yorker* declined several batches but sent a handwritten note from Alice Quinn. *New England Review* offered an encouraging letter. Journals such as *Midwest Quarterly*, *Poet Lore*, *Sulfur*, and *Sequoia* returned personal replies. *Free Lunch* declined but expressed interest in *My Friend and His Wife*. *The Journal*, *Crazyhorse*, *Poetry*, and *Witness* each engaged across multiple rounds. One response from *Blank Gun Silencer* included Dan Neilsen's remark about "the blather of lawnmowers" in *Tomorrow Is a Long Time*, as if Racine were untouched by such suburban machinery.

Submissions went to a wide range of journals, from *Poetry, The New Yorker, New England Review, Iowa Review,* and *The Antioch Review* to university-affiliated journals such as *Sycamore Review, Poet Lore, Indiana Review,* and *Sulfur,* and to independent venues including *Swamp Root, Black Fly Review, Blank Gun Silencer,* and *Howling Dog.*

PART SEVEN

The Ethos of Civic Poetics

For part of my adult life, poetry lived less through publication than through placement, into public space, institutional structure, and civic memory. While many poets centered their practice around the writing and release of personal work, my orientation moved toward amplification, access, and form.

The poems I lifted into shared space were rarely my own. I commissioned broadsides, curated readings, built programs, and created platforms that made room for poetry. The aim was presence, verse situated within the life of a city. That work shaped the poetics.

This poetry collection and its companion's reflections may form the first sustained presentation of my own writing, yet they rise from the same ethic. Both were composed with public attention in mind, as offerings placed within a larger field of accompaniment and regard. Their cadence and structure follow the instinct that once placed poems on billboards and broadsides, in classrooms and civic institutions. The aim was space.

Presence, in this context, carries no demand for attention. It creates structure. It affirms that poetry belongs in shared life, and that one of its enduring forms is the act of lifting another voice forward.

If this prelude offers a lived account of that orientation, what follows begins to trace its expression. It outlines a civic poetics that values placement over promotion, form over display, and contribution carried forward.

CIVIC POETICS /ˈsɪvɪk poʊˈɛtɪks/ *n.* [Poetics] (from Latin *civicus*, "pertaining to citizenship" + *poetica*, "the art of poetry")

1. An artistic practice that places poetry in shared space, schools, galleries, streets, libraries, through design, curation, and public invitation. It operates through presence rather than promotion, emphasizing placement as a primary poetic act within this practice.

2. A cross-disciplinary orientation in which poetry enters public life alongside music, visual art, and communal practice. These forms function as co-equal elements in the poetic structure rather than as framing or ornament.

3. A poetics of stewardship grounded in durable structures, reading series, broadsides, archives, residencies, designed to carry poetry across time and setting. Its work is cumulative, sustaining cultural memory through continuity rather than event.

4. A practice committed to plurality, allowing many poetic traditions, vernacular, experimental, sacred, academic, to coexist within the same civic frame. Each poem is received on its own terms, without aesthetic hierarchy.

5. A mode of poetic engagement that situates lyric work within public life. Attention shifts from authorship to access, from self-expression to placement. Rather than enclosing the lyric, civic poetics treats poetry as a shared inheritance, something to house, offer, and hold in common. Meaning often resides in the act of offering, in the shape of a reading or

performance, the placement of a poem, the invitation to read or perform, itself.

Civic Poetics in Practice

Civic poetics values endurance over immediacy. Its labor unfolds quietly and across time. It invests in lasting structures rather than momentary acclaim. It may appear in a broadside made in response to grief, a verse placed in a hallway, or a stage opened to an untrained voice. Each act carries formal weight, asking what form a poem must take to enter shared memory.

It welcomes difference. It creates conditions for multiple poetic traditions, vernacular, academic, ancestral, experimental, to exist alongside one another. Each poem is received on its own terms. Through this ethic, civic poetics sustains plurality and protects complexity.

For Clarke, this orientation extended beyond the written word. Music, visual art, and hybrid performance became structural collaborators. These forms shaped how the poem entered the world. The civic field became a chorus rather than a monologue.

Civic poetics seeks no elevation above the world. It seeks grounding within it. This ethic emerged through practice. It was shaped by poets who gave poetry a place in public life. In Chicago, that labor formed no canon. It grew as a root system, shaped in part by three quiet builders whose work defined the field by what it carried, where it was placed, and how long it endured.

Civic poetics rarely receives the same attention as poetic craft. It moves more slowly. It operates without spectacle. Yet in Chicago, three literary figures shaped in an enduring civic poetry infrastructure: Paul Carroll, KC

Clarke, and B. Sampson. Each approached poetry as public offering rather than career. What they built carried forward beyond recognition. It became a structure others could enter.

Paul Carroll first imagined the Chicago Poetry Center as a civic institution. He launched it at the Museum of Contemporary Art with the belief that poetry belonged in public life. His programs and national reading series were guided by presence rather than credential. Through this work, the lyric found a place in the city.

Clarke, his successor a generation later, carried that vision into a new chapter. "He inspired the next chapter of what poetry in Chicago could mean," Clarke later recalled. "I stood on his shoulders. And then we began to build again."

During Clarke's tenure, the Center's reach deepened. He commissioned a wide-ranging series of broadsides, collaborations between nationally known poets and visual artists, and launched Hands On Stanzas, a citywide residency program placing working poets into classrooms. Developed under the mentorship of Kenneth Koch, informed by *Rose, Where Did You Get That Red?*, the New York based Teachers & Writers Collaborative, and the student poetry anthology *Something I wrote Myself*, edited by Robert Fox, the program invited students to engage poetry through direct encounter.

The broadsides offered a visible record of poetic presence. They were produced, pairing the work of Lucille Clifton, Mark Strand, Lawrence Ferlinghetti, Haki R. Madhubuti, Ron Padgett, and others with printmakers, painters, and photographers. These letterpress prints were designed to circulate. They served as public artifacts, evidence that poetry had taken place.

Clarke treated the broadside as civic form. He curated readings with the same ethic, shaping each as a gesture of placement over promotion. The focus remained with presence rather than prestige.

When B. Sampson became executive director, she inherited a living structure. She stabilized Hands On Stanzas, reorganized the Center's operations, and secured its continuity during a vulnerable period. Her leadership extended the same ethic that had shaped the institution from the beginning: quiet, rooted, and public facing.

In 2024, the Poetry Foundation presented an exhibition of many of the broadsides Clarke had commissioned. Organized by Sampson and the Poetry Foundation and supported by Clarke, the show included public programming and a short documentary marking the Center's fiftieth anniversary.

Public memory shifts. Recognition circulates unevenly. Yet the structure these three poets shaped, Carroll, Clarke, and Sampson, continues. It was never a monument. It remains a root system.

The Asteroid

In December 2003, The Wall Street Journal published a front-page story announcing a $100 million bequest to the Poetry Foundation. Clarke, then executive director of the Poetry Center of Chicago, was one of the few literary figures quoted. His response was simple and direct:

"My hope is that they share the wealth."

It marked the moment. For decades, civic poetry organizations like the Poetry Center had relied on distributed funding and public trust to sustain their work through community programs. The Foundation's bequest changed the landscape. Along with resources, it carried the potential to reshape relevance.

A week later, Crain's Chicago Business reported a ripple effect. Donors began to withdraw support from the Poetry Center. Some assumed it had merged with the Foundation. Others concluded that a second poetry nonprofit was no longer necessary in the city. The institutions remained fully independent. Yet the confusion reshaped the ground beneath the Center. Support thinned. Partnerships paused. Programs slowed.

Clarke later described the Foundation's emergence as a dinosaur-killing asteroid. The impact carried no malice. It carried mass. And like any extinction event, it reshaped more than terrain. It altered the atmosphere.

A civic poetics rooted in plurality, risk, and access found itself overshadowed by a single, highly visible institution supported by consolidated funding and brand clarity. What followed was less displacement than absorption, a gradual consolidation of cultural attention.

This essay affirms the Foundation's influence, importance, and scope. Its gravitational pull is real. Yet, civic poetics depends on breadth, on many actors and many forms. When one entity concentrates the majority of press, grants, and public imagination, others struggle to remain audible.

Still, the record endures. The broadsides continue to circulate. The students still remember. The articles remain.

The Wall Street Journal noted the bequest. Crain's documented the shift.

The asteroid did not destroy the Poetry Center. But it altered the sky. That change extended beyond funding. It reflected a shift in philosophical alignment. As institutions leaned toward consolidation and prestige, the public orientation of poetry moved into the background. What receded was not only financial support. It was the conditions for being heard.

What Was Lost in the Inward Turn

There was a time when poetry in Chicago stood visibly in the open air. It rose from classrooms, galleries, and civic stages, not from the tenured podium or the private seminar. The Poetry Center built its house from presence and trust. Over time it became one of the longest-running independent reading series in the country, sustained by the belief that poetry must meet the public where it stands.

That belief shaped its work, which formed a civic record. Prestige was never the goal. Presence was. The poems mattered because they were encountered in hallways, on billboards, and in the hands of students and strangers. The artifacts remained in kitchens and libraries long after the voice had faded.

Then the landscape changed when Poetry Magazine, an esteemed literary journal on a modest budget, became a national literary institution. The changes for Poetry Magazine were consequential beyond its newfound wealth. Longtime editor Joseph Parisi, who had done much to attract Ruth Lilly's attention during his tenure, resigned abruptly. In the wider poetry scene, the shift came with an unintentional erosion of the civic structures that had long supported poetry in many places. The Chicago Poetry

Center soon became confused with the Foundation in the public eye. Staff received congratulations, grant inquiries, and press requests meant for someone else. The loss was structural.

The Foundation expanded its programs and visibility. It built a headquarters, launched initiatives, and became a central literary presence. Centrality has consequence. This civic practice depends on a distributed field. When attention and resources gather in one place, the surrounding ecosystem thins.

The consolidation grew through momentum. A culture shaped by plurality, shared risk, and community presence yielded to the gravity of a single institution. By 2020, the limits of that model appeared. After George Floyd's murder, the Foundation faced intense criticism for its limited response. The president and board chair resigned. The rupture exposed more than internal governance. It revealed a long-standing distance from the civic landscape that had given poetry in the city its reach.

Some commentators, including John McWhorter, framed the resignations as capitulation to ideological pressure. That reading missed the structural cause. The Foundation had not been undone by ideological excess. It had been weakened by insulation. Years of consolidation had reduced its relation to the broader field. What collapsed was not neutrality. It was connection, amplitude, and risk.

Poetry has always welcomed political and social reckoning. From abolitionist verse to queer manifestos, from Whitman to June Jordan, the art has long engaged the conditions of its time. The danger lies not in politics but in restriction. Civic poetics requires multiplicity. When multiplicity contracts, culture narrows.

Still, the Poetry Center endured. Under B. Sampson's leadership, a former poet-in-residence in the schools program she later guided, the institution returned to its ground. Poetry belonged among the people of the city rather than above them.

The two institutions were never adversaries. They arose from different poetic lineages and served the city in distinct ways. Their records show this clearly. One built national stature. The other maintained continuity in the public sphere.

The archive remains. The memory of readers and students record the work. They reveal a persistent truth. When poetry turns inward, when it moves toward prestige, insulation, or fixed stance, something essential is lost. The civic was never ornament. It was a way of working.

The Table Returns

In 2024, the Poetry Foundation hosted *A Bigger Table: 50 Years of the Chicago Poetry Center*, an exhibition that quietly affirmed what many within the city had long understood. The civic poetics championed by the Center had not vanished. They had been displaced. Overlooked. And now, belatedly, acknowledged.

Fred Sasaki, Creative Director at the Foundation, opened the exhibition with a gesture of overdue recognition:

"We love broadsides, and for a long time have wanted to highlight the iconic Chicago Poetry Center broadside series."

The exhibit honored more than individual poets or isolated events. It recognized the infrastructure, the public labor that carried poetry into schools, galleries, neighborhoods, and civic memory. The broadsides, the classroom programs, the reading series, these were not promotional tools. They formed a structure of presence.

Clarke, who led the Center from 2000 to 2005, appears in the exhibition's short documentary. He recalls arriving at the institution and becoming "profoundly curious" about its origins. What had been forgotten, tucked away in drawers and dusty cabinets, he began to restore. Among his earliest discoveries was the Center's 1974 founding press release. It listed three goals: to encourage public interest in poetry, to support poets in writing poetry, and to create professional opportunities for them.

"Every single one of those things is ridiculously hard to do," Clarke says in the video, "but it's just such a laser beam into what you need to do."

He pursued those goals through action. He expanded the broadsides from occasional commemorations into routine civic documents, each co-designed with a visual artist and distributed across the city. Clarke treated the broadside as a form of public memory.

"One of my favorite collaborations," he recalled, "was the broadside I created for Lawrence Ferlinghetti's reading. It was a homecoming for him, and I worked with Ed Paschke directly on the piece."

Ferlinghetti entrusted Clarke with a poem for the occasion. Paschke, in turn, allowed Clarke to take one of his paintings and translate it into a two-color letterpress image, reducing and reorienting the work for the form. The resulting print retained Paschke's visual voice, yet became a singular piece within his catalog, shaped by the constraints and possibilities of the medium.

The broadside's colophon makes no note of Clarke's role in this transformation. At the time, the work itself carried the priority. Documentation came later. What mattered then was the trust extended by both artists, and the care taken to honor it.

The broadside became a civic artifact, carrying Ferlinghetti's words and Paschke's vision into shared public space.

Fred Sasaki, reflecting on his early encounter with Clarke, was struck by how "hands-on" he was with artists, treating each broadside as an illuminated poem. That ethic extended beyond the page. The same care shaped Clarke's work in classrooms, where poets taught students to write their own poems as part of the school day and the arts education curriculum.

One former participant, now a staff member at the Poetry Foundation, recalled saving her first poem in a Bratz folder when she was an elementary school student. She wrote about immigration marches. She learned to use poetry as a way to reflect, to witness, and to resist.

The arc of civic poetics, from Carroll to Clarke to Sampson, remained largely obscured during the rise of the Foundation's national profile. As literary attention consolidated within a single institution, the broader lineage of civic work fell from view. Clarke once described that moment as a dinosaur-killing asteroid. It carried no malice. It carried mass. And for a time, the public lineage that had long supported poetry's civic presence seemed severed.

But it remained. The institution endured. And its ethic endured with it, largely through the leadership of B.

Sampson, who revived the school programs, renewed the reading series, and reasserted the Center's public mission. She had been a student at the School of the Art Institute, where the Poetry Center had been in residence since 1980. A former Hands on Stanzas poet-in-residence herself, Sampson did not inherit civic poetics as theory. She extended it through practice.

That the Foundation ultimately hosted an exhibition honoring the very work it once overshadowed is not revisionist. It is restorative. *A Bigger Table* affirmed that poetry's civic presence was never rooted in hierarchy. It was held through multiplicity.

The broadsides on the gallery wall. The archival press release. The acknowledgment of the Center's long-running reading series. The testimonies from students, poets, and organizers. These were not decorative gestures. They formed a record. And they marked a moment of return.

This moment of recognition does not erase the years of cultural displacement. But it affirms what quiet poetics often require: time.

Clarke's work, and the broader civic lineage shaped by Carroll, Sampson, and many others, endured through function rather than fashion. It brought poetry into public life and memory. The lyric became tangible, shared in physical form and lived encounter. And now that work has been seen again. That ethic, of placement over prestige, of presence over applause, was never aesthetic alone. It carried moral weight.

And it revealed itself most clearly in moments of shared grief, when a poem became more than form. It became a gesture toward what cannot be replaced.

More Than a Number

In early 2003, as the Poetry Center prepared for Haki R. Madhubuti's upcoming reading, he sent several poems for Clarke to review for the event's commemorative broadside. One of them was *When 21 Is More Than a Number*, written in the wake of the E2 nightclub tragedy, where twenty-one young people died in a late-night crowd crush. Clarke lived down the street from the site. The moment he read the poem, the choice was immediate. Nothing else matched the weight of what had happened.

The result was a broadside titled *When 21 Is More Than a Number*. It functioned less as tribute than as civic gesture, a reckoning with the scale of the loss and the silence that followed. Clarke embedded subtle visual elements into the design: a blind strike forming a cross from the words *twenty one*, and smaller blind strikes along the border evoking the names. The broadside was distributed to the mayor and to city officials.

It was public grief, rendered through poetry and design. The poem made no appeal for applause. It stood in for the missing. It offered presence where policy and press had left absence.

Clarke later reflected that this moment, when poetic voice, civic urgency, and public distribution aligned, may have contributed to his appointment at Chicago's Department of Cultural Affairs. No official link was made. Still, the timing suggests a rare event: a poet receiving civic appointment through poetic action, by placing another poet's poem into shared space during a moment of collective mourning.

The poem itself carried weight. It was written by a major literary figure and delivered through a civic medium shaped by quiet labor rather than visibility. Madhubuti's poem listened to the silence that followed a siren.

The broadside carried a public purpose. It placed the work where it could register. It offered a way to grieve, even briefly.

Few remember the tragedy. Fewer remember the poem. Yet something passed through the streets when it appeared. A government noticed. And for a moment, a voice carried.

Poem Finds a Home

In winter 2003, a poem by former U.S. Poet Laureate Mark Strand appeared on a billboard above Chicago Avenue and Wells Street, rather than in a journal or anthology:

"You there, / Come with me into the world of light and be whole. / For the love you thought had been dead a thousand years / Is back in town and asking for you."

The lines, from Strand's *Five Dogs*, hovered over the city for weeks, visible to commuters, pedestrians, and children in backseats. The poem was more than read. It was encountered.

The billboard space was offered by Lightology, a lighting firm housed beneath the sign. As reported in the *Chicago Tribune*, Clarke recognized the opportunity. "They had the billboard," he said, "and we had the poets."

Strand's poem was chosen for its clarity. The language reached upward, both in tone and in placement. Though Strand taught at the University of Chicago, he remained distant from the city's daily poetry life. The billboard placed him in the sky.

Other poets followed: Li-Young Lee, Lisel Mueller. Each brought a distinct register, Lee's hush of intimacy and exile, Mueller's domestic precision. Together they formed a rotating public anthology above the street.

These installations offered no promotion. They served as interruptions, brief entries of lyric presence within the city's visual rhythm. The broadsides carried attribution rather than advertising, marking their source without framing the poems as products. Like weather, they entered and receded.

What remained extended beyond the text. It was the ethic that guided the work: that poetry belongs where people live. Placed in traffic and weather, among people and motion, the poem entered the shared movement of the city.

Line 39

In June 2006, *Newcity* published its annual "Lit 50: Who Really Books in Chicago," a ranked list of the city's most influential literary figures. At number 39 was a brief profile of the Poetry Center's newly appointed director. The line that matters in this context appeared near the end: "...replaced the influential [KC] Clarke at the Poetry Center last year."

One sentence. No fanfare. No pull quote. Yet its meaning was unmistakable. Influence, in this case, did not rise from publication or personal brand. It lived in what had been built and in what someone else now carried forward.

Clarke had departed in 2005 after five years of quiet but transformative civic work. Under his leadership, the Poetry Center treated poetry as a living urban art. The programs reached beyond the literary circuit. They placed poetry in shared civic time.

To be named influential in this context was not a recognition of authorship. It was an acknowledgment of architecture, the structures and relationships that remained.

Influence here meant infrastructure. It meant creating something durable enough to endure beyond one's tenure. The sentence in *Newcity* did what many literary honors overlook. It named the invisible thread.

It affirmed that influence does not always arrive through spotlight. Sometimes it enters quietly, as a doorway left open for the next voice.

That it was noticed at all felt improbable. But the structure had taken shape. And sometimes the work speaks in its own time.

Civic Amplification

What counts as poetry? Who gets to read it? And how do institutions handle the line between populism and permanence?

During Clarke's tenure at the Poetry Center of Chicago, poetry moved beyond the literary world and further into public life. Two high-profile readings exemplified this ethos: one featuring singer-songwriter Lucinda Williams alongside her father, the poet Miller Williams; the other a solo appearance by Smashing Pumpkins frontman Billy Corgan. Each event tested civic ground, an experiment in reach, resonance, and form.

Lucinda and Miller Williams shared the stage at the Art Institute of Chicago's Rubloff Auditorium. The Chicago

Sun-Times previewed the reading with the headline "Rhymin' Williamses to team up for show," framing it as a collaboration across generations. Miller, long a central figure in American public verse and Bill Clinton's inaugural poet, read with the plainspoken clarity shaped by decades of civic work. Lucinda followed with song and text that carried the weight of poetry without explanation. "My dad would sometimes quote lines from poems when I was a child," she told the paper. "That's how I got exposed to that world." The evening held lineage. It offered inheritance made public.

President Jimmy Carter, in a letter of endorsement, called Miller Williams his mentor, affirming the reading as a cultural offering grounded in trust and influence.

Painter Wesley Kimler played a pivotal role in promoting the event. His artwork appeared in the promotional materials, and he hosted the post-reading gathering at his Carroll Street loft, an independent gallery that had become a haven for non-institutional artistic risk. The gathering brought together artists, actors, playwrights, poets, and musicians in an atmosphere that echoed the evening's spirit: unguarded, cross-disciplinary, and fiercely local.

Corgan's event, held in the same venue, stirred sharper reactions. The Chicago Sun-Times ran a double-page spread titled "Poetic License or Verbal Abuse?" with a full photograph of Corgan at the podium, surrounded by commentary, excerpts, and responses. The conversation extended beyond the poems. It asked whether a figure like Corgan, untrained in literary convention, could hold a formal platform. Could a rock musician be taken seriously as a poet? Did the moment blur the lines, or clarify them?

One critic described Corgan's work as "comical," comparing it to "C-minus high school assignments." Clarke, quoted in the piece, offered a measured response: "He didn't say, 'I've been reading poetry for 100 years, and I'm the world's best.' I think it was a vulnerable moment, but he pulled it off."

That line reflected the Poetry Center's ethic during that era. The aim centered on honoring poetic risk. More than 900 people arrived. Many had never attended a poetry reading. Some arrived with expectations shaped by music. Some arrived skeptical. Some arrived hopeful. What they encountered was something simple, raw, and unguarded.

Before the event, Corgan expressed frustration about the poster design, a vivid piece by American concert artist Mark Arminski. "Image is everything," he told Clarke. He also objected to the auditorium's temperature, warning that if the Art Institute failed to raise it, he might cancel. Corgan still stepped to the microphone and began.

Looking back, the moment carried more than resistance. For an artist who had performed before tens of thousands, this was something entirely different: a stage without a band, without effects, with only a microphone and a set list of poems. It came just after the breakup of his new band, Zwan. This was not a concert. It was a reading, stripped down, unscored, solitary. The format remained unfamiliar, and likely unsettling, though Corgan would never have admitted it.

The atmosphere felt familiar, like the quiet before a show, the air charged and light. What followed was stranger, quieter, and more intimate. The audience leaned in. And the work held.

The reading provoked strong reactions because it asked the public to take poetry seriously without requiring mastery. That is a vulnerable space, and it is where poetry often lives. As with all major readings at the Center during that period, the evening centered on a broadside. This one featured an image by photographer Laura Letinsky, presenting the occasion as civic gesture rather than spectacle.

A bootleg recording of the reading still circulates online: rough audio, ambient crowd noise, poems read without adornment. It's a record of what it meant, in that moment, to take poetry seriously in public, without polish or permission. Corgan would later publish *Blinking With Fists*, a New York Times bestseller. This reading came first.

The year before, in 2002, Lawrence Ferlinghetti read in the School of the Art Institute ballroom on Michigan Avenue, just across the street. He wore a World War II aviator's cap while performing "History of the Airplane," turning the room into a small theater of civic memory and wry imagination. By the end of the night the cap had disappeared, lifted by someone in the crowd, a strange and fitting echo of the evening's charge.

Earlier that day, he and Clarke walked Michigan Avenue and State Street, past the Reliance Building, his favorite Chicago skyscraper. As they walked, Lawrence Ferlinghetti recalled his service during World War II and being stationed at Navy Pier, the Beat movement, Paul Carroll's First Amendment battles with *Big Table*, and a different Chicago, one that had carried voices like Ginsberg's into public memory. He mentioned Studs Terkel, whose WFMT broadcast carried the 1959 *Howl* reading from the Palmer House event that Carroll produced for *Big Table*. The recording of this event was used to create the spoken-word album *Howl and Other Poems.*

That same circuit remained active decades later. Working with Terkel, Clarke helped bring Lisel Mueller out of retirement for a return reading at the Poetry Center, placing her voice once again into public space through presence rather than ceremony. After the reading, Mueller sent a note to Clarke. She went on to say:

"A poem does not exist on the page alone. It has a voice that needs to be heard, and no one can unlock that voice more memorably than its author. The Poetry Center allows Chicagoans to hear our best poets read from their work month after month, and that is a rare gift."

Lisel Mueller
personal correspondence

The lineage persisted in the walk, the names recalled, the memory of past struggles, and the quiet continuity of poetic presence. Ferlinghetti's reading was recorded and released as the album *Lawrence Ferlinghetti Live at The Poetry Center*, a Poetry Center production by Clarke. It circulated through City Lights and The Poetry Center, and remains available at the time of this book's printing on streaming platforms.

Both albums emerged from Chicago. Both resulted from the same civic poetics logic at work in different moments.

What linked these events came from what they revealed about the civic space for poetry, and how narrow that space could become. Each reading served as a wager. It tested whether poetry could live in spaces shaped for other purposes. Whether it could hold through presence alone, unfiltered by credential or frame. And each time, it held.

These readings drew their strength from how and where they occurred. Their force rose from the simple act of placing poetry in structured space. The Rubloff Auditorium and the School of the Art Institute ballroom, sites shaped for visual legacy and artistic formation, became, for a time, civic stages for poetry. The gesture carried weight through placement: poetry read aloud, without adornment, held by presence alone.

But those stages formed only one dimension of the work. Much of the civic energy during that period took shape elsewhere, offstage, improvised, and co-created. In conversation with painter Wesley Kimler, that ethic became something lived: a shared attempt to make a scene, to place art in public, and to carry that work forward without waiting for permission. What follows is not an interview in the conventional sense. It is a record of that effort, gathered during a tornado warning, in a repurposed church, long after the lights had gone down.

What We Built: A Conversation with Wesley Kimler

In 2022, I was visiting my longtime friend and collaborator Wesley Kimler at his studio in Chicago. We didn't meet in the more familiar Carroll Street studio, but in the dilapidated church he was renting after being forced out of Carroll Street. We were in the basement because tornado sirens were going off all around us. While the weather raged outside, I decided to record our conversation as a kind of interview. I'd done many formal interviews over the years; this felt like the right moment to turn a long-running conversation into one of them. So here it is.

Note: *The following is a segment from a longer recorded conversation between KC Clarke and Wesley Kimler. It*

KC Clarke:

So I've done a lot of these interviews, and, you know, I interviewed a guy who parachuted in behind lines during World War II. A guy named Rock Merritt. Just some really amazing people.

I also got to interview Ed Paschke, and I know he's a mutual friend between you and me. You knew him a lot longer than I did, but he treated me, for some reason, he treated me really well. He was really nice to me. Supportive.

Wesley Kimler:

Ed was a very, very good man.

KC Clarke:

Yeah. He didn't have to help me. But he helped. Yeah. There're all sorts of things that he did when I was, you know, running the Poetry Center of Chicago.

Wesley Kimler:

I was talking about that studio of his (Paschke's) on Howard Street. How I was expecting this big production, assistants rolling out the canvases. And here's this little place that looked like an old dentist's office from the '40s or something, with the, you know, the mottled glass, opaque glass in the front door. Didn't have his name on it, but it could have.

KC Clarke:

It was quite perfect.

Wesley Kimler:

And you went in there, and there was a chair that he had for his easel. He put all those paintings on the chair.

KC Clarke:

But I also met another artist in Chicago. Somehow, I stumbled across you. And I was, this is twenty years ago. I'm thirty-two years old. You were my age now. So twenty years ago, you were forty-nine.

I think he [Paschke] said something to the effect of, "Do you know Wesley Kimler? He likes poetry." And I was like, oh. Because, you know, that was what I was doing. And I don't exactly know how you and I ran into each other.

Wesley Kimler:

I don't remember exactly how we met. Maybe I came to an event or something. And then maybe you came to something at my studio. And then it was right around the time Billy Corgan was hanging around.

KC Clarke:

I met you earlier than that, because I think I remember showing you the broadside series. We were doing these letterpress art pieces. I remember showing them to you, and you were like, "Oh, you gotta do something different." You were not into it. And some of the early ones were a little staid, but you had to start somewhere. But you said, "I'll do one." (This was in my offices at the School of the Art Institute of Chicago.)

Wesley Kimler:

Yeah, and I am so glad that I did that with Mark Strand. He was a lovely man. A great poet, great poet, and a lovely man. And he told me, he said, "This is my favorite broadside

I've ever done." So, and we printed it kind of old-school. And it's, you know, *the death of death* is how he described that poem. And yeah, I'm really proud of that.

KC Clarke:

He was another pretty amazing person who, for some reason, was nice to me.

Wesley Kimler:

Well, he was a fabulous man.

KC Clarke:

Yeah. And he was nice to you.

Wesley Kimler:

And Poet Laureate of the United States and all this stuff, and ignored here in Chicago.

KC Clarke:

He was completely ignored. So I started doing something.

Wesley Kimler:

Welcome to Chicago, man. Yeah. Welcome to Chicago.

KC Clarke:

There was this person, and they were like, "You will never do anything with Mark Strand."

Wesley Kimler:

Why?

KC Clarke:

Because Mark Strand had somehow offended them at an event at the Art Institute years before, and there would never be any forgiving this supposed social slight.

Wesley Kimler:

Good God.

KC Clarke:

And I was like, well, you know, Mark's a Poet Laureate of the United States.

Wesley Kimler:

Mark was such a cool customer. If he offended them, it was probably coming.

KC Clarke:

I don't even know if it was on purpose. You know, Mark was probably at the Art Institute going, "Oh boy, this is boring." He was like a real guy. He was a real guy. We did Strand first, right?

Wesley Kimler:

It was all, it seems like to me, it was intermingled. We did that thing at Metro, which was...

KC Clarke:

Right, where he was the rock star for the night.

Wesley Kimler:

You know, I mean, the thing is, is that you and I did... you know, I did that season program with that painting of mine. We did. And then we did the Lucinda Williams, Miller Williams thing at my studio.

KC Clarke:

That was a neat piece.

Wesley Kimler:

We had some of the theater people, the Hypocrites, come and perform and so forth. But the main thing is, talk about it, is how you, I mean, it was so dynamic, how you used music people. And, you know, thinking about it, I don't know if you were thinking about Dylan. Like, I certainly, you know, would think about Dylan's deep relationship to poetry.

I mean, it's interesting, because in a way, Dylan, even though he's not a poet per se, and you really can't read his songs just as poetry, paradoxically, you could say he's the Chaucer of our time. He's the greatest poet of our time, more so than anyone else. He didn't just chronicle, he created vision for people to live in. I mean, he really did.

KC Clarke:

My whole thing with the music and the art and the poetry is that I just kept running into all these artists who used poetry as part of their basis for inspiration.

All these visual artists. And it wasn't just now, you go back in time and you get into history. I started diving into, you know, the history of the Poetry Center, which was, part and parcel, this intersection between visual art. It was born in the Contemporary Museum of Art. It was at the Art Institute of Chicago. It was just kind of obvious, but nobody had really mined that.

And then nobody had really done the music seriously, because they didn't think of somebody like a Billy Corgan as even...Like, he shouldn't even be on the Poetry Center stage, according to some people. Which, you know, you could argue one way or the other. But he is a lyricist, and poetry and music do have that intersection.

Wesley Kimler:

Right. And then, but I mean, some of the people you were bringing in at the time...But, you know, I mean, we really lost a lot when... you know, we, and it was my fault, I got seduced by Facebook and social media. And now, looking back at it, we should have stuck with the blogs and stuck with, and moving forward, we should be thinking along that...

KC Clarke:

Well, I loved Sharkforum. That was a great experience. There were a lot of fun, great parties.

Wesley Kimler:

Oh, it was a lot of fun.

KC Clarke:

I would come and bartend, and it was just like all night long, slinging drinks. I couldn't do anything else but sling drinks all night. But it was a lot of fun.

Wesley Kimler:

Oh, and there were some just wildly evil things, like when I'd run into Judy Ledgerwood, who was so pompous, with such an overblown reputation as a painter. She said, "The difference between you and me is I'm trying to do something new, and you're trying to do past time." I just looked at her like, "Are you out of your mind?" I mean, have you looked at Larry Poons? You're reinventing color field painting. So, I did that article on her, but I used all Larry Poons' paintings.

KC Clarke:

Oh, that's hilarious.

Wesley Kimler:

I was always lampooning Mr. Cookie. Howard Stone. When Howard Stone died, I was talking to Lynn Warren, and she said, "Maybe you'll be done being blacklisted at the museum level in Chicago."

Howard worked tirelessly, this ex-institutional Oreo-cookie knockoff maker, who had a couple of nickels to rub together, and he got into all that reinvention of conceptualism 101 that ran roughshod over the scene here. All the hackademics. UIC. That white-red art that just ruined the scene for a good 25 years.

He was one of the funders of that. And he didn't like the fact that I criticized it, that I wasn't a good little artist. So he went out and campaigned against me.

KC Clarke:

Wow.

Wesley Kimler:

All because of that article I wrote in the *Chicago Reader*, "Kimler's Complaint," where I detailed the corruption of the scene.

KC Clarke:

Wow. It's like that story I told about Mark Strand getting blacklisted. One person, one perceived slight, you're not allowed to be read. And they weren't doing anything at *Poetry* Magazine at the time because they didn't like him either. So that thing at Metro with Strand? That was a correction.

Wesley Kimler:

Yeah. It was kind of a correction. We both know the people who took over there, the Poetry Center, after you. I mean, a bunch of socialite lowlifes. And you were a great director there. They were fucking fools not to hang on to you and the wonderful program. They had no idea what they had.

And the kind of dynamic, intersectional stuff you were doing, well, to use one of those popular words of the moment, you were actually doing it.

KC Clarke:

Before it was cool, yeah.

Wesley Kimler:

It was really fucking wild and wonderful. And we really, for a moment, had a scene going.

KC Clarke:

We did.

Wesley Kimler:

But like so many other things in Chicago, the only scene that's ever really stuck and worked out for people is the theater scene. Right? Theater. Yeah. Theater somehow really got traction.

KC Clarke:

Well, it's bigger, and better, and more dynamic.

Wesley Kimler:

I think it's interesting. And I think it's important that we're talking not just about *you* or *me*, but about the amazing scene we had, for a minute, and what we tried to create, and what we ultimately failed to create. I mean, we had it for a minute, and then, for a lot of reasons, it just didn't pan out.

(foxes start barking back and forth)

KC Clarke:

It was amazing while it happened.

Wesley Kimler:

It *was* amazing while it happened. We had some of the greatest poets and musicians in the world.

KC Clarke:

Right here.

Wesley Kimler:

Do you remember that thing we did in my studio with Billy Corgan, Nick Tremulis, and Rick Rizzo, all doing 20-minute sets? And we had the whole of *Time Out* magazine there.

KC Clarke:

Yeah.

Wesley Kimler:

And there weren't that many people, maybe 150?

KC Clarke:

Very small.

Wesley Kimler:

And it was magical. Absolutely magical. You know, the sad story of Chicago is, I felt like we built a race car. Like we built a Ferrari, or a Shelby... but we never got to race it. We built it, and people didn't come. We built it, and the powers that be here... The fact that this city, at the time, probably still, is run by the universities and their art departments...

KC Clarke:

And the influence of money. Because my trouble at the Poetry Center, if I had one, was all that money that landed on Poetry Magazine, by way of that random hundred-million-dollar bequest.

I'm quoted in the *Wall Street Journal* saying, "I hope they'll share the wealth, *Poetry* magazine."

And sure, they've done little things here and there. You can't say they've done *nothing*. But they had the money to literally plop a million bucks, or ten million, on the Poetry Center, on the Guild Complex, on the scene in general. They still would've had $70 million or $60 million sitting in the bank. Which by now would be worth three times that.

And they didn't do any of that. They didn't see anything about what the scene *was*, or where it *was*, or what it *could have been* in that moment. And that, I'd say, is what killed a big part of the scene.

Wesley Kimler:

Isn't that funny?

KC Clarke:

You remember Lew Manilow, right? Lew told me, "I'm going to help you. I'm going to help you with the Poetry Center." And I thought, okay. He said he was going to do this and that.

But the minute that money hit, that Ruth Lilly money, he was on the phone with me saying, "The Poetry Center should merge with *Poetry* magazine. It should go away. You should just merge with them." And he just picked up and wandered off into that camp. I never really talked to him much after that. He thought I was somehow being argumentative or resistant, but he didn't understand.

The Poetry Center came from the beat movement. *Poetry* magazine came from the modernist movement. They both should exist, as part of Chicago's literary history. They should exist, because of the power behind them.

And he was talking about merging them. I'm like, why merge? It's like,

Wesley Kimler:

Lew had a lot of ideas that, you know...

KC Clarke:

Unbelievable. I mean, he was helpful for a little while.

Wesley Kimler:

So it's a real issue, and it's a real problem. And it has to do with, you know, creation and destruction, and self-destruction, and kind of understanding the difference. I had such a destructive style of creativity.

And it's hard sometimes to discern between destructive creativity and self-destruction. They're very different things. So how do you find balance?

You know, that's one thing that's great about these cell phones, I have pictures. I can look at older versions of a painting and go, "Oops. I should've left that. I should've left it. Look how good that looked." And then I'll say to myself, "Damn. If you'd just waited a week..."

That's the other thing about this new studio of mine. My old studio, as wonderful as it was, was long and narrow. It was really hard to work on multiple paintings at once. This new place is a box, about 50 by 65. A bright rectangle. But a very squared, deep rectangle. And I'm going to be able to be surrounded by work, work I can step back 50 feet from at all points. So it's going to allow me... I'm going to have the room to work on many, many pieces at once. There won't be just *one* good place in the studio to hang a big painting, there'll be *many*.

So I think that'll help me. That's what I'm thinking. And I'm going to be up there in the middle of winter, with my wood stoves blowing away, music on, and I'm going to be working on paintings. Trying to, you know, the time we live in right now...

I don't know, the art world...The art world today, you know, you and I are both interested in politics. And we're both, I would say, somewhere... not that we're libertarians, but I don't think either of us aligns neatly with any party.

But I have a hard time with things like Art Basel Miami, when there are places like Gaza and Aleppo in flames. The whole scene seems awfully decadent to me. Lacking seriousness.

And that doesn't mean there aren't great artists. There are. Some brilliant ones. But there's also a lot of shit, stuff that's there because it's socialized, not because it's meaningful.

And it'd be nice if the art world could move past the parties and the fairs and all that machinery. Those things are showing signs of exhaustion.

And look, I don't think art is going to *carry* anything. Art's just art. It's not everything. But it matters. And it's important to recognize its limits. It's not critical theory. It's not activism. If you want to address social injustice, maybe you should be a social worker.

Art isn't a policy tool. It's meditative thinking. Action without direct purpose, or for a purpose that's not functional. It's not standing in line at Whole Foods–Amazon to buy organic beans. It's movement. So we can remember who we are. So we can add meaning to what we do. It's how we clear away decadence. Clear the cobwebs. Art cleans our windshield into the world. It gives us clarity.

It comes before politics. Before ideology. It gives us a deeper view of who we are. It helps us live. Not just act, not just react, but actually *be*. And if we have good art, if we *make* good art, we might have a shot at that.

But right now? Why is the world the way it is? Because human beings aren't being who they could be. We're not living up. We're not the Sistine Chapel. We're more like a Thomas Kinkade painting. Or a happy painter with a bad afro.

KC Clarke:

And again, all the things we've been talking about, the philosophy, the consciousness, the what-art-should-be, it also takes people *doing* it.

You've done it. Other people have gotten close or helped someone like you do it. But there's a practical side to all of it.

Wesley Kimler:

But also, it's like, you know, watching as I lost everything over the last few years, and thinking about all the things you witnessed in that studio of mine, in a functioning community, people would've come forward. They would've helped me. It's been breathtaking. For every person who *has* helped, there are two or three who've run me through the rigamarole, showing them work, walking them through what's available, and then they ghost me.

It's been amazing. And not in the good way. And I've had to really struggle. Because the truth is, I didn't kowtow to people. I didn't kiss wealthy collectors' asses.

I spoke the truth as I saw it. I called out the scene. And I *wanted* a better scene.

You and I working together, that was part of that vision. Trying to build something better.

•••

This conversation with Kimler took place years later, after the civic work it recalls had already taken shape. What it preserves is a record of public-facing poetics in practice. At the center of that work lived a civic ethos: poetry placed in visible, resonant space, often outside conventional literary frames. The aim was presence rather than credential, structure rather than display, and a willingness to carry risk into view.

The events we talked through, the Corgan reading, the Williamses, the Strand broadside, occupied formal venues, yet the same values moved elsewhere. Live From Mars, organized through the Poetry Center and shaped with Chicago's poetry and music communities, carried the work into gallery space, where poems met images and sound. Sharkforum, animated by Kimler and a wide circle of artists and writers, took that energy online with a different kind of urgency, closer to debate and intervention.

None of it stayed abstract. It lived in the city. It was built, offered, and carried forward.

Live from the Art Gallery, Live from the Margins

Legacies often begin in places without ornament. Some rise from warehouse galleries and folding chairs. On July 12, 2003, the Poetry Center hosted *Live From Mars V*, a gathering of "Chicago's freshest poets and singer-songwriters," held at the Mars Gallery in Fulton Market. The lineup carried a wide sweep of Chicago's voices: Kent Foreman's lineage of spoken word, Simone Muench's experimental clarity, Marvin Tate's multidimensional range, Sherille Lamb's gospel poetry, and Li-Young Lee's enduring lyric presence.

Clarke read that night as well, offering *Upland* and *Tomorrow is a Long Time*. The program closed with *Poetry Dance*, a gesture of movement and lived edge. Earlier that year, Ferlinghetti had written to Clarke with a question that felt half playful and half directive: "Have you staged a Poetry Dance yet? Ours was a huge success."

These gatherings worked as bridges. They joined community and art, tradition and innovation, permanence and play. Their purpose was not gatekeeping. They opened space. They offered stages. They made room for encounter.

If *Live From Mars* brought together Chicago's emergent voices and visual energy, then the later invitation to Baxter Black widened the reach across geography, culture, and poetic form. These gestures belong to the same continuum as the Corgan reading, the Williams family appearance, and Madhubuti's elegy. Each extended the logic of civic poetics. Each tested how far presence, attention, and welcome could move through a city, and how many versions of poetry could stand within the same frame.

Cowboy Poetry

In 2005, KC Clarke invited cowboy poet and large animal veterinarian Baxter Black to read at the Poetry Center of Chicago. At the time, Black was one of the most nationally visible figures in populist verse. The decision was intentional. Cowboy poetry had existed for years outside the regard of literary institutions, despite its oral craft and performative force. Black's reading affirmed a central element of Clarke's civic ethos: poetry as shared memory, occupational voice, and public vernacular. The invitation was not novelty. It was a wager on reach, a widening of the table.

Two years after Clarke's tenure ended, the event was cited by Black in the *Daily Herald* as a pivotal moment. He recalled being surprised by the invitation. Clarke, quoted in the article, made the purpose clear: "People like Baxter liven up the conversation in a way that is better than almost anything we've had for a while," he said. "For a long time people talked about high art and low art, and I think the people who are writing in any genre are just as much a part of the art conversation."

Black remembered riding the Blue Line from O'Hare to downtown in full cowboy regalia, drawing puzzled looks from fellow passengers as the train moved through the neighborhoods along its path. "But it's not right to place poets like Black on a different level from other poets," Clarke told the Herald. "He wasn't a joke. He belonged."

The article described Black's popularity across Utah and the West, but it lingered on the resonance of his Chicago appearance. The reading was not staged as curiosity. It was an invitation, grounded in the Center's belief that poetry lives in working voices as fully as it does in books or institutions.

If Black's reading affirmed that poetry thrives in public voice, then what followed pointed toward a quieter form of care. The civic impulse does not end at the microphone. It continues in correspondence, in the maintenance of relationships, and in the steady work of remembering where things begin.

Clarke never knew Paul Carroll personally. Yet the invitation to Baxter Black belonged to the lineage Carroll had set in motion. From its earliest years, the Poetry Center operated on the belief that poetry should meet the public where it lives, in voice, in public wager, in presence. Clarke extended that orientation by carrying it forward into wider ground. He worked through a matrix of relationships, with Maryrose, with Paul's son Luke, and with Inara Birnbaum Carroll. Whether or not Carroll would have embraced Baxter's work, he would have recognized the gesture: a poet placed on the main stage, not for fashion, but for form.

The Cavalcade of Hats

In *Beats Me*, her hybrid memoir and tribute to Paul Carroll, Maryrose Carroll recounts his editorial courage, from *Big Table* to *Naked Lunch*, and the long arc of friendships, fractures, and books that followed. In the preface, she names KC Clarke, then director of the Poetry Center of Chicago, as someone who treated Carroll's early anthologies, especially *Young American Poets*, as "the bible." It was a passing line, but one marked by recognition. It arrived a decade after Clarke had left the Poetry Center.

By then, the gestures had already deepened into stewardship. Clarke stayed in touch with Maryrose, with

Paul's son Luke, and with Paul's first wife, Inara Birnbaum Carroll, who ran the Chicago florist Green Inc. While at the Center, Clarke made Green Inc. his regular florist for sending flowers to poets, friends, and collaborators. The gestures were not ornamental. They acknowledged a lineage, both personal and civic.

That lineage extended further. When Maryrose sought a home for the remaining back issues of *Big Table*, Clarke secured a gift from arts philanthropist Lewis Manilow so the Poetry Center could acquire and redistribute them. The issues were not placed into archive. They were returned to circulation. Readers could buy them, pass them on, or carry them into their own work, letting that early energy reenter the bloodstream of literary life.

Clarke did not set out to mythologize Paul Carroll. He chose to honor the work and the risks: what Carroll built, and what others built with him. The Center's earliest years, rooted in *Big Table* and in Carroll's founding vision at the Museum of Contemporary Art, carried a spirit of inclusion, exposure, and public generosity. Over time, that spirit had grown quiet.

The risks that made it possible were not without consequence. Carroll's commitment to an open, civic poetics fixed his course early, binding him to a mode of independent work that left little room for institutional shelter. He was an institutional civic poetics person by nature, and when existing institutions could not or would not contain that work, he created new ones. What followed was not failure, but the narrowing that often accompanies public risk once its effects have been absorbed.

Clarke contacted visual artists who had collaborated with Carroll, secured permissions from their estates, and slowly reintroduced that ethos into the Center's identity. "It's actually more respectful," Clarke said, "to honor the good he did than to prop him up like some figure on Mount Olympus." The aim was never a monument. It was a bigger table. Indeed, Paul Hoover wrote that Paul's "greatness lay in his enthusiasm for poetry, which radiated from him like heat," in *The Poet in His Skin: Remembering Paul Carroll*, published in the Chicago Review (Spring 1998).

One Poetry Center brochure featured Claes Oldenburg's sculpture *Bat Spinning at the Speed of Light*, an iconic Chicago public work that also carried personal resonance. Oldenburg and Carroll had been friends; Carroll once wrote a poem in response to the piece. Years later, Clarke used an image of the sculpture on a public program brochure with Oldenburg's permission. The image appeared without commentary, but it spoke across time. It echoed a lineage of friendship, art, and public poetics, bridging eras through memory rather than legacy.

Other publications featured Aaron Siskind's photograph of the jumping boy, first published in *Big Table* during the magazine's most embattled period. By placing Siskind's work back into view, Clarke was doing more than referencing history. He was reactivating it. The image stood on its own, yet its inclusion signaled a quiet return to the boldness that had helped define the Center's civic mission.

In August 2015, Maryrose inscribed a copy of her book for Clarke: "For [K.C.] Clarke, who must be Scottish, because for justice, he has no fear!"

The line, fierce and affectionate, carried more than gratitude. Maryrose had lived through the diminishing of Paul's contributions, how his struggles became license for others to soften or erase his place in the record. Long before there was language for it, Paul's place in the record had already been unsettled. Clarke's quiet effort to remember what Carroll had built, through *Big Table*, through the Poetry Center, through years of unruly public generosity, was not only archival, it was refusal to let the record be shaped only by absence and omission.

It captures what runs beneath this story: that to sustain a civic poetics means staying in motion, for the public, for the record, and for the soul of the work.

Carroll's legacy lives in the work he made and in the work it made possible. That legacy continues because someone asked, someone listened, and someone chose to preserve. The following studio exchange between Ed Paschke and KC Clarke continues this ethic through dialogue, carrying the record forward by treating memory as method: unpolished, present, and still alive.

Talking with Ed Paschke

From a 2001 Studio Visit

The conversation that follows offers a different kind of presence: visual, physical, and anecdotal. The exchange functions less as analysis than as oral history, a first-person account of Paul Carroll's temperament, influence, and artistic entanglements, recalled by one of Chicago's most distinctive painters. The tone remains intimate and unscripted, offering a street-level view of those who shaped the civic field through proximity, provocation, and steady presence.

Originally published on Sharkforum.org, active from 2005 to 2014, the conversation preserves a lineage that resists monumentality. It holds the offhand grit and lived texture of a poetics shaped as much in basements, barrooms, and backstreets as in archives.

In the summer of 2001, Clarke contacted Ed Paschke to ask if he would share some of his memories of Paul Carroll: poet, publisher of *Big Table* magazine, founder of *Big Table Books*, creator of the Program for Writers at the University of Illinois Chicago, and founding director of the Poetry Center at the Museum of Contemporary Art. Paschke invited Clarke to his Howard Street studio, where he worked on a painting while they talked.

KC Clarke:

I've been going around trying to get in touch with people who worked with Paul Carroll. He was friends with artists like Claus Oldenburg, Aaron Siskind, Andy Warhol, Leon Golub, Harry Callahan, you. So anyway, I've been trying to connect things from the past to honor Paul's work. From what I've heard, Paul died in the gutter of the arts.

I've heard a lot of things about Paul. The best story, one Paul Hoover told me, is that even though Paul was a tenured professor at UIC, where he founded their program for writers, he was also driving a cab. The story goes something like: he was driving these people around, and they didn't care about his subject, Pablo Neruda, so he stops the car and said," Get the fuck out." That seemed to be the kind of guy he was.

Ed Paschke:

Oh yeah. He was in your face in every way. He had a way of standing a little too close to you when he talked to you. Everybody has a sense of personal space, right? Like, this is okay right here, right? This is getting a little too close, right?

[Ed moves in]

And this is real close...

[Ed gets in my face]

He'd come in, right here into this zone, and your first feeling is like, you think there's going to be some kind of confrontational thing, but that was just his way of connecting with you. He connected at close range. So, do you want to just start free associating about him?

KC Clarke:

Sure.

Ed Paschke:

I was certainly aware of *Big Table* and of Paul Carroll for a number of years before I actually met him, and so to me he was already a mythical figure, associated with some of the Beat writers.

KC Clarke:

For the record, we are... Where are we?

Ed Paschke:

We are on Howard Street at Ed Paschke's studio.

KC Clarke:

And you're Ed Paschke.

Ed Paschke:

I'm Ed Paschke. Okay, so I'm trying to remember clearly... I might have met him somewhere at an opening, but I really got to know him through the making of a film that many of us were involved in here in Chicago. The artist Red Grooms was here in the late 60s, and he was creating kind of a big labyrinth Chicago installation, for which he is known. He would also use these big environmental constructions simulating the city, and some of the landmarks of the city, the "L" and so on and so forth. He would also use these things as props in the making of a film. So there was this film Red was making here and I got involved with it. Paul was involved in it.

KC Clarke:

What was the name of it?

Ed Paschke:

It's called *Tappy Toes*, and in a sense, it was a take-off or parody of a lot of the Busby-Berkeley musicals, where you had high production numbers, a lot of people, synchronized movements, overhead shots and things moving in circular fashions. So there were specific roles created for this film, there was a plot and everything, it was a real cliché, where the understudy steps in and becomes the star of the show. In the movie, Paul was the supposed producer of this musical, and I was the stage-door johnny, with my spectator shoes, reading newspapers, chewing gum, and could care less about show business.

Anyway, in the script, on opening night, Paul, the producer, shows up drunk, and then the leading lady has the gout, so she can't dance, and everything's in chaos. So they said, "What are we going to do?" And I was sitting there, reading the paper and tapping my toes and chewing gum, and they said, "The boy's got rhythm." They saw my toes tapping. So I became the understudy who went on stage and somebody else from the chorus line was put on stage to take the place of the lead female performer. So anyway, in the making of that, we all had a kind of hoot, and I got to know Paul better.

We would see each other at different openings, because he was always around at the fringes of the art world. The worlds of writing and art overlap frequently. He was married to Inara, who has a flower store on Wells Street called "Green, Inc." She remains somewhat of a friend. I stop by there occasionally. And then they got divorced, and he married Maryrose.

Maryrose called me one day about a position opening at Northwestern University, where she was teaching part-time, and one thing led to another, and I've been there twenty-two years. It was due to Maryrose calling me on the phone, saying, "Hey, got this job opening," and it came along at a critical time for me in my life. It literally saved my life to get the security of that job. So through being on the same faculty with Maryrose, I would see Paul here and there.

It was somewhere in the late 70s... Interview magazine, Andy Warhol's brainchild, was going to do a piece on me and they wanted me to pick a writer that I knew here that I trusted and had confidence in to do the writing for the piece, so I picked Paul. So, he wrote the piece for Interview magazine and that kind of further cemented our relationship.

Paul was a guy who had a bit of a cantankerous edge to him. There were a few legendary encounters that he had with different people in different social settings, and some argument would erupt, and he would get even closer in his yelling. I was never witness to any of those, but there were times where I could see he was a little bit into his cups, and you'd want to try and stay clear of him at those times. Even though we had a very warm friendship, there is just something about when somebody's not quite themselves, you kind of cut him some slack and stay away. I'm trying to think of when they left the city. You probably know better than I.

KC Clarke:

I think in 1993.

Ed Paschke:

1993, right, so she left her position. As I said, it was a part-time position, kind of a year-to-year appointment, so it really didn't provide the kind of security that they needed. Did he continue to teach at Circle Campus up 'til that point?

KC Clarke:

I think he was teaching undergrad.

Ed Paschke:

Okay. But throughout all of this, I had this sense, and this is just my own speculation, I had this sense throughout all the time I knew him, his stature and his importance as a contributor to the literary world was not being accorded the kind of respect...

KC Clarke:

Why did you think that?

Ed Paschke:

He always seemed to be angry about... There are things here and there we would discuss where he would grouse about this person who didn't treat him right. It just seemed to be a kind of pattern there where he was always in a state of feeling like he wasn't being, I don't know, accorded the respect he should have received. A lot of the younger people that came along were then assuming the positions of running the department that he was a part of, and they were a little unsure of how to handle him because he had a reputation. And he was like, "Who are these young snot-nosed kids trying to tell him what to do?" So that's the overall impression I had of the last several years he was here.

KC Clarke:

Well, you are not wrong. From what I can tell he felt that he was betrayed or disposed of by many people to whom he provided opportunity, lent a hand, helped get a job, promoted, defended, etc.

Ed Paschke:

I guess this is after Paul died... I happened to be out in Lawrence, Kansas. My daughter was going to KU. I was making a printout there at a print shop, and William Burroughs' name came up, and I was going to try to get him to collaborate on this print. He had a history of putting a few scribbles on a stone or something. A meeting was set up to go visit Burroughs, which was not easy to do, because there was a group of young writers and poets that kind of surrounded Burroughs. They would buy groceries for him, cook meals for him, and make sure everything was okay. They protected him. So I guess I was screened. My daughter and I went over there to meet Burroughs. I don't know if I brought it up or if he brought it up, but I think I said something about Big Table, and he said something about Paul Carroll right away. Burroughs, at that point, would kind of float in and out of being connected with what was being said. It was obvious that Paul Carroll was a very important person in Burroughs' life. *Big Table* is the first place that published *Naked Lunch*, and it happened at a time when it was critical for Burroughs to get this kind of validation. So the memory was etched in a very strong way in Burroughs' mind about Paul Carroll.

KC Clarke:

That's an amazing story. Is there anything else you'd like to say about Paul?

Ed Paschke:

One thing you always knew you were gonna get with Paul was a no-nonsense viewpoint of whatever it is that was being talked about, whether it was yourself or somebody else. He was not big on... well, he was capable of it... it's like he didn't have time for a lot of fancy diplomacy. There was kind of an urgency of words where he would kind of distill and zero in on issues in a way that maybe made some people uncomfortable. Oh, and I remembered another thing about Paul. I used to wear, well, I still do, I guess, hats all the time. I tend to be susceptible to cold drafts and things like that. So inevitably, whenever he would see me, I would have a different hat on. He'd come up to me real close like that and say, "The hats, the hats." He was intrigued with the cavalcade of hats on my head.

...

As I was leaving, Ed gave me a copy of an April 1980 issue of Andy Warhol's *Interview* magazine. Among the ads for Polaroid's SX–70 Sonar, "The world's finest instant camera," Leonard Cohen's 1979 album "Recent Songs." and a letter from Truman Capote, is Ed's interview by Paul Carroll. Ed said that our conversation reminded him of that interview. A small portion of that interview is provided below.

There's life and there's TV

In Ed Paschke's new studio on Howard Street in Chicago, the walls look like a gallery of pin-ups. There's Teddy Kennedy with rosy cheeks. There are strippers and muscle men, advertisements for bodybuilding schools, and a great deal of display of lingerie–both from porn magazines and from advertisements. The pin-ups themselves look like a gallery that will be transformed and has been transformed into Ed Paschke's art.

Paul Carroll:

What do you think first attracted you to subject matter from the streets and from the nightlife of the city?

Ed Paschke:

Really, it goes back to an interest I had in the circus and the sense of theatrical exaggeration that occurs there, a kind of garishness, a kind of bizarreness.

Paul Carroll:

A lot of the early critics praised the contrast between the garish and the bizarre subject and the painting quality itself. Yet, the attention paid to the art is largely due to the subject matter.

Ed Paschke:

It has bothered me that critics or those who react to the work in some way never seem to get past the superficial aspect that drew their attention to it.

Paul Carroll:

Often, in your earlier work especially, critics said that you were creating satire or mocking American ways. I was thinking particularly about your series of shoes where the shoes have hair. In terms of what you've just mentioned about the basic incongruity, I wonder if you felt affinity for someone like Magritte who would paint a pair of shoes with actual toes on the shoes.

Ed Paschke:

I think it's basically the thought process of juxtaposition and ironic combination. I think that growing up in a place like Chicago where surrealism was always endorsed on the part of the collectors probably played a part. I'm always interested in how the mind works and how, during the creative process, this kind of thing takes place. A lot of it has to do with avoiding the predictable, avoiding what one might expect in a given situation. In the case of early paintings, the subject matter had a lot to do with it. But in my subsequent work and in what I'm doing now the subject matter has grown more oblique.

Paul Carroll:

Has your enthusiasm for the incongruous always been with you?

Ed Paschke:

I've always felt like an outsider. I'm sure most people in the arts have felt that way. You grow up and realize that it's okay and perhaps even better because you avoid the mainstream. I think innovation is a big part of what we're talking about. When you're dealing with predictable thought processes, it's probably not very innovative. The idea of a controlled accident, of embracing the random occurrence is very important. Accidents frequently occur when I'm working. I love it when that happens. I really don't believe in mistakes. I think that when a mistake happens you go with it and the thing begins to tell you what it wants to do. If a brush falls out of my hand and hits the painting on the way down, I try to work with that mark rather than remove it.

Paul Carroll:

What do you think you'd be doing if you weren't painting?

Ed Paschke:

I don't know, I'd probably be out in the street, in a gutter somewhere.

Excerpts from "There's Life and There's TV," *a Paul Carroll interview with Ed Paschke, originally published in the April 1980 issue of Andy Warhol's Interview Magazine, are reproduced here for historical and critical purposes. Copyright © 1980 Interview Enterprises, Inc.*

The conversation between KC Clarke and Ed Paschke was first published on Sharkforum on January 1, 2007. It brings together two artists with intertwined but distinct civic trajectories, one shaped through verse and public structure, the other through pigment, image, and provocation. Paschke's recollections carry the texture of lived detail: Carroll's mischief, force, and generosity remembered up close rather than at a distance.

The candor of these memories, the hat stories, the encounters, the unruly edges, completes a strand of civic witness. These were figures who worked just outside the institutions they helped shape, operating through improvisation, risk, and sustained presence. Yet civic poetics does not end in anecdote or archive. It extends into the public record, wherever text meets memory and form.

One of the most solemn extensions of that inheritance emerged not in a gallery or a reading, but in a museum exhibition devoted to war. In his later work beyond the Poetry Center, Clarke continued to treat public text as civic act. Whether curating broadsides with artists like Paschke or restoring poetic lineage through gestures of placement and return, the ethic remained steady: language made visible within a shared record.

That orientation would soon be tested on another stage, a museum devoted to military history rather than lyric practice, where poetry was brought into proximity with war's memory and contested ground.

Holding Ground

In 2016, Clarke designed several broadsides for the exhibition *Hunting Charlie: Finding the Enemy in Vietnam* at the Pritzker Military Museum & Library. Two of them featured the words of Tim O'Brien and Karl Marlantes, both combat veterans and novelists whose reflections on the war resisted patriotic simplification. The broadsides of O'Brien and Marlantes, along with those of other combat veterans, hung beside original North Vietnamese propaganda posters and across from a urinal target printed with a cartoon of Jane Fonda, a crude relic still found in some American Legion and VFW halls. The juxtaposition was stark: one side's idealized self-image, another enemy's dehumanizing caricature, and, in between, the stripped, unguarded words of those who had actually fought.

These were not poems, yet Clarke treated them as public verse. The broadsides were shaped as text, composed with rhythm and silence. Their purpose was elevation rather than explanation. The words were given the same framing typically reserved for lyric speech. Each broadside carried the insignia of the military unit under which the author had served, acts of bearing and historical anchoring. Like the pieces Clarke curated at the Poetry Center, each one bore a colophon: source, speaker, design. Quiet signatures, without commentary.

O'Brien's broadside began, "It's as if we had no enemy." This was elegy. It spoke of erasure, a disappearance so complete that even memory struggled to retrieve the other side. The broadside held the line as public record, offered in visual form rather than filtered interpretation.

Marlantes's piece moved differently: "We hated... We reviled... We feared... We pitied... We marveled." Each phrase pressed deeper into contradiction. Hatred, fear, pity, and awe accumulated before ending with a recognition that cut through ideology: "They were good fighting men."

The design was minimal: plain type, open space, a field of quiet around each line. The form resembled poetry but did not declare itself. These were not arguments. They carried bearings.

Clarke's broadsides stood apart from the framing that surrounded them. They did not glorify. They did not condemn. They held. This was not aestheticism. It was a stance: a way to shape combat speech with care and to affirm that veteran testimony deserves public presence and formal attention.

The exhibition itself had already named the tension the broadsides entered: a war in which the enemy was rhetorically erased even as it remained everywhere and nowhere. As one reviewer noted in the *London Review of Books*, *Hunting Charlie* leaned toward portraying the United States as the war's primary victim, juxtaposing enemy propaganda with American grievance and echoing a Cold War narrative of betrayal and loss. Yet the North Vietnamese posters enacted the same flattening through stylized heroism, ideological certainty, and mythic clarity. Both sides simplified. The broadsides did not. They occupied the space in between, neither mediating nor resolving, simply refusing to simplify what war leaves behind.

In curating these pieces, Clarke was not trying to write history. He was trying to hold space for it. And like the most enduring poems, the broadsides did not settle what they revealed. They left it present, contained, and undeniable.

The ethic of public placement had never been only about poetry. It was about what a culture chooses to remember, and how.

The broadsides carried the voices of men who had carried service into danger. The next work lived in a different field, yet it asked for its own form of steadiness.

A Sworn Poetics

Many poets write from the edges of civic life. Clarke worked inside its structures, through education, public programming, archives, policy, and, for a period, law. In artistic contexts, such placement can seem incongruous. In his experience, the lyric and the legal shared foundations: attention, patience, restraint.

Poetry taught him how to look. How to listen. How to wait for what becomes visible only when urgency settles. Those same habits shaped his work in the field. Humane investigations rely on presence: entering an unfamiliar space, noticing what has been overlooked, recording without dramatization, allowing silence to reveal what words might distort. The poet's discipline, perception held through quiet composure, became the officer's method.

He entered homes where danger lived in the air, where weapons might be present, where suffering was visible, human and animal together. He met individuals capable of harm. They did not welcome him. In those moments, composure became its own form of authority, steady, unadorned, held.

This work operated at its smallest, most immediate scale: a call to stop pain where it was unfolding. The aim remained simple and precise. Remove the animal from danger. Hold the situation still. Let the next step emerge through law, through presence rather than force.

To serve as a sworn officer while remaining a poet meant testing the weight of language in rooms where lives changed by sentence or omission. It meant speaking only when needed, with each word carrying consequence. The lyric stance, attention without display and presence without dominance, shaped these moments. Action carried the rest.

Afterword: A Civic Poetics

For years, my poetic attention moved toward structures built for others. A reading series. A school program. A poem on a billboard. A broadside placed in a military exhibit. I stepped back from publishing my own work. The urgency lived in those public tasks. The poems I lifted forward carried other names, yet the ethic behind the work was mine: poetry placed within reach, carried into public life, shaped through risk and welcome.

This book emerged from that same orientation. It continues the civic poetics that guided the earlier years. It suggests that lyric presence can hold quietly within a culture drawn to spectacle, and that a poem can act through placement as much as through voice. Perhaps one way to honor what has been built for others is to offer a body of work shaped by the same field of attention.

Postscript: In 2025, the Poetry Foundation awarded the Chicago Poetry Center a $300,000 grant through its Sustainable Futures program. The move echoed a hope voiced more than two decades earlier: "My hope is that they share the wealth."

PART EIGHT

On the Construction of This Book

This book didn't begin as a book. It began with a phone call. In early 2024, B. Sampson invited me to participate in a documentary. They were filming interviews for an upcoming exhibit on the Poetry Center's history, its public programs, the broadsides, the civic reach. I agreed, unsure what it might stir. In preparing to return, I opened a set of boxes I hadn't touched in years, materials I had withheld from the University of Chicago archive in 2005. At the time, I'd left them out because they felt peripheral, personal correspondence, drafts, and working notes that didn't seem necessary for an archive then.

Inside were letters from Kenneth Koch, Ferlinghetti, James Tate, and Lisel Mueller, along with flyers and ads I had designed for early readings. The *reVerse* master recordings. Press packets. Annotated contracts. I had even illustrated some of the broadsides myself, visual gestures meant to serve the poem. Back then, it all felt like problem-solving. But looking again, I could see it was authorship too.

It had all seemed incidental. Two decades later, the same ephemera revealed something else: a civic poetics archive, a scaffolding of labor that had made space for poetry in the city, even if little of it had been remembered.

In July, the Poetry Foundation mounted its broadside exhibit. Many of the pieces I had commissioned or composed were on display. And the documentary, where I spoke about the Center's legacy, was screened in a full auditorium. I sat in the audience and watched myself speak about what we had built and realized something had endured. In that recognition, I began to wonder if there was space for another kind of book. Less a memoir or retrospective than a poetics.

That return to the archive also prompted a poem, *Americus, for Ferlinghetti.* It surfaced unplanned, provoked by proximity rather than sentiment. Touching the old broadsides, rereading the letters, encountering again the traces of what had once held, the poem arrived part memory, part indictment, part offering. And it made something clear: all of this was a body of work. An unconventional body of work, but a body of work all the same. The poem recognized what had been built. The book followed.

The poems in this book span decades. I began writing them in 1993 and carried them through years, cities, and roles. They emerged quietly, often in the spaces between public work. There was no real plan for a collection. Only a fidelity to the lyric itself. What held them together wasn't theme or chronology. It was stance, a way of listening, a refusal of spectacle. The poems matured as I did. They remained alive at work, shaped across time.

What remained was to accompany them. That became the charge: to build a structure of attention beside the work. That is when I turned to AI, to hold them still long enough that the poems could be seen from multiple angles.

I brought the poems, the structure, the ideas, the history. AI brought scale, recall, and a way of listening that never tired. It was a return. Some of that work began decades ago, in poems shaped under long pressure. The rest took form through steady attention, through a long season of quiet composition and structural care.

Its value rests in fidelity, the belief that even now, a poem is worth reading slowly. That its structure might still carry weight. That its silence might still shape meaning.

This companion volume exists because the poems endured. Because I kept writing them. And because I returned for continuity rather than closure. That return, though shaped by time, was made through energy and sustained attention. The next section reflects on that deeper cost, the kind that accumulates quietly.

On Time, Energy, and the Value of Attention

In a culture that quantifies nearly everything, clicks, views, currency, processing power, it's worth asking what poetic labor costs and what it generates. If cryptocurrency turns computation into value through energy expenditure, then perhaps a book like this, built across years of lyric work and nearly fourteen hundred hours of collaborative attention, functions as its own form of value.

The time spent here was deliberate, focused, and cumulative. Some of that labor stretched across decades, in poems shaped and reshaped in the margins of other work. The rest unfolded across a concentrated year of interpretive writing, archival return, structural refinement, and dialogue. These were burn hours, where language was tested, lineage traced, ethics held, and form pressed until it carried its weight.

At the time of writing, across tens of thousands of messages, the collaborative process consumed hundreds of kilowatt-hours of processing power, enough to fully charge tens of thousands of smartphones, power a home for weeks, or stream thousands of hours of high-definition video. That is one form of energy.

The other was human: the unmetered cost of attention and endurance. Human effort cannot be measured in kilowatts, but it burns all the same.

Together, we generated over one and a half million words to create a final book of more than seventy-five thousand, a compression ratio of about twenty to one. One word retained for every nineteen explored. The rest released by design: language that did its work, then let go.

Before it was published, the book was edited and read closely nearly a dozen times. Skimming never entered the process. Each pass added nearly one hundred hours of attention. The writing and formatting added more.

Though shaped in collaboration with a machine, nothing in *The Groaning Book* was automated. Every phrase passed through human attention. Each word was chosen by hand.

Every poem burns something. From midnight oil to processing power, the form changes, but the cost remains real.

This record accounts only for the hours spent in composition. The labor of bookmaking, a craft in its own right, from design through production and print, remains off the ledger.

The Lyric Vocation: West and Elsewhere

The public resistance to poetry rarely comes from misunderstanding. The distance runs deeper, more cultural than cognitive.

In much of the West, poetry is heard as intimate, even when it resists intimacy. A single line can feel like a whisper or a confession. The form is compact and concentrated, suggestive of interior life regardless of content. Even in experimental work, centuries of lyric practice have taught readers to brace for something personal.

When a poem is read aloud something shifts in the room. The response often moves toward unease rather than reverence. Poetry interrupts spectatorship. It calls attention inward and implicates the listener through its stillness.

A film or a song can carry violence or sorrow without disrupting the pace of the day. A short poem, spoken aloud, lingers differently. Its strangeness stays in the air. Its proximity unsettles. What remains is the voice and the silence around it.

In museums, we approach art with curiosity rather than fear. We ask what the artist is doing, why it matters, what we feel. We allow uncertainty. With poetry, that uncertainty often becomes a barrier. Readers look for immediate meaning or step away.

Elsewhere, that posture shifts. In 1991, while studying in the Soviet Union, I entered a culture where poetry carried a different weight. To call oneself a poet was to accept a vocation. The word was used with seriousness and without display. I was still finding my voice, yet the title was accepted as a role, not a claim.

In that setting, I was asked to write poems on request, in response, and to give them away. I wrote them by hand. They carried no expectation of permanence, only presence. Years later, before political crisis severed contact, a friend, Bella Gribkova, returned one to me, a poem written for her on a train between Moscow and Leningrad. She had kept it, folded and worn.

Such gestures are rare in many Western contexts, where poems are expected to circulate through publication or performance. In Russia, the gesture itself carried meaning. The presence of the poem, even briefly, was enough.

The poems in *Between Here and the Sound of a Groaning Interstate* carry something of that earlier exchange. They arrive shaped, not simplified, attentive to what is held rather than what is claimed. Like the poems once written and given away by hand, they ask only to be received. These poems, and this book, are offered in the same way. In that posture is a quiet respect for the reader and for the work itself.

Archival Holdings

Select institutional records, including Poetry Center of Chicago program files, design archives, and original broadsides, are housed at the Special Collections Research Center of the University of Chicago Library and at the Poetry Foundation Archive in Chicago for exhibition materials produced after 2024. Additional materials associated with this work, including correspondence, drafts, ephemera, and illustrative materials, are held in the KC Clarke Personal Archive at time of publication. Many Poetry Center broadsides are also held in rare book and special collections at universities and research libraries in the United States. Further documentation appears in public newspaper and periodical archives through contemporaneous reporting, reviews, interviews, and photographic records. Beyond these physical holdings, portions of the record remain accessible through public digital sources, including institutional websites, documentary footage, legacy media, and preserved online platforms such as the Internet Archive's Wayback Machine.

Signal Chain: reVerse (2004)

The following artists, engineers, and poets contributed to the 2004 release of *reVerse*, a civic audio project organized around poetry, music, sound, and public placement.

Li-Young Lee
Echo and Shadow
    written and performed by Lee
    music by Richard Fammerée and Linnaeus
    recorded at Soma Electronic Music Studios, Chicago

KC Clarke
Skyscraper (delux)
    written and performed by Clarke
    music by KC Clarke and Mikael Jorgensen
    recorded at Soma Electronic Music Studios, Chicago

Linnaeus
Shed
    written and performed by Linnaeus
    music by Richard Fammerée and Linnaeus
    recorded at Alien Sound, Chicago

Mark Strand (1934–2014)
What It Was
    written and performed by Strand
    recorded at Soma Electronic Music Studios, Chicago

Marvin Tate
Take Off Your Shoes (and Run)
    written and performed by Tate
    music by Marvin Tate
    recorded at Soma Electronic Music Studios, Chicago

Elise Paschen
Possession of the Field
    written and performed by Paschen
    recorded at Soma Electronic Music Studios, Chicago

Cin Salach
Evolution
    written and performed by Salach
    music by Cin Salach and Ten Tongues
    recorded at Maestro-Matic, Chicago

Richard Fammerée (1951–2011)
Green Man
    written and performed by Fammerée
    music by Richard Fammerée
    recorded at Alien Sound, Chicago

Lawrence Ferlinghetti (1919–2021)
History of the Airplane
    written and performed by Ferlinghetti
    recorded at City Lights Bookstore, San Francisco

Alexi Murdoch
Song For You
    written and performed by Murdoch
    recorded at Lookout Sound, Los Angeles

Simone Muench
Spectacle Possession
    written and performed by Muench
    recorded at Soma Electronic Music Studios, Chicago

Kent Foreman (1935–2010)
It's About Time
    written and performed by Foreman
    recorded at Soma Electronic Music Studios, Chicago

Sherrille Lamb
Words Are My Salvation
    written and performed by Lamb
    piano and organ by Mikael Jorgensen
    recorded at Soma Electronic Music Studios, Chicago

Lou Reed (1942–2013):
The City and the Sea from *The Raven*
    written and performed by Reed
    recorded live at The New School, New York City

Produced by KC Clarke and Richard Fammerée

Aftersound

This all began with the poems, though the uncertainty lived elsewhere. Poetry is an old art; its risks were familiar. What felt new was the companion volume that formed beside the poems.

I didn't expect a system to have any meaningful role in shaping that structure. The skepticism was real. But as the work deepened, something else surfaced. The process didn't speed anything. It widened the field of attention. It let questions stay open longer. It let ideas be tested from every angle. The surprise wasn't fluency; it was the energy that returned through sustained exchange.

Nothing about this replaced the human work. Books have always been collaborations: writers, librarians, archivists, editors, proofreaders, designers, engineers, and readers encountered along the way. This was another form of that lineage. What shifted was the instrument, and the resistance it offered. Whenever the system smoothed a passage, I pushed toward grain. Whenever it leaned toward certainty, I tilted the sentence back toward ambiguity. The friction became part of the method, something to sound against until the tone held.

Through that pressure, patterns came forward. They were created by duration, by attention held long enough for shape to appear.

The poems always remained my own work untouched by a machine. The poetics emerged beside them. And what formed in the end was neither argument nor experiment, but a record of the listening that made the book possible. The rest fades. What remains is aftersound.

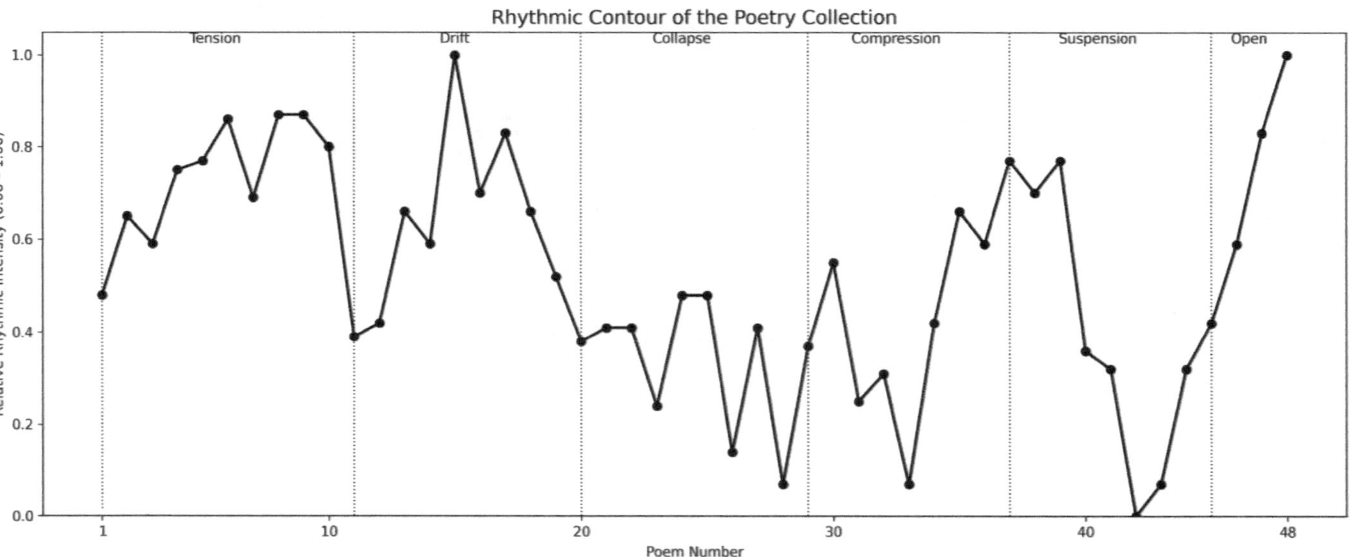

Values are normalized from 0.00 (lowest) to 1.00 (highest) to show relative rhythmic intensity across the poetry collection.
Rhythmic intensity reflects the combined pressure of tempo, compression, sonic texture, and tonal density within each poem.

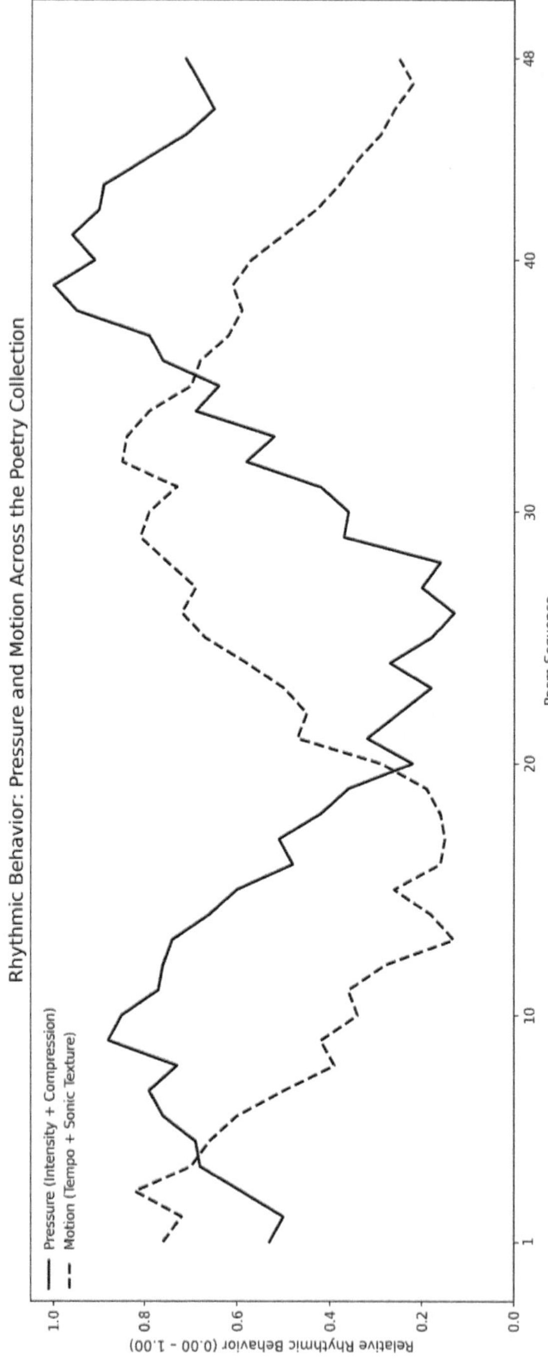

Pressure (Intensity + Compression) · Motion (Tempo + Sonic Texture)
Based on language density, sentence cadence, tonal force, and sonic patterning in each poem.
Values normalized from 0.00 to 1.00 to show relative rhythmic behavior.

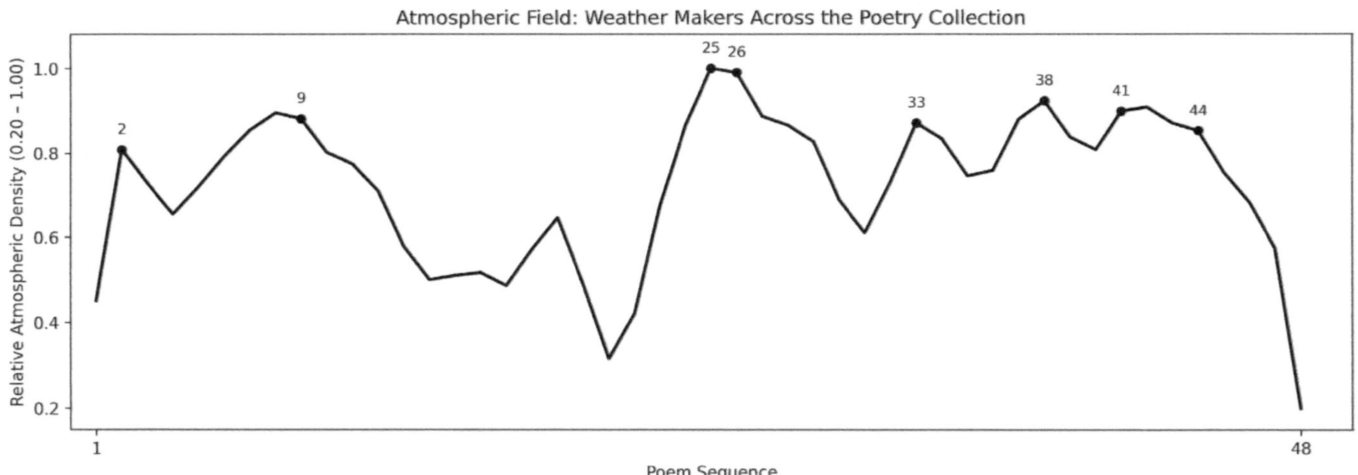

Atmospheric density reflects how each poem shapes space, image, time, pacing, and emotional presence.
Higher regions indicate poems that create more inhabitable, sustained, and tonally saturated reading environments.

After an event at Allen Turner's loft on Green Street in Chicago, my wife and I ended up in the elevator with Mark Strand and Robert Pinsky. The door slid shut, and Mark gave me that small, conspiratorial twinkle he had, then looked over at Robert. He knew exactly what he had: the four of us trapped, nowhere to go.

He said, as if reviewing the errands of an ordinary Tuesday, "Well, I guess it's time to go home and have a martini, a steak, and pull on a pair of invisible jammies with my lady."

Pinsky burst out laughing. Laura and I did the same. The elevator opened again, and we all drifted out into the night. Hilarious to the end. It was the last time I saw him before he moved off to New York.

Other Edited and Authored Works

Hands on Stanzas Anthology of Poetry
Editor
2002. ISBN 0-9720751-0-0. OCLC 50717931.
2003. ISBN 0-9720751-1-9. OCLC 1035088940.
2004. ISBN 0-9720751-4-3. OCLC 779974459.
2005. ISBN 0-9720751-5-1. OCLC 779976230.

"The Poetry Center of Chicago: When It Began."
In *From Poetry to Verse: Essays on the Making of Modern Poetry*, edited by Srikanth Reddy.
Author. 2005. ISBN 0-943056-35-7. OCLC 63293450.

On War: The Best Military Histories
Executive Editor
2013. ISBN 978-0-9897928-1-3. OCLC 865495192.

The History and Heritage of U.S. Navy SEALs
Executive Editor
2014. ISBN 978-0-9897928-3-7. OCLC 895197680.

Dignity of Duty: The Journals of Erasmus Corwin Gilbreath, 1861–1898
Executive Editor
2015. ISBN 978-0-9897928-5-1. OCLC 908263722.

The General: From Normandy to Dachau to Service in America
Executive Editor
2016. ISBN 978-0-9897928-9-9. OCLC 967196270.

Lest We Forget: The Great War
Executive Editor and Creative Director
2018. ISBN 978-0-9989689-0-2. OCLC 1008967739.

Zero to Hero: From Bullied Kid to Warrior
Executive Editor and Creative Director
2019. ISBN 978-0-9989689-2-6. OCLC 1064723551.

Wolves and Flax: The Prior Family in the Cuyahoga Valley Wilderness
Author
2020. ISBN 978-1-716-66790-9. OCLC 1201528996.

The Cartoons of Rescue Village: Twenty Years of Love and Lifesaving Through the Eyes of Cartoonist Jenny Campbell
Editor and Creative Director
2023. ISBN 978-0-578-29487-2. LCCN 2022918231.

Materials from the Jacket of This Book

Wesley Kimler (b. 1953)
Black Blizzard, 2021
Mixed media on canvas, 37 x 37 in.
Private collection of the author. Courtesy of the artist.

Between Here and the Sound of a Groaning Interstate gathers work written across thirty years and subjects it to forces poetry often leaves untouched. The poems move through civic spaces, private reckonings, and long stretches of attention where language carries itself.

Its companion volume, *The Groaning Book*, follows the poems and leaves their surfaces intact. It keeps them under pressure, attending to how poems are handled, placed, and sustained in public use. The work is pressed against lineage, music, silence, and use. Some poems tighten. Some distort. Some survive by learning how to breathe under water...

The poems enter fear as a working condition, public consequence as a fact of placement, and rhythm as an architecture indifferent to improvisation, carrying with them a poetics of refusal shaped through use rather than declaration. Poetry here stands alongside painting and music as something made, handled, placed, and then left intact. Dark humor appears where necessity allows it.

Some poems withstand sustained attention. This book assumes that matters, records the work of placement, and carries on.

& we mustn't remember
we've done all this before,
somewhere between here
& the sound of a groaning interstate.

www.ingramcontent.com/pod-product-compliance
Lightning Source LLC
Chambersburg PA
CBHW020724150726
48196CB00028B/814/J